SPECIAL PUBLICATIONS ON DEVELOPMENT No. 2

Barbados
Meeting the Challenge of Competitiveness in the 21st Century

Liliana Rojas-Suárez
Desmond Thomas
Editors

Inter-American Development Bank

Produced by the IDB Office of External Relations

To order this book, contact:
IDB Bookstore
Tel: (202) 623-1753
Fax: (202) 623-1709
E-mail: idb-books@iadb.org
www.iadb.org/pub

The views and opinions expressed in this publication are those of the authors and do not necessarily reflect the official position of the Inter-American Development Bank.

Cataloging in Publication data provided by the
Inter American Development Bank
Felipe Herrera Library

Barbados : meeting the challenge of competitiveness in the 21st century / Liliana Rojas-Suárez, Desmond Thomas (editors).

p. cm.
Includes bibliographical references.
ISBN: 1597820296

1. Competition—Barbados. 2. Labor market—Barbados. 3. Barbados—Commercial policy. 4. Tourism—Barbados. 5. Competition, International. I. Rojas-Suárez, Liliana. II. Thomas, Desmond. III. Inter-American Development Bank.

338.6048 B598 dc22 LCCN: 2006927264

Table of Contents

LIST OF TABLES

List of Figures

List of Schedules

Note on Spelling and Punctuation

Many international organizations employ a hybrid of the spelling protocols used in the US and those more commonly known in the United Kingdom, the Caribbean and elsewhere. The editors of this book have opted for this hybrid approach. For example words such as labour and behaviour retain the "u", as they would in Barbados or the United Kingdom but not in American writing. On the other hand, such words as utilize and harmonize keep the "z", as they would in the United States, and program is printed without the final "me" (programme) seen in British and Caribbean texts.

With regard to punctuation, we have adopted the protocols followed in the UK and the Caribbean. So, for example, where just a word or a fragment appears within quotation marks at the end of a sentence, the period is placed after the final quotation marks (as at the end of this sentence) rather than before, as would be the case in "American English".

Contributors

Andrew S. Downes is professor of economics and university director at the Sir Arthur Lewis Institute of Social and Economic Studies, University of the West Indies, Cave Hill Campus, Barbados. His research focuses on labour and human resource economics, applied econometrics, and economics of organizations. He also serves as editor-in-chief of the *Journal of Eastern Caribbean Studies.* He holds a doctorate in economics from the University of Manchester in the United Kingdom.

Anneke Jessen is Operations Specialist, with responsibility for Caribbean programs, in the Integration, Trade and Hemispheric Issues Division of the IDB's Integration and Regional Programs Department. Prior to joining the IDB in 1996, Ms. Jessen worked for five years as a Research and Project Coordinator at the Institute for European-Latin American Relations (IRELA), an EC-financed policy research and services organization in Madrid, Spain. Ms. Jessen holds a Masters Degree in International Economics and Latin American Studies from the Johns Hopkins University's School of Advanced International Studies (SAIS).

Dr. Auliana Poon, an economist and a tourism expert, is Managing Director and Senior Partner of Tourism Intelligence International.

Dr. Liliana Rojas-Suárez is a Senior Fellow at the Center for Global Development. She is also the Chair of the Latin American Shadow Financial Regulatory Committee. She was a Senior Advisor at the Inter-American Development Bank during the period September 2001–July 2004. From March 1998 to October 2000, she served as Managing Director and Chief Economist for Latin America at Deutsche Bank. Before joining Deutsche Bank, Ms. Rojas-Suárez was the Principal Advisor in the Office of Chief Economist at the Inter-American Development Bank. Between 1984 and 1994 she held various positions at the International Monetary Fund, most recently as Deputy Chief of the Capital Markets and Financial Studies Division of the Research Department. She has been a Visiting Fellow at the Institute for International Economics and has also served as a Professor at Anahuac University in Mexico and an Advisor for PEMEX, Mexico's National Petroleum Company. Ms. Rojas-Suárez has also testified before a Joint Committee of the US Senate on the issue of dollarization in Latin America. Ms. Rojas-Suárez has published widely in the areas of financial markets, macroeconomic policy and international economics. Ms. Rojas-Suárez holds a Ph.D. in Economics from the University of Western Ontario.

Dr. Clive Y. Thomas, the first person to be appointed Distinguished Professor at the University of Guyana, is Director of the Institute of Development Studies at that university. He has been a visiting professor with universities in Canada, the United States, Africa and the Caribbean and has consulted with several inter-governmental bodies including the United Nations Development Programme, the World Bank, IADB and the Pan American Health Organization. He has advised, or served on, numerous boards and committees, including the United Nations Secretary General's Millennium Project Task Force to monitor the implementation of the millennium development goals. He holds a doctorate from the London School of Economics.

Desmond Thomas is country economist for Jamaica, Barbados and the Caribbean Region at the Inter-American Development Bank. He was a lecturer in economics at The University of the West Indies from 1985 to 1995, and adjunct professor at the Universities of Trent and Ryerson in Canada from 1995 to 1997. As an academician, his research interests included open-economy macroeconomic management, with a focus on the development problems of small developing countries. His professional experience also included service as economic advisor to the President of Guyana and statistician at the Caribbean Community Secretariat. He holds a doctorate in economics from McGill University.

Christopher Vignoles joined the Inter-American Development Bank in 2003 as Consultant in the Integration and Regional Programs Department, where he focuses on trade and integration-related research and programming in the Caribbean Community (CARICOM). He has authored a series of papers on trade performance and integration in Trinidad and Tobago, Jamaica, the OECS countries and CARICOM as a whole. He has also worked as a Trade Specialist at the Caribbean Regional Negotiating Machinery in Barbados and the MERCOSUR Secretariat in Uruguay. Christopher has a Master's degree in International Affairs from the University of California San Diego and a Bachelor's degree from the University of San Diego.

Foreword

This book is part of the non-financial engagement, aimed at identifying development priorities, that is a critical part of the work of the IDB in its borrowing member countries. It is a contribution to efforts to engage expert minds, the Authorities, other international development agencies and other stakeholders in dialogue to deepen understanding of the problems and agree on appropriate actions. In part, it reflects a recognition of the importance of tailoring development assistance to specific country needs and the particular circumstances of the small, middle-income Caribbean countries. In the specific context of the Caribbean, it is part of a series of publications that started with *Revitalizing the Jamaican Economy: Policies for Sustained Development* and includes a similar book on Trinidad and Tobago that will be published along with this one.

This publication on the quest for a more competitive Barbados economy is timely. *Barbados: Meeting the Challenge of Competitiveness in the 21st Century* comes at a moment when the sustainability, indeed the survivability, of small island nations—from the Caribbean to the Pacific—often represents a daunting and formidable challenge. The material within these pages shows that Barbados, a Caribbean country with just over a quarter of a million people, embodies many of the classic vulnerabilities of an island with a small open economy, yet aspires to developed-country status, and is already well advanced on the road to achieving the MDG targets.

Viewed in this light, this book raises the question: Is Barbados the little island that can? The authors have approached that question mainly from the point of view of international competitiveness, one of the pillars, along with macroeconomic and financial stability, required for accelerated and sustained growth. Barbados requires such growth not only for the economic leapfrogging that it desires but also for the maintenance of current social and economic standards that it needs.

Starting with a wide-ranging macroeconomic diagnosis, this monograph examines the strengths and competitiveness challenges facing Barbados from the points of view of the institutional and private sector constraints and environment for competitiveness, labour market conditions and trade policy framework and performance. It also narrows the focus to take a sectoral perspective, examining the leading tourism industry. To convey a sense of the public-policy complexities, the book also includes a brief analysis focusing on the agricultural sector.

This publication is the culmination of an extensive process of study and dialogue involving many contributors. It has resulted from the active support and guidance of Ciro De Falco, Executive Vice President of the Bank and former manager of Regional Operations Department 3, Dora Currea, Division Chief, RE3/OD6, and Fidel Jaramillo, Regional Economic Adviser for RE3. The Barbados Authorities also provided critical support and cooperation through the whole process of research, consultation and review. The book has benefited from the research and analysis of a fine group of authors with an impressive mix of scholarship and practical expertise. It has also benefited from the insightful contributions of peer reviewers and other participants of two conferences in Washington and Barbados that provided opportunities for the scrutiny and discussions of experts and stakeholders. A considerable debt is owed to the authors, peer reviewers, stakeholders and other participants in the workshops for their expert contributions and gift of their time. To all of them I express my appreciation and thanks.

I would also like to acknowledge the contributions of Desmond Thomas, country economist, RE3/OD6, who coordinated the process from start to finish, and Liliana Rojas-Suárez, consultant, for her highly effective moderation of the workshops and expert guidance of the editorial process. Finally, this publication owes a considerable debt to the detailed editorial review of Francesca Castellani, Michael Hennessey, Maria Jordan of the IDB, and the consultant, Frank Campbell.

Alicia S. Ritchie
Manager, Regional Operations Department 3
Inter-American Development Bank

Chapter I

Introduction: Meeting the Competitiveness Challenge

Liliana Rojas-Suárez and Desmond Thomas

A. Introduction

For a small island developing country, Barbados, on an overall basis, displays strong social indicators. It has a per capita income close to US$16,000,[1] a poverty rate of only 13 percent and a literacy ratio approaching 100 percent. With numbers like these, it performs at a high level not only in relation to other Caribbean countries but also among countries in the emerging markets group.

Its 30th place ranking on the UN Human Development Index (HDI), based on 2003 data, places it among the more advanced economies in the latter group. Significantly, this HDI ranking is nine places higher than its *per capita* ranking, underlining the weight of the social dimension in its overall development. Not surprisingly, achievement of developed-country status is a clear goal among Barbadian policymakers.

The sustained high rates of economic growth necessary to reach the levels of per capita income in industrialized countries have, however, remained elusive. Over the last three decades, growth rates have been modest and, at times, even negative. For example, while growth averaged 1.8 percent during the 1980s, the balance-of-payments crisis of the early 1990s was associated with negative growth (averaging –4.3 percent during the period 1990–92). A new economic cycle brought growth averaging 3 percent annually over the 1993–2000 period. This positive result, however, was interrupted by a severe recession in 2001–2002 when the economy suffered a cumulative contraction of 2.1 percent. Analysts have attributed this downturn to uncertain international economic conditions aggravated by the September 11th terrorist attacks in the USA. Since then, the economy has once again recovered, achieving 4.4 percent growth in 2004.

[1] On a purchasing power parity basis.

Accelerated growth is needed to enable Barbados not only to move up the development ladder, but to *maintain* the country's solid social indicators. For example, while the unemployment rate has fallen to a national low of 9 percent, this rate is still unacceptably high. The figure is higher still among youths in their most productive age groups. Barbados also requires higher competitiveness and growth to respond to the challenges of a more liberalized international economic environment and the deepening Caribbean integration expected with the establishment of the CARICOM Single Market and Economy (CSME). As will be discussed below, recent developments point to the appearance of macroeconomic imbalances that need to be corrected in order to avoid stresses on economic activity that risk deterioration in living standards.

Broadly speaking, the achievement of high, sustained growth in a very small open economy such as Barbados rests on two pillars. The first is macroeconomic and financial stability, which, to a large extent, is reflected in the capacity to maintain exchange-rate stability. The second, related pillar is the ability to compete in the ever-changing global environment. These two pillars are certainly interrelated: The avoidance of real exchange-rate misalignment is clearly a factor in the maintenance of competitiveness in *any* economy. However, in the case of small island economies, it is useful to analyze these two pillars separately, since, as will be discussed below, for many of these economies keeping a fixed-exchange-rate regime is optimal. This approach contrasts with the usual prescription for a large number of developing countries, where exchange-rate flexibility is deemed to be the optimal system. Thus, for Barbados the challenge is to improve competitiveness *in the context of a fixed-exchange-rate regime.*

The interaction between these two pillars for sustained economic growth becomes apparent when we analyze their respective determinants. Indeed, as will emerge from the discussion below, a number of economic and social conditions needed to strengthen macroeconomic stability are also required to fortify national competitiveness. The rest of this introductory chapter deals with these two pillars and their interrelations.

Section B examines the conditions for macroeconomic stability in Barbados as a small open economy with a fixed exchange-rate anchor. That section focuses on three issues: (a) banking-sector strength and exchange-rate stability, (b) debt sustainability and (c) external liquidity as a factor of economic stability. Section C deals with the competitiveness challenge, highlighting the role of (a) strong institutions that foster a healthy investment climate, (b) adequate labour-market conditions where the link between productivity and remuneration is underlined, and (c) export diversification within the constraints imposed by the small size of the economy, with attention being paid to the potential of the tourism sector and to the prospects for other products within the services sector. And Section D concludes the chapter with an outline of the organization of the book in terms of the remaining chapters.

B. The Economics of a Small Economy: How Does Barbados Perform?

By their very nature small island economies tend to be very open, as they need to import a large proportion of their consumption basket and their capital inputs. Therefore, they also need to export a significant portion of their national product in order to provide import finance on a sustainable basis. Barbados is no exception. With its 272,000 inhabitants and a GDP of US$2.8 billion in 2004, the so-called "openness ratio", i.e., the ratio of exports plus imports to GDP, reached an average of 109 percent in the period 1990–2002. This ratio is comparable to other Caribbean islands and much larger than the Latin American countries.[2] As discussed by Worrell et al. (2003), small size also limits export diversification, since the limited availability of skilled labour and resources only allows for the achievement of efficient scale in a few industries.

These features of small island economies impinge on policy design and, in particular, on the choice of an adequate exchange-rate regime. In the very small Caribbean island states—specifically Bahamas, Barbados and the members of the Organization of Eastern Caribbean States (OECS)—a peg to the US dollar is the preferred exchange-rate system. There are two important arguments supporting this choice. The first is that, owing to the geographic proximity to the United States, combined with the small size of the country, the direction of a significant proportion of trade, especially from the import side, to the United States is cost-effective. The second related argument is that the high level of trade openness of the islands might result in a significant pass-through from changes in foreign prices and the exchange-rate to the domestic inflation rate. A stable exchange-rate system, therefore, is a contributor to price stability and, therefore, to economic growth.

These two arguments supporting an exchange-rate peg hold in the case of Barbados. With respect to the direction of trade, imports from the United States account for almost 45 percent of all imports, making the US the major import partner for Barbados (see Jessen and Vignoles in Chapter IV).

With respect to the issue of the pass-through, Bynoe-Mayers (1997) provides evidence of an important pass-through effect in a number of Caribbean countries.[3] Countries that have devalued have experienced high inflation with little effect on the real exchange-rate. By keeping a fixed-exchange-rate system since the 1970s, Barbados domestic inflation has been able to converge to the inflation in the United States. Figure I-1 provides evidence of the long-term convergence between inflation rates in Barbados and the United States. After a surge in inflation in the years 1973 and 1974, inflation in both countries has declined progres-

---

[2] The average value of the openness ratio for a sample of countries in Latin America and the Caribbean reaches 61%. Barbados' openness ratio is comparable to that of the following Caribbean economies: Trinidad and Tobago (93%), Jamaica (99%), St. Kitts and Nevis (103%), Dominica (108%), St. Vincent and the Grenadines (108%) and St. Lucia (125%).

[3] Thomas (1996) deals with this issue for the case of Jamaica.

sively and at the same pace.[4] Moreover, inflation rates tend to move together in the short term, as evidenced by the simple correlation analysis shown in Figure I-1.

Figure I-1. Yearly Inflation in Barbados and the United States*
(percent)

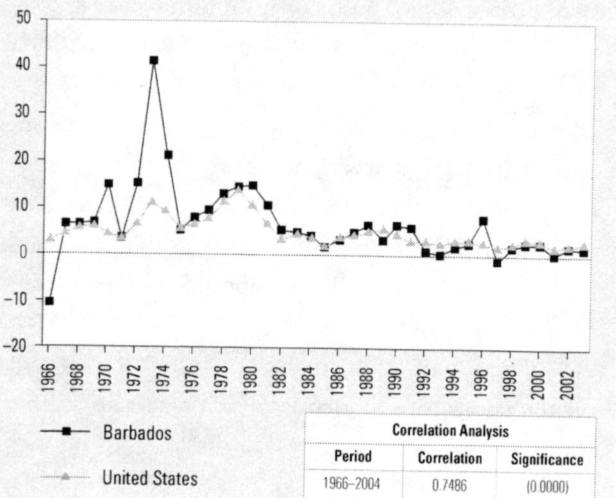

Correlation Analysis		
Period	Correlation	Significance
1966–2004	0.7486	(0.0000)
1976–2004	0.8943	(0.0000)
1980–2004	0.8674	(0.0000)

* Inflation in Barbados is corrected by variations in the nominal exchange rate, to better reflect Purchasing Power Parity.
Source: IMF, International Financial Statistics (October, 2005).

The advantages of a fixed-exchange-rate in Barbados, however, do not eliminate the risks associated with this system. As is well-known, a serious risk lies in a speculative attack against the domestic currency if investors deem the amount of foreign-exchange reserves relative to the outstanding obligations of the country to be insufficient. Barbados faced this risk during the balance-of-payments crisis of 1991. During this episode, foreign-exchange reserves declined significantly and a devaluation of the exchange-rate was avoided only through a comprehensive fiscal adjustment and the support of an IMF Stand-by Arrangement, complemented by a structural adjustment loan from the Inter-American Development Bank. While Barbados was able to keep its exchange-rate parity to the US dollar, this episode underlined the need to maintain at all times domestic policies conducive to exchange-rate stability.

Given the importance of exchange-rate stability for macroeconomic and financial soundness in a small open economy, a key issue to address is whether Barbados meets the necessary conditions for exchange-rate sustainability.

There are three key conditions for the sustainability of a fixed-exchange-rate system and, therefore, for macroeconomic stability in Barbados:[5] (a) a strong banking system;

[4] Regarding the performance of Barbados in the early 1970s, Downs (2001) notes that it "could be attributed to the world commodity shortage that brought significant increases in the prices of agriculture products and the 'oil crisis' of 1973–74 that resulted in the quadrupling of oil prices. The short-run macroeconomic consequence of the increase in international commodity prices was a reduction in domestic and foreign demand and hence a fall in aggregate domestic production", pp. 8–9.

[5] These conditions are further discussed in Rojas-Suárez (2003).

Table I-1. Key Indicators of Banking System Strength in Barbados

	2001	2002	2003	2004
Capital Adequacy Ratio (Indigenous Banks)	18.2	18.8	25.0	17.9
Non-performing Loans/Total Loans	5.0	7.9	9.3	7.5
Loan Loss Provisions/Assets	1.3	0.9	1.2	0.9
Return on Assets	2.2	2.7	2.0	2.2
Foreign Currency Deposits/Total Deposits	1.9	5.8	4.1	6.6

Sources: IMF (2005) and Central Bank of Barbados.

(b) the absence of public-sector debt problems; and (c) a sufficient accumulation of liquidity both by the government and the banking system.

The three conditions are linked by a common thread: the need to avoid pressures on the balance of payments and the exchange-rate arising from adverse external shocks, whether in the form of a reversal in capital inflows or an adverse shock to the terms of trade.

Bank Strength and Exchange-Rate Stability

The adverse effects on macroeconomic stability and growth derived from the high volatility of capital flows to Latin American and Caribbean countries are well documented.[6] Also well established is the fact that a weak banking system can drastically reduce a government's ability to defend its exchange-rate parity following a sudden reversal of capital inflows and the consequent pressures on the balance of payments. The fundamental reason is that defending the exchange-rate from a speculative attack on the currency usually requires increases in interest rates, which in turn can contribute to further deterioration of an already weak banking system. So, in the presence of an adverse external shock to the balance of payments, a weak banking system might force governments to face a policy dilemma—a choice between keeping a stable currency and preventing a banking crisis. In contrast, a strong banking system would be more resilient to changes in exchange-rates and interest rates, allowing greater flexibility for policy action.

An analysis of the Barbadian banking system shows that the strength of the banks is compatible with exchange-rate and macroeconomic stability. A number of financial soundness indicators presented in Table I-1 show that banks are well positioned to deal with potential adverse shocks. As shown in the table, capitalization ratios for the locally incorporated banks are very high, and banks display healthy profitability (as indicated by the return-to-assets ratio). Moreover, at less than 7 percent, the ratio of foreign currency deposits to total deposits implies that banks' currency exposures are very limited.

[6] See, for example, IDB (1995).

Table I-2. Barbados and Other Caribbean Economies: Non-performing Loans as a Share of Total Loans
(percent)

	2001	2002	2003	2004
Barbados (end-period)	5.0	7.9	9.3	7.5
ECCU (end-period)	13.1	13.7	13.9	12.0
Guyana (end-period)	38.2	37.2	23.3	18.8
Jamaica[1]	9.6	8.0	4.9	3.9
Trinidad and Tobago (end-period)	3.4	3.8	2.0	—

Source: IMF (2005).

[1] Fiscal year ending March 31.

In addition, the ratio of non-performing loans to loans has declined during 2004 and, as noted by Chase et al. (2005) this ratio and that on loan loss provisioning are on par with those in other emerging markets. Indeed, as shown in Table I-2, the ratio of non-performing loans to loans in Barbados is lower than that in a number of other Caribbean countries, including Guyana and the countries in the OECS. However, Jamaica and Trinidad and Tobago outperform Barbados on the basis of this indicator.

Finally, the results from the stress tests conducted by Chase et al. (2005) confirm that the Barbadian banking system can withstand significant adverse external shocks. For example, in their calculations, a 15-percent drop in tourism receipts will increase the ratio of non-performing loans by 2 percentage points but will leave the system highly capitalized and still profitable. Similarly, if the shock were to translate into important balance-of-payments pressures, the authorities would be able to increase domestic interest rates to defend the exchange-rate parity without fear of inducing severe financial disturbances in the banking system.

Debt Sustainability

As the many experiences of debt-cum-exchange-rate crises in emerging markets demonstrate, high government debt ratios work against macroeconomic stability, especially in fixed-exchange-rate regimes.[7] The problem is that if a country faces a large stock of debt, then an adverse external shock, such as a significant increase in the US interest rates, would require the government to increase the transfer of resources abroad in order to meet debt-service obligations on a timely basis. To the extent that these larger outflows of financial resources translate into a decrease in international reserves, pressures on the exchange-rate may ensue.

[7] In the Latin America and the Caribbean region, examples of unsustainable public debts leading to exchange-rate crisis abound, e.g., in Mexico (1982), Ecuador (2000) and Argentina (2001–02).

This problem cannot be alleviated by placing part of the debt in the domestic market. The reason is that, under a fixed-exchange-rate system without stringent capital controls, increases in the foreign interest rate also lead to increases in domestic rates (through the well-known interest-parity condition) and, therefore, to higher cost for servicing the domestic debt. Unless the net government expenditure is adjusted, higher interest payments on the public debt will further fuel the fiscal deficit increasing the government's financing needs. As investors' perceptions regarding the sustainability of the fiscal stance become less favourable, pressures on the exchange-rate are exacerbated.

In contrast to the situation in the banking system, Barbados does not score very well on public-debt ratios. In order to help the economy recover from the economic recession of 2001–2002, the government implemented an expansionary fiscal policy that has resulted in significant fiscal deficits and a growing debt-to-GDP ratio. As Figure I-2 demonstrates, by end-2004, Barbados' total public-debt ratio significantly exceeded the average for Latin America and Caribbean countries as well as for emerging markets.

Figure I-2. Public-Debt Ratios in Barbados and Selected Areas
(percent of GDP)[1]

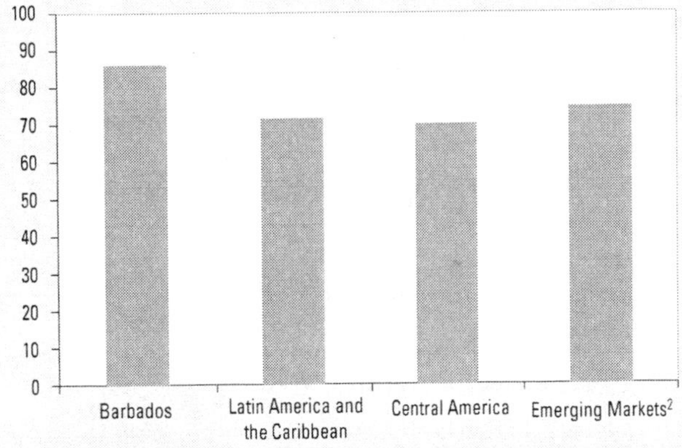

Source: IMF (2005).
[1] Figures refer to unweighted averages. Data for Barbados refer to end-year figures for FY 2004/05. Entire sample comprises 24 countries for Latin America and the Caribbean.
[2] Refers to 2003 data for 25 countries from the IMF Fiscal Affairs Department's emerging markets database.

At current levels and under the authorities' fiscal targets, public debt in Barbados is still sustainable. Two factors are contributing: The first is that the recent rebound in economic activity, projected to continue in 2005–06 supported by public and private investment towards the cricket World Cup in 2007, can certainly help to improve Barbados debt ratios. The second is that the authorities have expressed their intention to gradually adjust the fiscal stance, and have in fact reduced the fiscal deficit to its target level of 2.5 percent of GDP.

Notwithstanding these qualifications, an important caveat is in order: The current high debt ratios do impose a vulnerability on the Barbadian exchange-rate system that needs to be dealt with sooner rather than later. As experience in many emerging markets with high debt ratios has demonstrated over and over again, an unanticipated adverse shock can quickly turn a sustainable debt position into an unsustainable one. An important market signal to take into account is Standard and Poors' downgrade of Barbados' external credit ratings in August 2004 when ratings for both domestic and external debts were lowered.

Liquidity as an "Absorber" for External Shocks

In the absence of the "shock absorber" function of flexible exchange-rates, access to large amounts of liquidity denominated in foreign currencies provides a credible mechanism to defend a fixed-exchange-rate system in the presence of adverse shocks. While foreign-exchange reserves constitute the most important form of liquidity for exchange-rate stability, the access of private banks to external sources of liquidity can also significantly contribute to the stability of the exchange-rate peg.

The assessment of the Barbados situation with regard to this issue is not very encouraging. As a result of an expansionary monetary stance in 2003–04, the stock of official reserves declined significantly in 2004, and is projected to decline further in 2005. According to a recent IMF report, under a *baseline* (passive policy) scenario, gross international reserves could slide to only 2.9 months of imports coverage in 2005, a sharp decline from the almost six months of coverage achieved in the period 2002–03. Moreover, two classic indicators of exchange-rate vulnerability–the ratio of broad money to reserves and the ratio of gross official reserves to short-term external debt–show signs of deterioration as displayed in Figure I-3. The first indicator gives a sense of exchange-rate vulnerability to a run against the currency. Clearly, the higher the ratio, the higher the vulnerability since the stock of local money that can be used to buy US dollars from the Central Bank

Figure I-3. Indicators of External Vulnerability (*percent*)

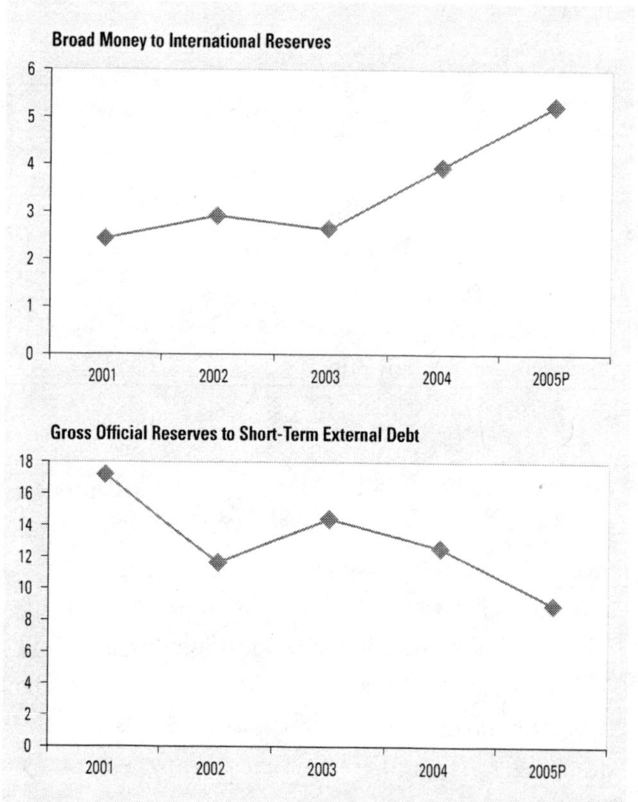

Source: IMF (2005).
Note: P = projected.

is larger. As shown in the chart, the deterioration in this ratio was significant and the ratio was projected to reach in 2005 a value twice as high as that achieved in 2001. The second indicator provides a signal of the country's capacity to rollover existing short-term external debt. Data on the recent evolution of this indicator do not provide a positive outlook since the ratio is projected to almost halve in 2005 relative to its value in 2001.

Good news comes, however, from the domestic private banking system. Because of the dominant participation of foreign banks in Barbados, one may reasonably expect that local branches and subsidiaries have, at least to a certain degree, access to credit lines in foreign currency from their parent institutions. To the extent that foreign banks perceive that local branches do not face a solvency problem in the presence of balance-of-payments pressures, to that extent foreign-currency liquidity might continue to be available to Barbadian banks, helping to mitigate the loss of official international reserves.

So, what can we conclude from the analysis so far? At the time of this writing, financial indicators do not point to severe pressures on the exchange-rate, but yield mixed results. While the sound banking system strongly supports macro and exchange-rate stability, public-debt and foreign-liquidity ratios show recent deterioration worth noting. As discussed in the introduction, macroeconomic stability is one of the pillars for sustained economic growth in Barbados. Maximizing the credibility of the chosen exchange-rate system is, therefore, imperative. Regaining the previous, more favourable international credit ratings for Barbados' external debt and rebuilding the stock of international reserves can only support the efforts of the authorities to encourage the private-sector investments (domestic and foreign) needed for growth.

We now turn to the second pillar for economic growth: improved competitiveness.

C. The Competitiveness Challenge: Institutions and Markets

As discussed in the introduction, achieving sustained and high rates of growth in Barbados requires, in addition to macroeconomic stability, important improvements in the country's capacity to compete in a more liberalized global environment. This is now more important than ever given the trend towards declining preferential trade treatment.

In a fixed-exchange-rate economy such as Barbados, international competitive advantages cannot be obtained through changes in the *nominal* exchange-rate. Instead, the major sources of competitive gains are:

(i) strong, efficient institutions that support the workings of the markets and, therefore, encourage a good investment climate;
(ii) adequate functioning of labor markets; and
(iii) improved productivity in sectors with the potential to compete internationally.

All these factors can contribute to an improvement in the equilibrium *real exchange-rate* (the relative price of tradable to non-tradable goods), the summary statistic for assessing competitiveness.

Institutions for Growth: Strengths and Deficiencies

By establishing the *rules of the game* determining the interaction between economic agents, economic and political institutions determine a country's capacity to use its resources effectively and productively. Indeed, sound institutions lie at the foundation of growth. As discussed by Clive Thomas in the next chapter, recent advances in the literature have produced a number of indices that attempt to measure different aspects of a country's institutional quality. Two of the most well-known sets of indices, the Governance Indicators identified by Kaufmann, Kraay and Mastruzzi (2005) and the Heritage Foundation/Wall Street Journal Index of Economic Freedom (Miles, Feulner and O'Grady, 2005) complement each other effectively. The former assess the quality of governance, defined as: "the traditions and institutions by which authority in a country is exercised for the common good"(Kaufmann, 2005).[8] The latter set of indices measure the degree of government interference in the activities of the market economy.[9]

Based on these two sets of indicators, Tables I-3 and I-4 compare the quality of institutions in Barbados over the last decade and the country's performance relative to that in other emerging market groups and in industrial countries. In both tables the first rows present the actual scores obtained for every indicator, while the last four rows show the differences in scores between Barbados and selected areas of the world.

The overall message from Table I-3 is that Barbados is a strong performer worldwide in terms of governance. The scores presented in the first five rows of the table range from –2.5 to +2.5, with higher values denoting better performance. By 2004, Barbados' performance surpassed the average of Latin American and Caribbean countries and emerging markets economies in *all* governance indicators. Barbados particularly stands out in *political stability* and *rule of law*, where the difference in scores with the emerging markets group is very large.

---

[8] According to their authors, the governance indicators can be grouped into three dimensions: The political dimension includes the process by which authorities are selected, monitored, and replaced; the indicators of *voice and accountability* and *political stability* belong to this dimension. The economic dimension refers to the government's capacity to manage its resources effectively, and to implement sound policies; the indicators of *government effectiveness* and *regulatory quality* belong to this dimension. Finally, the institutional respect dimension refers to the respect of citizens and the state for the country's institutions; the indicators of *rule of law* and *control of corruption* belong to this category. See Kaufmann (2005).

[9] Economic freedom is defined as "the absence of government coercion or constraints on the production, distribution, or consumption of goods and services beyond the extent necessary for citizens to protect and maintain liberty itself" (Miles et al., p. 58).

Table I-3. World Bank Governance Indicators[1]
(scores)

	Voice and Accountability		Regulatory Quality		Rule of Law		Political Stability		Government Effectiveness		Control of Corruption	
	1996	2004	1996	2004	1996	2004	2002[2]	2004	2002[2]	2004	2002[2]	2004
Barbados	1.23	1.17	0.36	0.91	−0.28	1.21	0.82	1.52	1.30	1.18	1.29	0.81
Caribbean	0.78	0.65	−0.04	0.29	−0.09	0.32	0.27	0.60	0.11	0.13	0.24	0.20
Latin America and the Caribbean	0.39	0.40	0.25	0.15	−0.17	−0.05	0.02	0.11	−0.14	−0.08	−0.07	−0.03
Emerging Markets	−0.01	0.00	0.26	0.07	−0.01	−0.10	−0.06	−0.20	0.04	0.07	−0.14	−0.12
Industrial Countries	1.48	1.34	1.38	1.45	1.74	1.62	1.15	1.08	1.80	1.69	1.80	1.84
Differences in scores between Barbados and:[3]												
Caribbean	0.45	0.52	0.41	0.63	−0.20	0.89	0.55	0.92	1.19	1.05	1.05	0.62
Latin America and the Caribbean	0.84	0.77	0.12	0.76	−0.12	1.26	0.80	1.41	1.45	1.26	1.36	0.85
Emerging Markets	1.24	1.17	0.10	0.84	−0.27	1.31	0.87	1.71	1.27	1.11	1.43	0.93
Industrial Countries	−0.25	−0.17	−1.01	−0.54	−2.02	−0.42	−0.33	0.44	−0.49	−0.51	−0.51	−1.02

Source: Kaufmann, Kraay and Mastruzzi (2005).

[1] Scores are expressed on a −2.5 to 2.5 scale, where higher scores mean better performance.

[2] Data for Barbados were not available for 1996. Figures for Barbados and all country groups are for 2002.

[3] Difference = Barbados score − area score. A positive difference implies Barbados performs relatively better.

As a result of Barbados' achievements in the quality of governance, the gap with industrial countries is not very large as is demonstrated by the relatively small difference in most scores. Indeed, and quite impressively, the score for the indicator on political stability outperforms that for the average of industrial countries.

On a less positive note, however, the gap between Barbados and industrial countries for the indicator of control of corruption is large and increasing. (The score for Barbados declined from 1.29 in 2002 to 0.81 in 2004.). However, a caveat with respect to this result is in order. A more detailed reading of the methodology shows that the standard error of the statistical estimation of the indicator is twice as large for Barbados as the one for all the countries in the sample (0.34 in Barbados compared to 0.19 for the entire sample) which, of course, reduces the accuracy of the indicator.[10] Indeed, an alternative measure of perceptions of corruption, the Transparency International Corruption Index ranks Barbados in

[10] The indicators are estimated using an unobserved components model (see Kaufmann, Kraay and Zoido-Lobatón (1999) for a fully detailed explanation of their methodology). For the purpose of this paper, it is enough to note that the authors condense information coming from a wide array of individual sources, assuming that they are different measures of the same concept (in this case, Corruption). Unfortunately, sources of information for Barbados are few when compared to other countries. The precision of the estimation is positively related to the quantity of information available; i.e., errors become larger when the number of sources is reduced.

the 24th position out of 159 countries in 2005, signaling Barbados' strong position in this area as well.

Leaving aside the deterioration in the indicator of control of corruption, the other governance indicators in Barbados have either remained relatively stable in the period 1996–2004 or significantly improved. The sharp improvement in the indicator of rule of law from –0.28 to 1.21 testifies for the country's capacity to improve performance in a short period of time.

Table I-4 presents the overall Heritage Foundation/Wall Street Journal Index of Economic Freedom and six of its components. The scores rank from 1 to 5, with 1 signifying an economic environment or set of policies most conducive to economic freedom, while a score of 5 signifies a set of policies that are least conducive to economic freedom.

While, on an overall basis, the Index of Economic Freedom places Barbados' performance above the average for emerging market economies, a more detailed analysis of the index components reveals mixed results. Consistent with the soundness of the governance indicators discussed above, the country's performance on the indicators of *property rights* and *regulation* was excellent in 2005 (better than those of all categories of developing countries and at par with those of industrial countries). Most importantly, the significant improvement of the country's performance since 1996 is what accounts for the elimination of the gap with industrial countries.[11]

Also, because of its strong banking system (see Section B above), Barbados is very well positioned among emerging markets in the *banking and finance* indicator. With a score of 2, the country enjoys a favorable position relative to emerging market countries in Latin America and elsewhere, and is very close to the standards of industrial countries. Likewise, the authorities' commitment to support a market-based economy has given Barbados a strong score in the area of *informal markets* and has placed the country above the average of emerging market economies. Of significant importance is the sharp improvement recorded by Barbados in this indicator: from 1996 to 2005, the score halved from 4 to 2.

In contrast, Barbados ranks poorly in the indicators of *fiscal burden* and *government intervention.* With a score of 4.5 in both indicators, the country performs worse than the average of all categories of developing countries considered in the table. This outcome leads to two conclusions. The first is that the results are consistent with the deterioration in the fiscal accounts discussed in Section B and with the need to correct macroeconomic disequilibria as a precondition to the fostering of economic growth. The second is that the results point to the existence of institutional weaknesses in the public sector, an issue stressed by Thomas in Chapter II.

---

[11] In fact, in 2005, the difference in scores between Barbados and the average of industrial countries has taken a negative value for these two variables, indicating that Barbados has outperformed some industrial countries.

Table I-4. Index of Economic Freedom Components[1]
(scores)

	Index of Economic Freedom		Fiscal Burden		Government Intervention		Banking		Property Rights		Regulation		Informal Market	
	1996	2005	1996	2005	1996	2005	1996	2005	1996	2005	1996	2005	1996	2005
Barbados	3.20	2.40	4.50	4.50	5.00	4.50	2.00	2.00	3.00	1.00	3.00	2.00	4.00	2.00
Caribbean	3.23	3.06	3.79	3.87	3.44	2.50	2.88	2.71	2.50	2.86	3.13	3.43	3.63	3.57
Latin America and the Caribbean	3.14	3.04	3.52	3.47	2.71	2.56	2.65	2.64	2.81	3.32	3.31	3.44	3.69	3.56
Emerging Markets	3.20	3.00	3.87	3.33	3.00	2.62	2.73	2.84	2.73	3.32	3.23	3.38	3.54	3.44
Industrial Countries	2.20	2.02	4.18	3.64	2.66	2.50	2.14	1.78	1.36	1.22	2.55	2.48	1.36	1.41
Differences in scores between Barbados and:[2]														
Caribbean	−0.02	−0.66	0.71	0.63	1.56	2.00	−0.88	−0.71	0.50	−1.86	−0.13	−1.43	0.38	−1.57
Latin America and the Caribbean	0.06	−0.64	0.98	1.03	2.29	1.94	−0.65	−0.64	0.19	−2.32	−0.31	−1.44	0.31	−1.56
Emerging Markets	0.00	−0.60	0.63	1.17	2.00	1.88	−0.73	−0.84	0.27	−2.32	−0.23	−1.38	0.46	−1.44
Industrial Countries	1.00	0.38	0.32	0.86	2.34	2.00	−0.14	0.22	1.64	−0.22	0.45	−0.48	2.64	0.59

Source: Miles, Feulner, and O'Grady (2005).

1 The Index of Economic Freedom is the simple average of 10 individual components, of which only 6 are shown in the table. Scores for each individual component range from 1 to 5. A score of 1 signifies an economic environment or set of policies that are most conducive to economic freedom, while a score of 5 signifies a set of policies that are least conducive to economic freedom.

2 Difference = Barbados score − area score. Thus, a negative difference implies that Barbados performs relatively better.

In his comprehensive diagnostic analysis for improved competitiveness in Barbados, Thomas identifies deficiencies in public-sector management as an important constraint on the maximization of firms' performance and competitiveness. For example, based on a recent World Bank survey, customs delays and weak administration were assessed as important factors impinging on foreign investors' perceptions of the business climate. Moreover, the potential for the improved competitiveness of small and medium-sized enterprises (SMEs) is curtailed by limitations in the operations of institutions and other business-development services run by the Government. An important insight advanced by Thomas is that, in a number of cases, an important Government consideration for supporting SMEs has been the sector's potential for generating jobs. Thomas' concern is that this consideration resembles a "welfare-oriented" view of the SME sector rather than the vision of a dynamic, pro-growth sector acting as an incubator for the development of sound businesses.

Thomas identifies some other institutional features that need improvement in order to provide a more favourable business environment for SMEs. A lack of entrepreneurial/business skills is identified as a major weakness in Barbados. So is inadequate access to formal sources of financing. Investment and business planning is also hindered by insufficient survey and other data. In general, there is a need to strengthen the provision of business-support services and training to promote small-business growth.

Additional insights on public-sector institutional constraints to competitiveness are presented by Weigel (2005). For example, long delays in obtaining titles to land and limitations in the ability to use land as collateral have been identified as barriers to private investment. Similarly, while the judicial system is identified as honest and fair (consistent with the results in the governance indicators), court decisions in commercial cases, especially foreclosures, are seen as extremely long. In addition, the tax system is seen as complex and opaque, acting as a discouraging factor for private sector investment. Finally, Weigel identifies the need to simplify what is now a very complicated government structure for investment promotion and to review the assumptions about the effectiveness of tax incentives in encouraging investment.

Improving the Labour Market to Enhance Competitiveness

Undoubtedly, one of Barbados' biggest strengths with regard to competing in a more liberalized global economy lies in the quality of its labour force. Its strong social indicators are the mirror image of this quality as good health and education conditions are key determinants of workers' capabilities. The HDI, a summary statistic of social and economic indicators, illustrates this point. Not only does Barbados rank 30th out of 177 countries in 2003, but, as Figure I-4 illustrates, its position has improved continuously over the last three decades.

A number of social indicators are displayed in Table I-5. Basic indicators related to health (life expectancy and attended births) and education (average years of schooling) show

Figure I-4. Barbados: Human Development Index

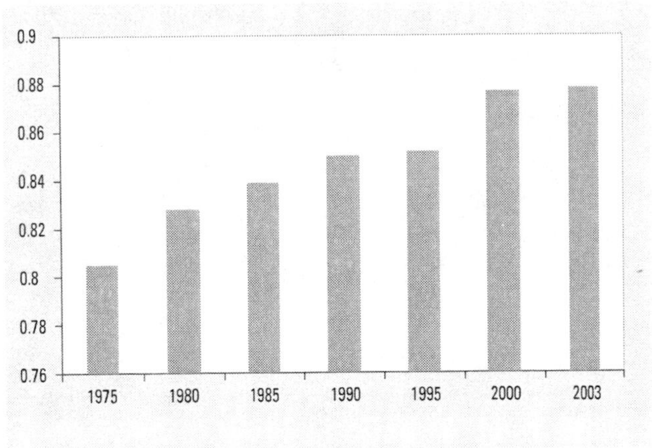

Source: UNDP, Human Development Report (2005).

Barbados to be better positioned than the average for emerging markets and close to the levels attained in industrial countries. One hundred percent of the population has access to basic services, such as water and sanitation (not shown in the table).

While the overall quality of the labour force is supported by the soundness of basic social indicators, Barbados' employment performance reveals important deficiencies. Table I-5 shows three social indicators related to employment. The percentage of labour force with tertiary education only reaches 12.4 percent, a much lower number than the average for emerging market countries and just half the percentage reached in industrial countries. Long-term unemployment, defined as the percentage of the unemployed population who have been out of work for a year or longer, reached 55 percent over the period 1990–2002. This ratio is the highest among the group of countries presented in the table. In addition, youth unemployment, a problem of similar dimensions in Barbados as in other Caribbean countries, reached an average of 30.5 percent in the period 1990–2002,

Table I-5. Social Indicators

	Life Expectancy (years)		Attended Births (% of total)	Average Years of Schooling[1]		Labour Force with Tertiary Education (% of total)	Total Youth Unemployment (% of labour force 14–24)	Long-Term Labour Unemployment[2]
	1990	2003	Average (1990–2003)	1990	2000	Average (1990–2001)	Average (1990–2002)	Average (1990–2002)
Barbados	74.9	74.8	95.5	7.9	8.7	12.5	30.3	55.3
Caribbean	69.4	70.9	90.6	5.7	6.2	9.3	30.3	42.1
Latin America and the Caribbean	68.8	71.2	83.9	5.5	6.2	13.4	22.3	30.7
Emerging Markets	68.0	70.0	80.2	6.1	6.6	17.9	20.3	31.9
Industrial Countries	76.2	78.8	99.4	9.0	9.6	24.7	13.8	32.0

Sources: WDI and Edstats; Barro-Lee data set (http://devdata.worldbank.org/edstats/td10.asp); International Labour Organization.

[1] Average years of schooling of adults (aged 15+) is the years of formal schooling received, on average, by adults over age 15.

[2] Long-term unemployment refers to the number of people with continuous periods of unemployment extending for a year or longer, expressed as a percentage of the total unemployed.

Table I-6. Barbados: Labour and Competitiveness Indicators

	Unemployment Rate (%)	Labour Productivity Index (1995 = 100)	Real Wage Index (1995 = 100)	Change in Real Unit Labour Cost (%)
1995	19.7	100.0	100.0	−1.7
1996	15.6	99.2	100.6	1.4
1997	14.5	102.2	99.0	−4.4
1998	12.3	105.3	104.3	2.3
1999	10.4	103.5	106.6	3.9
2000	9.3	103.3	108.3	1.7
2001	9.9	95.6	109.2	9.0
2002	10.3	96.9	112.5	1.7
2003	11.0	98.4	113.9	0.3

Source: Downes, Chapter III in this book.

ten percentage points higher than the average for emerging markets and more than twice as high as the average for industrial countries.

Why does Barbados, a country with otherwise strong social indicators, face these important employment problems? Chapter III by Andrew Downes provides answers, and advances recommendations for dealing with this issue. In his assessment of the labour market, Downes shows that labour productivity has been declining while real wage rates have been increasing. The combination of these two factors has resulted in an increase in real unit labour costs, a loss in Barbados competitiveness on the international markets and the persistence of unemployment.

In addition to the disconnection between labour productivity growth and real wage growth at the aggregate level, Downes identifies a number of problems adversely affecting both employment and competitiveness. For example, there is a mismatch between the years of schooling and the ability of workers to participate in the labour force since a significant proportion of the adult population does not have any form of certification. Moreover, there is a need for better coordination between the skill mix demanded by economic activities in Barbados and the training provided by the educational system. Downes identifies these as signs of dysfunction in the Barbados educational system. An additional problem is that labour-market regulations have created non-wage labour costs that undermine the competitiveness of goods and services.

Some of Downes' main recommendations for improving competitiveness and employment are to:

(i) promote the use of performance-based pay;

(ii) rationalize the use of severance payments and unemployment insurance funds to avoid "double dipping" and to reduce excessive non-labour costs that hurt firms' competitiveness;

(iii) increase the funding of training in new skill areas and in supervisory management;
(iv) improve the labour-market information system to better connect demand for and supply of labour; and
(v) speed the process of labour legislation with the objective of increasing the flexibility of the labour market while providing necessary social safety nets.

But even if Barbados improves its macroeconomic fundamentals, strengthens institutions where needed and improves the functioning of its labour markets, meeting the country's competitive challenge requires revisiting the performance of its export sector and encouraging appropriate diversification. The latter issue is the subject of analysis in the remainder of Section C.

Enhancing and Diversifying Exports in Key Sectors

Exports are, and need to be, the engine of growth in Barbados. As argued in Section B, the structural features of a small open economy like Barbados require a very dynamic export sector capable of creating jobs and providing resources to import essential goods and services for consumption and investment.

However, as a result of the competitiveness problems discussed throughout this chapter, the recent behaviour of exports has not been encouraging. Tourism receipts, the main source of external revenues in Barbados, have been growing at a moderate pace averaging 4 percent per year since the early 1990s. Also, as indicated in a recent IMF paper (IMF, 2005), Barbados' shares of both tourism arrivals and expenditures in the Caribbean have been declining. These developments combined with a stagnant merchandise export sector have resulted in a significant deterioration of the current account balance. From a position of surplus in the early and mid-1990s, the current account turned into widening deficits, which reached 10.5 percent of GDP in 2004.

A comprehensive analysis of the trade sector in Barbados is undertaken by Jessen and Vignoles in Chapter IV of this book. The authors point to a high concentration in merchandise exports: In the period 1999–2002 the top 20 products exported—led by sugar and spirits—accounted for 75 percent of the value of total exports. This high concentration of exports makes the country quite vulnerable to external shocks. And, indeed, the country is currently facing a severe adverse shock in the form of the phasing out of preferential treatment in the European market with respect to its main merchandise export products, especially sugar. As the study by Chesney in this book shows, the loss of this preference undermines the long-term viability of the sugar industry in Barbados given the high production costs that render this sector uncompetitive. Moreover, while the paper by Chesney advances a number of recommendations for improving the performance of the agricultural sector, including alternative ways of utilization of sugar, it is highly unlikely that agricultural products can become "champion exports" for Barbados.

How, then, can the country achieve much needed export diversification? Small size does limit the range of diversification that is possible in a small island economy. Nonetheless, efforts are needed to explore fully the potential scope to diversify within existing sectors that have been key sources of exports and to develop a few new sectors with the potential of becoming new sources of exports.

Several of the authors in this book (Jessen and Vignoles, Thomas, and Poon) agree that the potential for export diversification lies in the service sector. Significant diversification of products can be achieved within the already well-established tourism sector. As Poon (Chapter V) points out, maintaining the focus on the traditional provision of "sun, sand and sea," is not enough. Poon identifies the potential for developing the health, wellness and honeymoon markets as sources for future growth and enhancement of the tourism sector. Exploiting those niches, however, requires improvements in complementary infrastructure, such as hospitals, health facilities and spas. Most importantly, improving competitiveness in the tourism sector implies keeping operating costs down. As Poon indicates Barbados does not get high scores among visitors and tour operators in the area of "value for money." The Dominican Republic, Mexico and Jamaica stand as strong competitors offering high-value products at lower prices. These issues, of course, relate to the deficiencies in the labor market discussed above.

Another prominent possibility for export diversification within the services sector is the development of the information and communications technology (ICT) sector. As Thomas indicates in Chapter II, the Government of Barbados has the vision of making the country "the centre of excellence for ICT in the Caribbean." Table I-7 highlights some indicators of technological development. Perhaps the largest advance by Barbados relative to other Caribbean countries is in the much lower Internet cost, which approaches the cost in industrialized countries. The use of Internet lines and the availability of telephone mainlines have also grown faster in Barbados than in the Caribbean region as a whole. As Thomas notes, however, Barbados still has a lot of ground to make up to become a world-class ICT country. An important immediate step the country needs to take is the development of an adequate database for measuring and tracking ICT usage and performance.

Thus, Barbados faces a mixture of favourable prospects and major challenges in a changing international economic environment. Urgent action is needed to accelerate the pace of growth to raise living standards and curb vulnerability. On the face of performance in recent decades, Barbados' main prospects evidently lie in the growth of its service sectors. Barbados needs to do all that is necessary to strengthen the competitiveness of its lead tourism sector as the core that will spin off other business activities in both the service and merchandise sectors (such as entertainment, on one hand, and food and beverages on the other). It also has a good track record of growth in the off-shore financial sector to build on,

Table I-7. Indicators of Technological Development

	Internet Cost (US$ per 20 hours of use)	Internet Users (per 1,000 people)		Personal Computers (per 1,000 people)		Telephone Mainlines (per 1,000 people)	
	2003	1996–97	2002–03	1996–97	2002–03	1996–97	2002–03
Barbados	25.90	5.7	241.2	64.1	104.1	386.2	495.6
Caribbean	33.83	10.2	144.7	42.1	108.6	225.8	275.5
Latin America and the Caribbean	31.66	7.0	104.0	30.8	77.0	160.8	196.7
Emerging Markets	24.85	9.1	128.9	37.3	95.3	156.5	195.9
Industrial Countries	21.03	90.0	426.1	241.5	435.1	544.3	587.6

Source: International Telecommunication Union's World Telecommunication Development Report database.

and good prospects with respect to other business and professional services. The country has good experience with diversification, having shifted dramatically, and with good results, from an economy based on sugar production up until the 1960s to a tourism-based economy today. Its high level of human capital development through education and training provides a fertile resource to support diversification and growth, provided the proper steps are taken to promote appropriate macroeconomic, institutional and investment conditions.

D. Some Conclusions—and a "Preview" of the Book

The discussion in this introductory chapter has focused on the different dimensions of the competitiveness challenge in Barbados. Two main conclusions flow from this analysis. The first is that a variety of indicators point to the need for prompt corrective actions to be taken to contain and reverse the losses that Barbados has been suffering in its competitiveness losses in the international economy. The second is that Barbados is well positioned to meet all facets of the problem.

Its strong institutional framework, particularly in the key area of governance, combined with its sound social indicators, places it "ahead of the pack" among emerging market economies in terms of the ability to implement necessary reforms. An additional factor supporting the country's capacity to deal with outstanding issues is the maintenance of a tripartite social contract involving government, labour and the private sector. By institutionalizing consensus building, this social contract provides a central tool for advancing policy changes needed to improve the country's competitiveness.

In the rest of the book, experts on the competitiveness issues in Barbados discuss at length the different aspects of the subject and advance specific proposals and recommendations. The book follows roughly a sequence in which the overarching macroeconomic and institutional aspects relating to stability, productivity and international trade conditions are presented, followed by an examination of practical challenges in the area of tourism and by an annex that explores some public-policy issues as they relate to the agricultural sector.

In Chapter II, Thomas provides a comprehensive assessment and diagnostic of the competitiveness issues facing the country. His wide-ranging analysis provides an umbrella for the more specific areas of discussion in the ensuing chapters. In Chapter III, Downes tackles the issues of labour-market conditions and reform that are fundamental aspects of the competitiveness effort. In Chapter IV, Jessen and Vignoles address another area of fundamental importance, especially in the context of a small open economy, that is, prevailing performance and conditions, and imminent changes, with respect to international trade and their implications for Barbados. Finally, Chapter V examines the prospects for the tourism sector, and presents proposals for raising competitiveness and diversifying the attractions and activities within the sector. And, as already noted, the annex looks at some public-policy issues from the perspective of the Barbados experience in the agriculture sector.

It is our hope that the rich content of all these papers will serve not only to shed light on Barbados' quest to meet the challenges of an increasingly open global economy. We hope they will also generate policy discussions in other small countries facing similar challenges.

References

Bynoe-Mayers, Nola, 1997, *Measuring the Real Exchange-Rate Using GDP Deflators*, Central Bank of Barbados Economic Review, June.

Chase, Karen, Kevin Greenidge, Winston Moore and DeLisle Worrell, 2005, *Quantitative Assessment of a Financial System—Barbados*, IMF Working paper WP/05/76, International Monetary Fund, Washington, D.C., April.

Downes, Andrew, 2001, *Economic Growth in a Small Developing Country: The Case of Barbados*, paper presented as part of the GDN/LACEA project on Economic Growth in Latin America and the Caribbean, September.

Inter-American Development Bank, 1995, *Economic and Social Progress in Latin America: Overcoming Volatility*, Washington, D.C.

International Monetary Fund, 2005, *Barbados: 2005 Article IV Consultation—Staff Report; and Public Information Notice on the Executive Board Discussion*, Washington D.C. August.

Kaufmann, Daniel, 2005, *Myths and Realities of Governance and Corruption in the World*, in Economic Forum Global Competitiveness Report 2005–06, chapter 2.1.

Kaufmann, Daniel, A. Kraay, and M. Mastruzzi, 2005, *Governance Matters IV: Governance Indicators for 1996–2004*, World Bank, Washington, D.C.

Kaufmann, D., A. Kraay, and P. Zoido-Lobatón, 1999, *Aggregating Governance Indicators*, World Bank Policy Research Working Paper 2195, October.

Miles, Marc A., Edwin J. Feulner and Mary Anastasia O'Grady, 2005, *2005 Index of Economic Freedom: The Link between Economic Opportunity and Prosperity.*

Rojas-Suárez, Liliana, 2003, *What Exchange-Rate System Works Best in Latin America*, in The Dollarization Debate, edited by James Dean and Dominick Salvatore, Oxford University Press.

Sahay, Ratna, *Stabilization, Debt, and Fiscal Policy in the Caribbean, 2005*, IMF Working Paper, WP/05/26, Washington D.C., February.

Thomas, Desmond, 1996, *Estimating a Monetary Model of Inflation Determination in Jamaica*, Trent University, Working Paper 96–01, Ontario, Canada, February.

Weigel, Dale, 2005, *Barbados: Strategy to Support Private Sector Development*, mimeo, Washington, D.C.

Worrell, DeLisle, Harold Codrington, Roland Craigwell and Kevin Grenidge, 2003, *Economic Resilience with an Exchange-Rate Peg: The Barbados Experience, 1985–2000*, IMF Working Paper WP/03/168, Washington D.C., August.

CHAPTER II

Productivity and Competitiveness

Clive Y. Thomas

A. Introduction

This chapter provides a diagnostic assessment of competitiveness issues in Barbados along with recommendations for improved productivity and international competitiveness. The analysis has been framed against the background of both steady moderate growth and a reduction in employment over the period 1993–2000, which were interrupted by a major downturn in 2001–02. Positive growth resumed in 2003–04, and analysts have attributed this resumption to a major rebound in tourism combined with the underlying strength of the economy. The durability of the recent revival, however, is still uncertain as Barbados faces important challenges arising from external considerations as well as a number of domestic imperatives posed by population preferences. Overcoming these challenges requires marked improvements in competitiveness and productivity.

The remainder of this section introduces the theoretical issues centring on competitiveness, and reviews the debates over its meaning and relevance. It also outlines the perspective adopted in this chapter and indicates the different approaches taken in recent diagnostic assessments of competitiveness in the region. Section B identifies the main structural features of the economy, reviews the macroeconomic situation and outlook, and draws some broad diagnostic conclusions based on the foregoing. Section C offers a diagnostic assessment of Barbados' competitiveness performance and standing at the macro level, utilizing a number of indicators, which are grouped as global, country-specific, and "other". Section D then offers a diagnostic assessment of microeconomic considerations, focusing at the firm level on three major areas: 1) the investment climate, 2) the operation of small and medium-sized enterprises (SMEs), and 3) the ubiquitous importance for enterprise development of e-readiness and capability as summed up in the operations of the information and communications technology (ICT) sector. This selection was guided by concurrent assessments of tourism, agriculture and the labour market being undertaken in other chapters in this book. Finally, Section E presents conclusions and policy recommendations.

Meaning and Relevance of Competitiveness

Debate

There have been sharp differences in the literature over both the meaning and the assessment of the relevance of the notion of competitiveness when applied to national economies as distinct from firms/enterprises or even the sectors of a national economy. Some of these differences have been attributed to the origins of concerns over national competitiveness in business schools, where, it is claimed, the focus is on corporate strategic analysis in the "typical" context of zero-sum games or winner-take-all situations. Several economists have pointed out that, in contrast, synergies are obtained when national economies participate in global trade when compared to the situation that obtains when the participants are individual firms/enterprises. They add that these synergies have not been adequately captured in some of the formulations on national competitiveness. In neoclassical economics, particularly its theories of comparative advantage and economic growth, these different approaches seem to recall both age-old controversies, such as that between Adam Smith and the Mercantilists, and more recent ones arising from the emergence of the "new" endogenous growth theories.

Alongside such differences, there are other areas of contention. One that is important for our purpose is the effectiveness of different measures and indicators used to determine competitiveness. Disagreements exist over the use of price (exchange-rate, wage rate) versus non-price (productivity) indicators; hard data (objective time series) versus soft data (opinion surveys); economic indicators versus non-economic ones such as governance and institutions; aggregated data (exchange-rates, total factor productivity) versus disaggregated data (sectoral and individual firm measures) or macro versus micro evaluation; and broad (comprehensive) versus narrow (specific) measures. There are other derivative concerns related to comparability, such as the reliability of data sets; the weighting schema to be employed when aggregating component indicators; and the resultant problems of standardization of measures and indicators across countries and over time.

Approach

The approach to these concerns employed in this chapter has been guided by *four* considerations. First, while acknowledging the importance of the issues raised in these debates, we hold the view that, *empirically, the competitive circumstances facing Barbadian enterprises at the broad national level today are substantially different from, and far more urgent than, those in which many of the firms had in fact emerged a few decades ago*. In those early days, competitiveness issues both at the macro and the firm level were not treated as a matter of the highest priority. Given the then available means of transport and communications, the country's geographic location and its small market, it was felt that these factors constituted sufficient "natural" protection and "economic distance" to provide local firms/enterprises with significant comfort levels. Additionally, state protectionist policies supported local industry uncritically.

In today's environment however, economic distance has shrunk, protectionism has been drastically reduced, and market liberalization has proceeded at an unprecedented pace. Consequent changes in firm functions, structures, and operations have been profound. Technology, research and development (R&D), innovation, support services, competition for market share, and other best practices have become integral to the survival of firms/enterprises. As a result public policy focuses heavily on such considerations as innovation, product quality, support services, functionality, and portability. It also acknowledges the existence of "drivers of change" and the fact that lagging countries, sectors, firms and enterprises will lose ground both absolutely and relatively if their separate and collective performances do not improve.

Second, *Barbados has both to compete with other nations and to be internally competitive. This means creating the conditions/environment/framework/policies for its enterprises to be competitive, whether they operate locally or abroad, and for the country also to be able to attract investors who will produce for the domestic markets and/or for export.*

Third, *competitiveness concerns are considered to be comprehensive in scope, with productivity gains fundamental to the improvement of the welfare of Barbadians. These concerns encompass policies, programs, and actions that focus on relations/ linkages between investment, productivity, international insertion, economic growth, economic development and enterprise development.* The broad environment within which these activities occur would include:

- (i) the legal and regulatory framework [including trade agreements, competition policy, consumer protection, judicial process, property rights, taxation, ICT competitiveness, standards, government effectiveness and so on];
- (ii) firm/enterprise support organizations [private sector networks, government ministries];
- (iii) the macroeconomic situation and outlook; and
- (iv) finance and credit.

This approach recognizes, therefore, that:

> An economy is now understood to be more competitive where the business environment is conducive to the sustained growth of productivity and per capita income, in a context of integration into the world economy. (IADB, 2003, page 11)

This IADB 2003 document also expresses the view (formally adopted by the IADB) that "countries compete primarily with themselves to be more competitive".

Fourth, having adopted a broad approach that incorporates the multi-faceted nature of competitiveness issues, the chapter is further premised on the view that *the more indicators of competitiveness there are, the greater is the likelihood of satisfactorily assessing these issues with regard to Barbados.* From this perspective there is, and can be, no single definitive indicator or set of indicators of competitiveness. Indeed each indicator used in this chapter has its own limitations to which attention will be drawn when presenting them. Where appropriate and available, competitiveness indicators for Jamaica and Trinidad and Tobago are also provided for purposes of comparison. Both of these countries have recently had major diagnostic appraisals of their competitiveness and policy reviews supported by the IADB (Downes, 2005 and OTF Group Inc., 2004). At the regional level, there are as well two other studies, which have helped to inform this work. One is the Report of the Caribbean Trade and Investment Group (CTAG) 2001 and the other an IADB 2004 Report.

B. Context, Development, and Outlook

This section provides a review of the background, major developments, and outlook for the Barbadian economy.

Main Structural Features

Barbados is a small and very open economy heavily dependent on trade in goods and services as well as on foreign capital inflows (see Table II-1). Analytically, the main structural features of the economy reveal several reasons why there should be continued concerns about productivity and competitiveness. First, because of heavy dependence on exports, the performance of the export sector in a competitive global environment is critical to the overall performance of the economy. Second, the "strength" of the linkages between the export sector and domestic production structures is crucial, as it is through these linkages that broad-based development effects are transmitted with export expansion. Third, since independence, Barbados' colonial export structure has been substantially diversified. It has moved away from traditional agricultural exports, mainly sugar, and has developed services, mainly tourism and travel.

In particular, the decline of the sugar industry has been rapid. Starting in 1965, when it contributed as much as 20 percent of GDP, its share has been halved during each succeeding 10-year period, reaching a low of 2 percent of GDP by 2004. The services sector, which contributed 56 percent of GDP in 1965, however, increased to 74 percent by 2004, reflecting the expansion of travel and tourism. The share of the manufacturing sector has remained unchanged at 10 percent for most of this period, and was at 8 percent in 2004 (see Table II-1). Other services are being promoted as a replacement, for example off-shore finance, while the main product (tourism) is being configured to target the "high-end" of the regional and global tourism and travel markets:

> Our objective is to develop Barbados as an upscale destination, without the introduction of mass attractions like casino gambling or a variable exchange rate. (Ministry of Finance, 2002 as cited in ECLAC, 2003)

Additionally, the Green Paper on Tourism in Barbados states:

> The new legal and regulatory framework and policy being developed for tourism are designed to inter alia ... sell Barbados as a high quality destination, not only to visit but invest in. (Ministry of Tourism, 2001)

Fourth, Barbados' small size means the absence of a domestic capital-goods sector, domestic machinery and equipment producers, local basic raw materials suppliers, and strong manufacturing and food-processing sectors. Not fully appreciated, however, is the fact that the country's import dependence is as significant as its reliance on exports for directly providing jobs, sustaining economic well-being, and enhancing economic growth and development. In this regard, various measures of its "food import capacity ratio" reveal that the ratio of the value of food imports to food exports is 1.2; the ratio of food imports to total merchandise exports is 0.7; and, the ratio of food imports to the total exports of goods and services is 0.08. As a result of such high import dependence, the long-run trend towards the liberalization of trade (imports) is likely to increase competitive pressures on domestic producers. Further, it can be anticipated that these pressures will intensify over the near to medium term as Barbados is currently engaged in far-reaching external trade and financial negotiations in several theatres, including the World Trade Organization (WTO), the Free Trade Area of the Americas (FTAA), economic partnership arrangements with the EU under the Cotonou Agreement, and the formation of the CARICOM Single Market and Economy (CSME).

Fifth, when one combines the lumpiness and indivisibilities of economic and social infrastructure investments with the strong pressures on government resources to satisfy a multiplicity of pressing demands in all sectors, in the context of the limited absolute size of savings that can be generated from a small economy such as Barbados (GDP of US$2.8 billion at current prices in 2004), then, irrespective of its domestic savings ratio, inflows of foreign savings will continue to be essential if living standards are to be maintained and economic growth sustained. Over the past decade and a half, however, Barbados, like most other developing countries, has faced a situation of declining official development assistance (ODA) and has been forced to rely increasingly on foreign direct investment (FDI) as a source of foreign savings. Further, because of its income level, it has formally graduated from concessional lending by international agencies, and now sources government financing in the open market.

Sixth, owing to a number of reasons—political, cultural and economic and including as well other structurally induced considerations—government in Barbados has played a major role in guiding the performance of the economy. This is amply demonstrated in the seemingly strong consensus in favour of: (i) its responsibilities for promoting macroeconomic stability; (ii) its sectoral policies and programs (agriculture and tourism); and (iii) its cross-cutting efforts directed at improving economic performance through general cross-sectoral policies, whether they be export promotion or productivity and competitiveness-enhancement strategies, or its role in complementing areas of education, research promotion and institutional building.

Table II-1. Basic Indicators, 2005 or Most Recent Year

Indicator	Measure
Population (thousands)	272
Area (sq km)	431
Density (per sq km)	624
Annual Rate of Growth (%), 2003–04	3.2
HDI (2005 Report)	0.878
HDI Ranking (from 177 countries), 2005	30
Safe Water Access (%)	100
Adult Literacy (%)	100
Primary School Enrollment (%)	100
Average years of schooling	9
Gender Parity Index	100
Life Expectancy (years)	77
Pop. per Physician	749
Pop. per Hospital Bed	136
Telephone Subscribers (per hundred)	124
Revenue (per line, $US), 2001	1,380
Outgoing Traffic (minutes per subscriber)	625
Daily Newspapers (per thousand), 2001	200
Readers (per thousand), 2001	748
Television Sets (per thousand), 2001	325
Personal Computers (per hundred), 2005	13
GDP Per Capita ($US, PPP)	15,700
Unemployment (% of labour force)	9.6
Income Inequality (Gini coefficient)	39
Openness (%)	108
Pop. below Poverty Line (%)	13
Inflation (%), 2003–04	1.5

Sector (% of GDP)	1965	1975	1985	1995	2004
Sugar	20	10	5	2	2
Services	56	65	70	80	74
Manufacturing	10	10	10	10	8

Sources: Various official statistics and UNDP, World Bank, and CITU reports.

The government is also expected to be responsible for major capital projects to provide business, social and physical infrastructure in order to lower the cost of doing business as well as to provide the legal-regulatory-institutional-incentive framework within which economic activity takes place.

For a small developing country, Barbados has achieved impressive levels of social development and broad technological capability (see Table II-1). Its technological capability indicators of ICT infrastructure and access, and availability of computers and Internet are good for a developing country. In the UNDP's Human Development Report 2005, Barbados ranked 30 out of 177 countries and so is classed as a country that has achieved a high level of human development. Its performance in the areas of government effectiveness, rule-of-law, transparency and accountability, has been equally impressive in terms of global comparisons. (Some of these indicators will be presented in Section C.)

Barbados also has a strong international and regional reputation, and plays hosts to a number of important multilateral organizations and initiatives, such as the Caribbean Development Bank (CDB), the Caribbean Regional Negotiating Machinery (CRNM), CARICOM's CSME Unit. It has hosted the first Small Island Developing States (SIDS) Summit in 1994, with the SIDS+10 Summit taking place in Mauritius (2005).

The Green Paper on Social Policy in Barbados (Thomas 2002) identifies a number of institutional strengths for the country including:

- A long tradition of economic and social policy and planning as well as state activism on development issues, a tradition that is widely shared by all the significant political parties and social agents.
- A long tradition of political stability as reflected in the "seamless transfer of political power" after national elections, since its independence.
- A strong media network noted and respected for its "independent stance" and its consistent promotion of public education and dialogue on matters of national interest.
- A well-developed and well-informed network of civil organizations and interest groups, which has "played an important catalytic, advocacy and monitoring role" (Downes 2001).
- An extremely small and thus relatively inconsequential underground, illegal, parallel economy.
- A strong tradition of continuous and participatory review, adaptation, and re-engineering of economic and social policies and programs. Generous resort has been made to such time-tested modalities as public consultations, commissions of inquiry, and the formation of task forces.
- A unique tradition among developing countries of harmonious industrial relations founded on agreed protocols among the social partners (labour, business and government).[1]

[1] In 1993, a time of serious economic pressures, the three social partners—business, labour and government—after a considerable period of stress, formulated an exceptionally durable tripartite process with the establishment of

Despite these positive achievements, the structural challenges posed by the broader environment in which the economy functions should not be underestimated. The Uruguay Round/World Trade Organization (UR/WTO) liberalization has impacted the traditional export sector through the threat of imminent preference erosion and has affected domestic producers through competition from imports.[2] These pressures have been reinforced through regional commitments that Barbados has had to fulfill, for example, introducing the Common External Tariff (CET of CARICOM), en route to the formation of the CSME. As we saw, well before the UR/WTO process, diversification of exports had started with the development of travel and tourism. Notably, financial services were added later and these became the second largest and fastest growing sub-sector in the country's services exports. However, the OECD actions and measures on Harmful Tax Competition have interrupted the growth of this sector. Added to these pressures is the number of theatres in which external trade and financial negotiations are simultaneously taking place with the expectation of their finalization in the near to medium term.

These institutional factors apart, there are also immense challenges posed by globalization *per se*, especially in areas such as: 1) technology (especially education, training, skills-upgrading, transfer and adaptation); 2) the emergence of a new global division of labour, new patterns of consumption, and advanced production processes; 3) cultural impacts (especially those affecting behaviour and expectations); 4) the re-definition of the state (dismantling of its productive sectors and the growing importance of macroeconomic management and of its regulatory/supervisory/incentives roles); and 5) the re-configuration of enterprises and the re-definition of entrepreneurship and business leadership.

In all these areas, Barbados' enterprises—which are small, have limited comparative technology capability and are undercapitalized—face enormous challenges. The stresses therefore, which are being put on the human, technical, financial, organizational, and institutional capacities of the state are also being placed on private businesses and, for that matter, on civil society groups and the wider society.

---

the first Protocol on Prices and Incomes and the formation of a National Productivity Board. The latter became subsequently (1996) the National Productivity Council. Since 1993 there have been four Protocols [1993–1995; 1995–1997 (extended to 1998); 1998–2000 (extended to 2001); and 2001 to date]. Each succeeding Protocol has deepened the consultation process and introduced further activities aimed at enhancing competitiveness and productivity. Of note, the Second and Third Protocols covering the years 1995–1998 were both signed in periods of prosperity, so that the arrangement is not crisis-driven. The first Protocol focused on 1) maintaining parity of the currency, 2) securing growth through competitiveness and enhanced productivity, 3) wage restraint, and 4) economic restructuring. The second Protocol added price restraint along with public- and private-sector reform to improve competitiveness. The third Protocol further added support for a number of ILO Conventions. And, the fourth Protocol has sought to deepen all these processes.

The National Productivity Council is a statutory body financed by the Central Government with its directorate comprised of the Social Partners. The objective was to make it an autonomous self-financing body by the end of 2005.

[2] As we shall see, Barbados has sought to pursue a process of "controlled liberalization".

The Macroeconomic Situation

The Barbadian economy suffered significant reverses in the period 1991–92, when real per capita GDP declined by about 11 percent. The period 1993–2000 saw the economy grow at an average rate of 2.7 percent per annum. For the period of the "9/11 crisis" (2001–02), the economy recorded a negative rate of growth of real GDP of 0.2 percent per annum. There was a resumption of growth (3 percent) in the period 2003–04. For the entire period 1991–2004, therefore, economic growth has shown significant volatility, with quite high coefficients of variation and standard deviations at both the overall and sectoral levels (see Table II-2).

The sectoral data in Table II-2 reveal the expected strong influence the tourist sector has had on overall growth as can be seen from the similar patterns in the two periods of negative growth (1991–92 and 2001–02) and the period of positive growth (1993–2000). Not surprisingly, the greatest annual fluctuations in growth rates (ranging from –26% to +54 %) occurred in the declining sugar sector during the period 1995–96. Generally, the measures of variation by sector are so large that they instantly reveal the intrinsic vulnerability and fragility of the growth process.

Table II-2. GDP Growth, Sectoral Growth, and CPI Changes

		Sectoral Growth Rate				
Year	GDP (Real) Growth Rates	Tourism	Sugar	Construction	Wholesale and Retail	CPI
1991	–3.90	–5.40	–5.10	–7.80	6.20	6.00
1992	–7.20	–1.90	–17.50	28.20	–7.90	6.10
1993	0.80	4.00	–10.40	2.00	2.40	1.10
1994	4.60	9.40	7.70	6.10	6.00	0.70
1995	2.40	1.00	–26.00	9.80	0.20	1.90
1996	3.20	1.70	53.60	4.00	3.30	2.40
1997	4.60	2.00	9.30	14.00	8.70	7.70
1998	6.20	6.20	–25.70	16.90	12.20	1.20
1999	0.50	0.30	10.90	10.00	–8.00	1.60
2000	2.30	9.20	9.70	1.00	1.30	2.40
2001	–2.60	–5.90	–14.70	6.90	–3.10	2.80
2002	–0.50	–2.70	–10.00	7.70	1.20	0.20
2003	2.00	7.30	–19.00	0.80	4.10	1.60
2004	4.00	9.30	–5.40	3.60	4.90	1.40
Avg.	1.17	2.46	–3.04	7.37	2.25	2.65
Std. Dev.	3.70	5.12	21.56	8.83	5.90	2.34
Coe. Var.	3.16	2.08	–7.09	1.20	2.62	0.88

Source: Data supplied by the Caribbean Centre for Monetary Studies (Dec. 2005).

Table II-3. Growth Volatility by Decades

Country/Region	Period				
	1960s	1970s	1980s	1990s	1961–2000
Barbados	4.9	4.1	4.4	3.8	4.6
Jamaica	2.4	7.4	4.3	2.1	4.6
Trinidad and Tobago	3.8	5.1	5.9	2.6	4.9
CGCED Group	4.5	6.1	4.9	3.5	5.0

Source: World Bank, CGCED (2002).

A comparison of its decadal growth volatility with that of other CARICOM countries and the CGCED group of countries is shown in Table II-3.

The export sector has played the leading role in this volatility. Because of the decline of the sugar sector and other lesser contributory factors, total merchandise export growth in Barbados over the past decade has been low, averaging 1.4 percent per annum or about one-quarter the global rate of 6 percent per annum. For the longer period 1985–2004, domestic export sales (and volumes) have been exceptionally volatile—ranging from an annual decline of –45 percent in 1987 to an annual increase of about 27 percent in 1996. Similarly, the value of re-exports sales ranged from 50 percent in 1995 to –38 percent in 1986. Overall, the value of total exports (f.o.b.) fluctuated from –42 percent in 1987 to +32 percent in 1995 (see Table II-4).

Compared to the performance of exports, merchandise imports grew more substantially, achieving 6 percent per annum over the past decade, a rate more than four times faster than exports. Imports, however, also fluctuated considerably, ranging from +25 percent in 1995 to –25 percent in 1992. The gap between merchandise exports and imports widened as is shown in the graph in Figure II-1. For the period 2002–04, this gap averaged about US$970 million, which was about 2½ times the size of the merchandise trade gap in 1985–88. Overall, the current account deficit/resource gap in the balance of payments averaged just under 6 percent of GDP for the period 1999–2003 but rose to 10.5 percent in 2004. As we noted, this volatility has been clearly reflected in the volatility of GDP growth, which is a matter of major concern for the efficiency and the competitive standing of the economy.

Services exports constitute 80 percent of the value of Barbados' total exports of goods and services and 42 percent of its GDP. More broadly, services contribute about 74 percent of GDP and about 77 percent of employment. Even so, these figures understate the impact of the services sector because they do not capture fully the role of the sector as an input (directly and indirectly) into the production of goods and the determination of the competitiveness of firms.[3]

[3] The direct and indirect impacts of travel and tourism are discussed in the next section, where we introduce tourism satellite accounts as an indicator of the competitiveness of the sector.

Table II-4. Annual Change in Merchandise Trade for Barbados, 1985–2003
(percent)

		Export		
Years	Import (cif)	Total (fob)	Domestic (fob)	Re-export (fob)
1985	−7.8	−9.4	−14.0	3.7
1986	−3.3	−22.0	15.3	−37.7
1987	−2.3	−42.1	−45.0	−24.9
1988	12.4	9.6	6.1	7.5
1989	16.4	6.1	1.4	16.9
1990	4.0	14.5	0.9	42.0
1991	−0.7	−3.6	−3.7	−3.5
1992	−25.4	−8.3	10.0	−34.7
1993	10.1	−1.6	4.9	−17.5
1994	6.5	−2.9	−4.3	1.1
1995	25.4	31.6	25.4	49.8
1996	8.2	17.5	26.5	−4.4
1997	19.4	0.8	−1.8	9.2
1998	3.6	−7.7	7.2	9.1
1999	7.4	2.0	1.1	0.6
2000	4.3	3.2	−4.0	24.8
2001	−7.6	−4.8	−7.0	0.4
2002	0.2	−6.9	−5.6	−9.7
2003	11.6	3.4	−1.1	13.5
2004	18.2	11.4	10.5	12.3

Source: Central Bank of Barbados, Economic and Financial Statistics.

Between 1990 and 2001, the total value of Barbados' services exports increased by slightly over two-thirds, from US$650 million to US$1100 million. The annual rate of growth was about 4.7 percent compared to a worldwide growth of the sector of 5.9 percent for the same period (Table II-5).

The lion's share of the sector is comprised of travel and tourism, which together contributed 71 percent of the total value for the entire

Figure II-1. Visible Trade for Barbados, 1985–2003

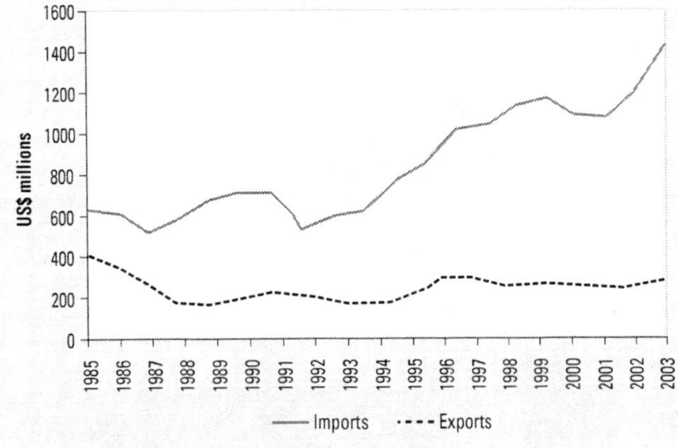

Source: Government statistics.

Table II-5. Services Exports

Year	% Change
1991	−5.5
1992	0.2
1993	11.4
1994	18.0
1995	6.5
1996	7.0
1997	3.5
1998	6.7
1999	0.6
2000	5.9
2001	−0.5

Source: Jessen and Vignoles (2004).

Table II-6. Services-to-GDP Ratios

Category	Ratio
All Services	.74
Wholesale and Retail	.19
Tourism	.15–.16
Business and General	.16–.17
Government	.14
Transport and Communication	.08

Source: Government statistics.

Figure II-2. Industrial Production Index
(period averages, 1982=100)

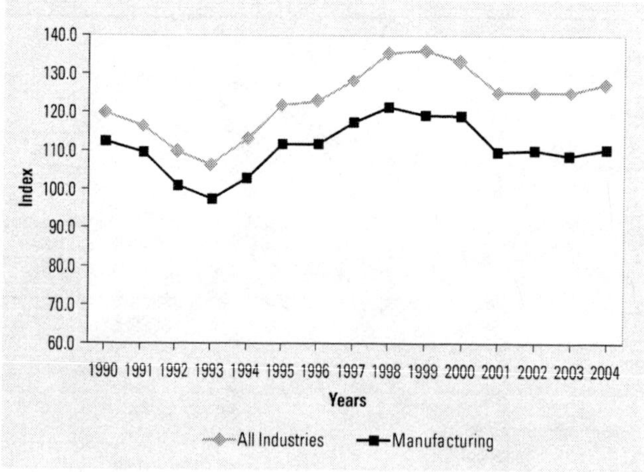

Source: Barbados Statistical Service.

period 1990–2001. Next in importance is the commercial services sub-sector (24 percent). The government and transportation sub-sectors remain small (3 and 2 percent respectively). The travel and tourism sub-sector has shown steady growth, averaging 3 percent during the entire period (1990–2001). Data on the recent composition of the services sector of GDP are shown below (Table II-6).

The present outlook of the export sector is clearly cause for concern. And, although a significant share of Barbados's exports has been sold in preferential markets, its export dynamism has not been appreciable. A major competitiveness concern that has arisen is that Barbados' dependence on preferential treatment might have (unwittingly!) helped to solidify the position of non-dynamic, non-responsive production entities in its economy.

The macroeconomic data also reveal that the rate of inflation has declined from an average annual growth of 3.7 percent in the period 1991–97 to just over one percent for the period 1998–2004. The Index of Industrial Production (Figure II-2) reveals the decline in activity observed in the early 1990s, the rise thereafter until the end of the 1990s, and the slowdown of 2001–02. The manufacturing index closely patterns this overall industrial trend.

Turning to the present macroeconomic outlook, we find it dominated by three features, namely:

- The emergence in recent years of significant debt vulnerability.
- Signs of recovery following the economic slowdown of 2001–02.
- Efforts by the authorities to: (i) consolidate the recovery; (ii) promote the structural reforms already in process; and (iii) keep in focus the need to enhance growth and competitiveness through the reforms and through promotion activities for the tradable export sector (merchandise and services).

Barbados has operated a fixed-exchange-rate system tied to the US dollar since 1975. This commitment has placed a premium on sound economic management, strong preventative measures, and a proactive policy stance by the authorities in order to both anticipate and cope with external shocks and to prevent an erosion of the country's competitive position through incorrect policies. Given the structural features of the economy, it is often the case that the authorities have to contend with the possibility of *two particular biases emerging as they seek to manage the macroeconomic environment.* One of these is a *deflationary bias* in its counter-cyclical policy. This can impede/slow the growth of the economy's potential output and employment in "normal periods". The other, in danger of being manifested when the economy is undergoing "stress", is the likely emergence of *a bias by the authorities toward unsustainable compensatory increases in public spending*, leading quickly to the emergence of debt vulnerability. Different episodes of economic difficulties for the periods 1991–92 and 2001–03 give some indication of how both of these biases can emerge and operate in day-to-day practice. (For details on these episodes, see Worrell, 2003 and Sahay, 2004.)

The Barbadian authorities have practised a modified form of "capital-management techniques" advocated in UNCTAD publications, which has been combined with a "controlled process" of import liberalization. This approach has helped to reduce some of the excesses experienced elsewhere because it combines user-friendly capital-account controls with strong prudential and regulatory oversight of the domestic financial sector. Nonetheless, in our view the present debt situation in Barbados appears to be overshadowing other considerations, and the rest of this sub-section will therefore treat this issue, as it is unlikely to simply go away.

The Debt Scenario

Government spending rose in response to the recession indicated earlier, which had started in 2001. This was brought on in large measure by the then worldwide downturn in economic activity along with the 9/11 events and their aftermath. This downturn affected tourism substantially. The recession occurred one decade after the economy had recovered from the earlier major 1991–92 balance-of-payments crisis and had subsequently enjoyed a period of moderate sustained growth (1993–2000, when real GDP increased at 2.7 percent per annum). For this period the overall fiscal deficit and current account balance-of-payments deficit averaged –1.5 and –1.8 percent of GDP respectively.[4]

Data from recent IMF Article IV Consultations (2004 and 2005) reveal, however, that the central government deficit (broadly defined so as to include extra-budgetary spending) rose from about 2.3 percent for financial year (FY) 2000–01 to about 13 percent for FY 2002–03. In this period, as the deficit quadrupled, the central government debt-to-GDP ratio rose from 64 percent in March 2001 to 74 percent by March 2002 and 78 percent in March 2003. For each of the years ending March 2004 and 2005, it was 75 percent. For the overall public sector, the debt rose from 74 percent to 87 percent of GDP in the period March 2001 to March 2002. During 2004, the total debt-to-GDP ratio remained approximately the same, but the overall deficit narrowed to –6.4 percent and 5.9 percent for the years ending March 2004 and March 2005 respectively.

The primary balance on the government's account (which excludes interest payments on accumulated debt) is considered a better proxy of government's effort to produce a fiscal surplus. In the context of debt vulnerability, this is perhaps the most critical indicator. Further, based on this supposition, we can in fact say that the required surplus (effort) will be higher, the higher is the outstanding debt, and the higher is the interest rate on the debt. And, the effort will be lower, the higher the rate of growth of real GDP and the greater the appreciation of the real exchange-rate. The central government primary account balance, which was 1.9 percent in 2000–01 worsened to –4.3 percent in 2002–03. It then improved to an estimated –1.6 percent in 2003–04, and further improved over FY 2004–05 to –1.3 percent.

Based on government's targets (the "baseline scenario"), the IMF (2004) estimated an expected decline in the central government debt-to-GDP ratio by the end of 2008, but this it considers still "high" at 69 percent. For total government debt the ratio remains at 87 percent through 2009. Because of this, the IMF has called for a more robust effort directed at: (i) increasing government revenues; (ii) limiting government expenditures;

[4] This combination of circumstances led to a downgrade of Barbados' external credit rating and long-term domestic credit rating (Standard and Poor's).

(iii) reducing government transfers to parastatal bodies; (iv) increasing charges on government-supplied utilities; and (v) utilizing privatization proceeds to write down the debt.

These would, the IMF estimates, eliminate the deficit in three years and bring the debt-to-GDP ratio down to 50 percent by 2011.

However, the authorities claim, in response, that:

(i) the debt is denominated locally and the external debt has not shown significant change;
(ii) the government has high "credibility" and therefore the risk to the domestic debt is inconsequential;
(iii) further, their working relationship with the unions and the private sector through the Protocols has created an atmosphere for medium-term industrial harmony; and
(iv) they are pursuing their own efforts at the deliberate speed required by the circumstances to eliminate the primary deficit and had projected a primary surplus of 0.5 percent of GDP by 2004–05, and a reduction of the central government debt-GDP ratio to 60 percent by FY 2016–21, even though the total debt-GDP ratio would remain at 87 percent.

One also gets the feeling arising out of discussions that the authorities anticipate a sustained global upturn and they do not want to be caught restraining the economy at a time when it can benefit from a rise in global activity.

Diagnostic Conclusions

Based on the foregoing analysis as well as discussions and interviews with Barbadian officials and other stakeholders, three broad diagnostic conclusions are drawn at this stage of the chapter. First, the technical/economic relations and conditions that flow from the small open nature of the Barbadian economy, its historical evolution, and the manner of its present insertion into the regional, hemispheric, and global economy express the opportunities as well as the constraints and challenges it faces as it seeks to enhance its competitiveness. As the flow chart below shows, clear linkages can be discerned between:

export dynamism ⇉ production structures directed at the domestic market ⇉ foreign exchange availability to finance indispensable imports ⇉ capital inflows ⇉ the structural insufficiency of domestic savings even at "optimal" rates and, ⇉ production compatibility with the dynamic components of global and domestic demand.

Second, in the 1991–92 and the more recent 2001–02 episodes of economic downturn and balance-of-payments pressures the two dilemmas that face macroeconomic management in Barbados in the context of a fixed-exchange-rate are clearly revealed. On the one hand there is the propensity to a deflationary bias when times are "normal" and on the other there is a propensity to rising government expenditures leading to debt vulnerability when times are stressful. These contradictory impulses complicate efforts to pursue sound macroeconomic management, a necessary requirement for a positive impact on national competitiveness.

Third, several conclusions derive from our brief review of the performance of the external sector and its outlook, including:

- the slow growth of merchandise exports;
- the stagnation and decline of its major component, sugar;
- the consistent but still only modest growth of the services sector;
- the failure of overall export dynamism to perform at the average rate of the global economy;
- the high product concentration of export trade and the need for diversification of both its merchandise and services exports;
- the high volatility of all components of export, although this is less so in the case of travel and tourism;
- the limited diversification of export markets;
- the country's reliance on preferential market access and the strong threat of preference erosion;
- the growing merchandise trade gap and the significant level of the resource gap/current account deficits, in the absence of large-scale capital inflows; and
- the positioning of merchandise exports in the non-dynamic components of global demand.

C. Barbados' Competitiveness Indicators

Group 1: Global Indicators

What do the competitiveness indicators show in Barbados? We examine this question by firstly looking at certain international indicators prepared by intergovernmental organizations for purposes of worldwide comparison and ranking. These are classed for convenience as global indicators. There are two principal trade indexes in this category, namely the ***trade performance index*** and the ***revealed comparative advantage measure***. Both of these are considered in the separate chapter by Jessen and Vignoles, and the main conclusions of that discussion have informed the diagnostic assessment and policy recommendations in this chapter. In particular we stress the observation that Barbados does not have a dynamic and

Table II-7. Score and Ranking in Core Group Sample (93 Countries), CIP Index

	2000		1990		1980	
Country	**Score**	**Rank**	**Score**	**Rank**	**Score**	**Rank**
Barbados	0.249	44 (61)*	0.251	30	0.296	29
Jamaica	0.137	78 (119)*	0.144	73	0.141	71
Trinidad and Tobago	0.217	53 (74)*	0.170	67	0.209	48

Source: UNIDO (2004).

*Ranking based on full sample (155 countries).

competitive merchandise export sector and that far too large a share of its exports fail to reach the "Champions" category; are underachieving in terms of supply to dynamic markets; or, face stagnant and declining markets.

An important set of global indicators highlighting Barbados' competitiveness standing in industry is provided by the recent *UNIDO's Competitive Industrial Performance Index (CIP)* and UNIDO's *Industrial cum Technological Advance Index (ITA)*. The CIP covers 155 countries for the period 1980–2001. Based on data availability, UNIDO also has within this group of 155 countries a core group sample of 93 economies. Barbados is included. Other CARICOM countries are also included, thereby allowing comparison with two key ones: Jamaica and Trinidad and Tobago. The CIP Index is calculated from six industrial indicators (bracketed below) structured as four performance indicators:

(a) Manufacturing Value Added (MVA) Per Capita (1), indicating the ***level*** of industrialization;
(b) Manufactured Exports Per Capita (2), indicating the ***capacity*** to be competitive and keep abreast of technical progress;
(c) Industrial Intensity, which is the arithmetic mean of the share of MVA in GDP (3); and the share of medium and high-technology (MHT) activities in MVA (4);
(d) Export Quality, or the arithmetic mean of the share of manufactures in total exports (5); and the share of MHT products in manufactured exports (6).

Each component of the CIP Index is normalized by its range in the year in question, with the highest (lowest) value given by the best (worst) performer in the sample. All four indicators are weighted equally.[5] The results for Barbados and two other CARICOM countries in the score and ranking of the core group sample are shown in Table II-7.

[5] "Individual indices of performance *lij* were obtained through standardization according to the general formula

$$I_{I,,j} = \frac{X_{I,,j} - \min\left(X_{i,j}\right)}{\max\left(X_{I,,j}\right) - \min\left(X_{i,j}\right)}$$

Data on changes in the rankings by period are shown in Table II-8. Data on the behaviour of the components of the CIP Index for the period 1980–2000 are also shown in Table II-9.

The Index presented here uses "hard" (quantitative) data only and does not include "soft" (qualitative) data. According to UNIDO it has been expressly designed: "to provide policy makers and analysts with information to locate countries in the evolving global scene, comparing performance to direct competitors, countries ahead (the role models) and a little behind (future competitive threats)" (UNIDO, 2004).

As regards rank stability, UNIDO reports that statistical tests for the sample show some "churning" but that overall positions are fairly stable and the magnitudes of change small. This, it suggests, reflects the fact that capacity building in these areas takes time and so does changing ranks. However, it is recognised that ranks can be lost quickly if economic shocks, natural disasters, or policy mishaps precipitate them.

Because of data limitations, labour productivity is not explicitly measured in the CIP and this could be a major constraint on the usefulness of the measure. This crucial element for competitiveness measures is acknowledged and its absence, UNIDO further claims, is tempered by the consideration that regression analyses across a small set of developing countries for which data are available establish on average that labour productivity for the manufacturing sector and the CIP are positive throughout, and show a systematic trend for the period 1980–2000.[6] An important observation to note is that these measures constitute only a starting point for assessing Barbados' performance or for that matter, that of any individual country although the comparisons may be revealing. In truth therefore,

---

where $X_{I,.j}$ is the jth country value of the ith performance indicator. Therefore the highest country in the ranking has a score of 1 and the lowest a score of 0.

The CIP index was then constructed as

$$CIP_j(\alpha)=\left(\frac{W_1 I^{\alpha}_{1,j}+W_2 I^{\alpha}_{2,j}+W_3 I^{\alpha}_{3,j}+W_4 I^{\alpha}_{4,j}}{W_1+W_2+W_3+W_4}\right)^{\frac{1}{\alpha}}$$

where W_i are the weights given to the individual indices and α is a parameter to control how variations and weights of the individual indices affect the CIP index.

With $W_1 = W_2 = W_3 = W_4 = 1$ and α also set to one the general formula became

$$CIP_j \equiv CIP_{j(1)} = \frac{1}{4}\sum_{i=j}^{4} Ii, j$$

[6] UNIDO reports that in the initial year the correlation was 0.213 and insignificant, but strengthened and became significant by 1990 (0.438) and by 2000 had attained a high level of significance (0.611). This is interpreted to mean that the CIP Index has been embracing the effects of improved labour productivity.

Table II-8. Changes in Ranking (Core Group Sample), CIP Index

Country	1990–2000	1980–1990	1980–2000
Barbados	–5	–10	–15
Jamaica	–5	–2	–7
Trinidad and Tobago	14	–19	–5

Source: UNIDO (2004).

Table II-9. Components of the CIP Index

Country	MVA Per Capita			Manufactured Exports Per Capita			Industrialisation Intensity			Export Quality			CIP Index		
	1980	1990	2000	1980	1990	2000	1980	1990	2000	1980	1990	2000	1980	1990	2000
Barbados	0.083	0.072	0.056	0.084	0.049	0.020	0.328	0.248	0.275	0.689	0.636	0.646	0.296	0.251	0.249
Jamaica	0.037	0.043	0.026	0.012	0.008	0.005	0.364	0.347	0.286	0.151	0.178	0.230	0.141	0.144	0.137
Trinidad and Tobago	0.057	0.044	0.059	0.282	0.065	0.085	0.168	0.170	0.211	0.327	0.400	0.510	0.209	0.170	0.216

Source: UNIDO (2004).

they point to the need for even more data particularly with regard to: 1) the "drivers" of industrial competitiveness, 2) the policy framework within which enterprises operate, 3) the investment climate, 4) the institutional environment and 5) governance.

UNIDO has empirically established that certain "drivers" seem to account for the behaviour of the CIP Index in countries (and hence competitiveness). They have identified in this work: skills (as proxied by tertiary-level enrolment in technical subjects, science, mathematics and computing, and engineering); technological effort (as proxied by R&D financed by productive enterprises); investment FDI (total FDI); technological licensing (royalties and technical fees); and, modern infrastructure (ICT proxied by telephone maintenance). It should be noted that these drivers do not seek to fully 'explain" competitiveness, but meet two criteria, namely, 1) they capture the main structural factors that are expected to affect industrial performance and 2) they satisfy the test of data availability for comparative purposes. To the extent that these hold true, the results of this work provide significant pointers for the policy recommendations that follow in this chapter.

The question has been posed as to why countries do well/fare poorly in measurements using the CIP Index. The explanation offered by UNIDO is that while many factors explain this, one stands out, namely, the ability to tap into global value chains. This, however, can only be achieved *either* by building up local capabilities of domestic enterprises or by attracting export-oriented FDI. Notably, there has been in recent times, a growing "convergence" between the two approaches. UNIDO also observes a strong positive correlation between the CIP index and GDP per capita. It is even suggested that an increase of 0.01 of the former would lead to a rise of between US$250 and US$300 (1990 prices) in GDP per capita.

Quite recently, UNIDO extended this work in its just released annual report (November 2005). Utilizing the same six industrial indicators for the period 1990 to 2002, it has grouped them into an "industrial advance indicator" (the product of indicators 3 and 5 above) and a "technological advance" indicator (the product of indicators 4 and 6). These are then combined to produce the Industrial cum Technological Advance Index (ITA) referred to above. The results for Barbados along with selected CARICOM countries are shown in Table II-10 below.

Table II-10. Industrial-cum-Technological Advance (ITA) Index

	ITA Index		Industrial-Advance Index		Technological Advance Indicator	
Country	**1990**	**2002**	**1990**	**2002**	**1990**	**2002**
Barbados	0.130	0.158	0.520	0.496	0.250	0.318
Jamaica	0.033	0.035	0.228	0.223	0.146	0.151
Trinidad and Tobago	0.047	0.063	0.351	0.477	0.135	0.133

Source: UNIDO (2005).

The table shows that Barbados outperforms the other CARICOM comparators indicated. As UNIDO observes, overall the countries that it surveyed showed results ranging from a maximum of slightly over 0.5 to virtually zero. Barbados' rating on the ITA exceeded the average for all developing regions except East and South East Asia, which ranged between about 0.225 and 0.325 for the years 1990 and 2002 respectively. No other developing region averaged above 0.1 except South Asia at about 0.110 in 2002.

The three remaining global indicators presented here emphasize governance, institutional, and regulatory-framework issues, all of which are crucial for ensuring an enabling environment for competitive enterprises to thrive and effective macroeconomic policies to emerge. The first of these is the *Index of Economic Freedom* which is an annual compilation of the Heritage Foundation. In the compilation, each country is graded in 10 factors on a scale from 1 to 5, using equal weights. Countries with the smallest scores (1–2) are deemed to have the freest economies; and those with a score around 3 are less free; those with a score near 4 are excessively regulated; and, those with a score of 5 are classed as the most "economically repressed". The higher the score the greater is the presumed need for "significant economic reform to achieve sustained increases in economic growth". In this sense, the Index is intended to be a broad measure of competitiveness in the global economy. The latest scorecard for Barbados (as well as Jamaica and Trinidad and Tobago) is shown below (Table II-11).

As a general observation, this measure mixes "hard" and "soft" data and is based on the presumption that complete deregulation is best for the economy, which in turn further presumes pervasive government failure. Some believe that in this way the measure ignores the real risks of market failure in economies like Barbados with small and intrinsically "un-

Table II-11. Performance Indicators: Index of Economic Freedom, Barbados and Selected CARICOM Countries

Performance Indicators	Barbados	Jamaica	Trinidad and Tobago
Overall Score	2.35	2.81	2.49
Overall Rank	32	60	40
Trade Policy	4.0	4.0	2.0
Fiscal Burden	4.5	4.1	3.9
Government Intervention	2.0	2.5	2.0
Monetary Policy	1.0	3.0	2.0
Foreign Investment	3.0	1.0	2.0
Banking and Finance	2.0	2.0	2.0
Wages and Prices	2.0	2.0	3.0
Property Rights	1.0	3.0	2.0
Regulation	2.0	3.0	3.0
Informal Market	2.0	3.5	3.0
Category	Mostly Free	Mostly Free	Mostly Free

Source: Heritage Foundation (2005).

competitive" markets, particularly in the sense that market size may not permit the desired multiple firms for a competitive equilibrium. Based on the Index, Barbados is classed as mostly free, as are the other two CARICOM comparators, but achieves a better score and ranking than they. In the area of property rights and monetary policy, it achieves the best score, but does not do well in terms of trade policy and fiscal burden, a fact that follows our expectations based on the presentation above. This reinforces the need for attention to be paid to these concerns.

Most trade indicators are based on merchandise trade data but the *WTTC Competitiveness Monitor* reports a Results by Country table, which presents information for 200 individual countries using eight indices of services (tourist) competitiveness. The measure includes a number of institutional and framework indicators.[7] For each of the eight indices, the values range from 0 to 100 and indicate the level of performance relative to other countries, with 0 representing the lowest level of achievement and 100 the highest. The range is established from the actual data. For the 212 countries, therefore, the most competitive would be at number 1 and the least competitive would rank at 212. The results are classed into three broad categories: above average, average and below average performance. With the use of the traffic light metaphor, these are then classed as green, amber and red respectively.

The results for Barbados are shown in Table II-12, along with those for the Bahamas, Jamaica and Trinidad and Tobago, for purposes of comparison. The major observation here is that of the eight indices, for Barbados four are above average, two are average and one is below average. For the remaining one, the WTTC did not have adequate data from which to make a report for Barbados. However, the poorly performing price competitive index here is a matter of some concern, even though we have observed in the previous section that Barbados has deliberately targeted the "high end" of the tourist market.

---

[7] The indicators are the following:

1. Price Competitiveness [This is computed using the Hotel Price Index (HPI) or room rate per night in current US dollars and the Purchasing Power Parity Index from the World Bank's World Development Indicators.]
2. Human Tourism [This uses a number of indicators to measure the level of tourism impact on a country and the level of tourism participation in the industry.]
3. Infrastructure [This uses as indicators roads, access to improved sanitation facilities, drinking water and rail transport.]
4. Environment [This measures the level of government awareness towards environmental issues and uses as proxy indicators, population density, CO_2 emission, and ratification of environmental treaties.]
5. Technology [This is measured by indicators such as Internet hosts, telephone mainlines, mobile phones, high technology experts, and a technology index.]
6. Human Resources [This uses a large number of indicators such as life expectancy at birth, adult literacy, primary, secondary and tertiary school enrolment, travel and tourism direct employment, unemployment, urban-rural population distributions, male-female employment, and unemployment, and population growth.]
7. Openness [This focuses on tourism openness, trade openness, and the level of taxation on international trade.]
8. Social [This covers a range of indicators including the level of human development, daily newspaper coverage, television sets, recorded crimes, and personal computer availability.]

Table II-12. WTTC Competitiveness Index

	Barbados		Bahamas		Jamaica		Trinidad & Tobago	
Category	Index Value	Rank	Index Value	Rank	Index Value	Rank	Index Value	Rank
Price Competitiveness	42	86	24	105	58	51	47	74
Human Tourism	N/A	N/A	N/A	N/A	N/A	N/A	24	83
Infrastructure	70	15	67	20	53	56	60	39
Environment	43	115	50	83	22	149	23	147
Technology	89	49	77	61	41	103	54	89
Human Resources	73	40	71	43	47	91	59	70
Openness	62	80	80	10	53	94	66	64
Social	70	51	71	44	54	90	64	66

Source: World Travel and Tourism Council, Competitiveness Monitor (2004).

Kaufmann, Kraay and Mastruzzi (2003) present estimates of *six dimensions of governance* (voice and accountability, political stability, government effectiveness, regulatory quality, rule-of-law, and control of corruption) for 199 countries and territories. These estimates are based on several hundred individual variables that measure perceptions of governance and are drawn from the work of 18 different organizations using 25 separate data sources. These data are available at two-year intervals for the period 1996–2002. Estimates of the indicators are normally distributed with a mean of zero and a standard deviation of one in each period, implying that virtually all scores fall between –2.5 and +2.5. The higher the score the better the outcome. The results for Barbados along with comparators for Jamaica and Trinidad and Tobago for the most recent year (2002) are shown in Table II-13. Again Barbados' scores are well above those of other countries in the region, ranging from 0.81 (political stability) to 1.43 (rule of law). Its score for government effectiveness is 1.36, compared to –0.07 for Jamaica and 0.47 in Trinidad and Tobago. None of the two other CARICOM countries cited managed to achieve a measure of one in any of the indicators, with Jamaica achieving minus numbers for four of the six measures. This is a further indication of how

Table II-13. Governance Indicators

	Barbados	Jamaica	Trinidad and Tobago
Voice and Accountability	1.39	0.51	0.56
Political Stability	0.81	–0.09	0.03
Government Effectiveness	1.36	–0.07	0.47
Regulatory Quality	1.14	0.32	0.65
Rule of Law	1.43	–0.38	0.34
Control of Corruption	1.29	–0.46	–0.04

Source: Kaufmann, Kraay, and Mastruzzi (2003).

well Barbados has been performing within the context of the region where it has to compete in the recently formed Caribbean Single Market and Economy (CSME).

Group 2: Country-Specific Macro Indicators

The second set of indicators is derived from various sources and provides country-specific measures, generally at the macro level. Microeconomic indicators are treated later in the chapter.

i. Labour Productivity

The nexus between productivity and competitiveness has been well established. Average productivity or the amount of output per unit of input is the most basic indicator of how well an economy is performing. Increases in productivity represent a sustainable basis for improvements in welfare and in the standard-of-living. Some economists believe that, in the long run, this is the most fundamental determinant of economic well-being. Productivity can be measured in a number of ways and this sub-section begins with the measure of labour productivity in Barbados for the whole economy in Table II-14 as well as for key sectors in Figure II-3.

Data availability limits the measures of labour productivity to the ratio of the number of workers employed (total and sectoral) to the relevant GDP measure. It would have been preferred

Table II-14. Labour Productivity Index
(1991 = 100)

1991	100.0
1992	99.4
1993	101.6
1994	100.5
1995	99.4
1996	99.3
1997	99.4
1998	98.5
1999	101.2
2000	98.0
2001	93.6
2002	94.8
2003	89.3
2004	99.4

Source: Author's calculations (real GDP per worker).

Figure II-3. Sectoral Labour Productivity in Barbados, 1982–2002
(real GDP per person employed)

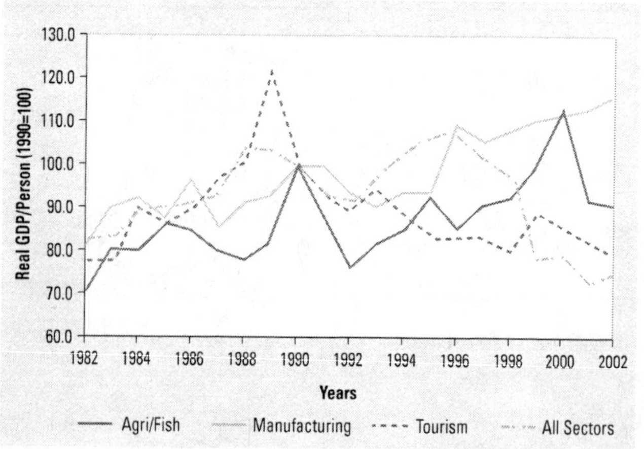

Source: Government statistics.

to use the number of person hours worked rather than numbers of persons employed. Further, changes in labour productivity capture the effects of changes in the contribution to output of other inputs than hours worked or the number of workers. The table reveals a general tendency towards a decline in overall labour productivity measured as real GDP per person employed between the years 1991 and 2004. Between 1991 and 1996, the decline was slight, with two years of minimal increases and three years of minimal declines with reference to the base year. In 1997 there was an increase of nearly 3 percent. Between 1998 and 2003 however, the productivity index declined by about 11 percent, with the decline in 2003 being particularly steep. In 2004 it recovered.

Figure II-3 shows the sectoral and overall performances for the years 1990 to 2002 for which the data were available at the sectoral level. These show the steepest decline between 1990 and 2002 in the tourism sector—a decline of 23 percent. Indeed tourism GDP per person employed in 1989 was more than 40 percent above the level of 2002. Agriculture, despite its woes, showed a less steep decline (9 percent). The manufacturing sector recorded a gain of 15 percent.

ii. Real Unit Labour Cost

The unit labour cost (ULC) is the ratio of the cost of full worker compensation (that is including all benefits) per unit of worker output per period to the output per worker per period (that is labour productivity). The ULC would therefore rise when compensation increases faster than productivity or if compensation remains the same (or falls) and labour productivity falls faster. It is, in other words, the net effect of changes in worker compensation and changes in worker productivity. The measure excludes other production costs, which means that the composition of inputs could affect the measure. Usually, the measure also faces difficulties of data availability, and especially the frequency for which these are required. As a rule, the available data are better for manufacturing output than for services.

With these caveats, very rough estimates of the ULC for Barbados are shown in Table II-15. We previously noted the decline in real GDP

Table II-15. Unit Labour Costs
(1991=100)

	Real GDP Per Worker (Index)	Real Wage Rate (Index)	Unit Labour Cost (Index)
1991	100.0	100.0	100
1992	99.4	92.8	93
1993	101.6	93.3	92
1994	100.5	93.3	93
1995	99.4	93.9	94
1996	99.3	94.4	95
1997	97.4	93.0	95
1998	98.5	96.5	98
1999	101.2	97.7	97
2000	98.0	99.1	101
2001	93.6	99.6	106
2002	94.8	102.4	108
2003	89.3	101.9	113

Source: Author's calculations.

per worker, and the table further notes that movements in the real wage rate have not been enough to offset the adverse effect of this decline on the ULC. The real wage index fell significantly (7 percent) between 1991 and 1997. In that period, the ULC declined by 5 percent. The real wage index increased between 1997 and 2003 by about 10 percent, and, with the decline in labour productivity after 1999, the ULC rose by over 16 percent between 1999 and 2003.

Like the previously considered indicator (labour productivity), this one also suggests a worsening of Barbados' competitiveness, mainly owing to the estimated decline in labour productivity, which has been quite marked since 2000.

iii. Real Effective Exchange Rate (REER)

The REER is the geometric weighted mean of the ratios of a country's domestic price level to that of its trading partners, with the price levels stated at their nominal exchange-rate value in a common currency. The weights are usually based on the share of bilateral trade flows (for both goods and services) in a country's total trade, with the base year preferably selected for its price stability and external balance sustainability. In reality the weights should be shares of bilateral trade with competitors, but country trade shares are used as a proxy in economies like Barbados where these data are not readily available. Similarly, the CPI is used as a proxy for the price movements between countries. In Barbados there is, however, a high correlation between exchange-rate movements and price-level movements. Therefore these two variables are not independent. Furthermore, when used as a proxy, the CPI has practical limitations such as time lags in the availability of data; its failure to isolate the effects of taxes, subsidies and administrative controls on prices; and its exclusion of the prices of many services as well as capital and intermediate goods.

These qualifications, which are similar to the others highlighted when referring to other indicators, have to be borne in mind, as a country's REER is a commonly used indicator of its competitiveness. The inflation rate in each country is assumed to "represent" the trends in domestic costs and therefore the competitiveness of the country's products. It is also an indicator of the country's international buying power, which bears directly on the level of welfare that can be obtained for the country's workers and consumers through trade. Thus, to take an example, if the Barbados dollar, measured in foreign currency, declines taking into account inflation differences, the prices of its exports decline and those of its imports rise so that living standards would fall, and vice versa. It should be noted, however, that a cheaper Barbados dollar relative to other currencies would be welcomed from the perspective of the individual exporter, as it would make the price of that exporter's products more attractive relative to those of its competitors in other countries. It should be constantly borne in mind also that there are many other factors that affect competitiveness, such as the macroeconomic environment, institutional arrangements, and business outlook, which the REER does not capture.

Data on Barbados' REER are presented in Figure II-4. An increase in the index represents an appreciation of the REER and a decline. Over the period 1990–2004 the REER exhibited conflicting trends. First, there was a small improvement over the years 1990–1993, then a decline between 1993 and 1996, and a further rise from 1996 to 2001 and thereafter, a substantial decline between 2001 and 2004. Barbados has operated a fixed-exchange-rate system with the US dollar since July 1975, and the appreciation since the mid-1990s reflect in significant measure the appreciation of the US dollar. The sharp depreciation of the US dollar in 2004 would have helped reverse the situation in Barbados.

Figure II-4. Real Effective Exchange Rate Index *(1990=100)*

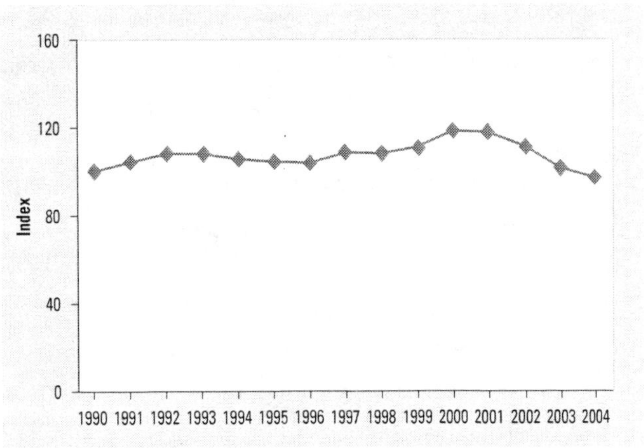

Source: Author's calculations.
Note: End of Period. An increase along the vertical axis signifies appreciation; a decrease, depreciation.

iv. Total Factor Productivity (TFP)

We have already noted the strong nexus between productivity and competitiveness. Unlike labour productivity measures, which focus on the input-output relation of one factor (labour), TFP measures seek to capture the contribution to output of everything except labour and capital. While movements in capital per worker affect output, so do other elements in the production process, such as organization, technology and innovation, and serendipity—all of these make for better use of all inputs. TFP therefore seeks to capture the effects of the latter set of elements on economic growth and improved welfare. In growth accounting decomposition exercises, the residual factor is what contributes to growth of real GDP, which cannot be captured by changes in the contributions of labour and capital inputs to output growth.

There are severe data problems encountered in arriving at this decomposition for small economies such as Barbados with their imperfect markets for goods, services, and productive factors. This is particularly important, since the conventional assumptions in these exercises include constant returns to scale and the requirement that factors are paid the value of their marginal product—a situation which theoretically exists only in competitive markets. If these assumptions held, then factor shares in real GDP would reflect their marginal contributions to output. Sometimes we also find that traditional "universal" shares of 0.3 for capital and 0.7 for labour are assumed. Often, too, the capital stock is derived from the perpetual inventory method. In Barbados, depreciation rates of 6.5 percent for building and construction and 14.8 percent for machinery and equipment are applied. Import prices are also used as deflators, and labour input is usually adjusted for the level of education attained.

Four sets of studies for different time periods have been done for Barbados: World Bank (1994) and (2005), Boamah (2004) and Downes (2004). The results are shown in Table II-16. The first World Bank study covered the period 1979–1990. It showed that with an average annual rate of growth of real GDP of 2.2 percent, the contribution of TFP was negative (minus 1.4 percent per annum). The second study (World Bank 2005) shows for the period 1991–2000 that the contribution of TFP was positive at 0.68 percent. Boamah's study covered selected years (years of positive growth of GDP) for the period 1964–1993 and this shows that, with an annual rate of growth of real GDP of 4.96 percent for the whole period (of positive growth), TFP contributed at the annual rate of 0.99 percent. Downes' study covered the period 1966–1999. This was broken into four sub-periods: 1960–73, 1975–80, 1982–89 and 1992–99—all years of positive growth. The result showed in every instance except the first period (1966–1973) that the TFP contribution was negative. For the period as a whole, with an annual rate of increase of real GDP of 2.88 percent, the TFP contribution was –1.34 percent. In the 1960–73 period when the TFP contribution was positive (1.43 percent per annum), the annual growth of real GDP peaked at 5.77 percent.

As Downes (2004) observes, the negative value and increasing contribution of TFP since 1975 is an area of particular concern. And, although sensitivity tests reveal that the

Table II-16. Results of Growth Decomposition: Total Factor Productivity Measures

Period/Source	GDP Growth	GDP Growth Due to Factor Accumulation	Contribution of Capital Goods	Contribution of Labour Growth	TFP
World Bank (1979–90) average	2.2	3.6	3.3	0.3	–1.4
World Bank (1991–2000)	1.93	1.25	0.39	0.86	0.68
Boamah (1964–93) average	4.96	3.93	1.48	2.45	1.03
Downes:					
1960–99	2.88	4.20	2.86	1.34	–1.34
1960–73	5.77	4.35	3.60	0.75	1.43
1975–80	5.02	6.20	3.45	2.75	–1.18
1982–89	2.83	4.12	3.05	1.07	–1.30
1992–99	2.83	4.00	1.44	2.56	–1.17

Sources: World Bank (1994, 2005), Boamah (2004), and Downes (2004).

Table II-17. Growth, Investment Ratio, Factor Contribution, and TFP Comparison

	Barbados	Latin America	East Asia	Africa
1980s				
GDP Growth	0.9	1.3	5.9	3.0
I/GDP Rates	19.5	18.7	28.9	18.6
Capital Stock Growth	7.1	2.6	8.5	4.8
Labour Force	1.1	2.7	2.7	2.8
TFP	−0.6	−2.6	−0.4	−2.7
1990s				
GDP Growth	2.1	3.3	5.1	3.2
I/GDP Rates	15.7	32.3	19.2	21.4
Capital Stock Growth	3.4	3.7	8.0	3.3
Labour Force	2.6	2.7	2.7	2.8
TFP	−1.4	−0.6	−0.8	−1.7

Sources: IADB (2003), Central Bank of Barbados (various issues), and Downes (2004).

contributions of physical capital and labour (human capital) are dependent on the values of the factor shares, the roles of physical and human capital in economic growth in Barbados are significant.

Some broad comparisons are drawn with other regions for which data are presented in a recent IADB study (2003) and shown in Table II-17 for two periods of the 1980s and the 1990s. In all the other developing regions, including East Asia for both periods, the contribution of TFP was negative. Barbados' ratio was far less negative than that for the Latin American region as a whole and just slightly worse that that of East Asia. It, however, worsened in the 1990s, with improvements being recorded in the Latin American region.

v. Investment Ratio

Because of the importance of investment in physical and human capital to growth in Barbados, data on these two indicators are briefly reviewed. Other things being equal, the investment/GDP ratio is linked to the growth performance and competitiveness of the economy. The significant role of physical capital accumulation in driving economic growth was revealed in the previous sub-section where we sought to identify the contribution of TFP. Data for the long period 1980–2004 are shown in Figure II-5. For the period of the 1980s, the investment ratio averaged 19.5 percent. While this was above those for the wider Latin American region and Africa, it was substantially below the rate of 30 percent that obtained in East Asia. By the 1990s, the Barbados rate had been reduced by about one-fifth to 15.7 percent while that of East Asia was more than double this rate (32.3 percent). Indeed the investment ratios for the other two regions (Latin America and Africa) had grown significantly. Over the period 2000–04, the investment ratio has averaged just under 18 percent, revealing a recovery that had started in 1997. The effects of the recessions in 2001–02 and 1991–93 are, however, revealed in the noticeable declines in these periods.

Figure II-5. Gross Domestic Investment Ratio *(percentage of GDP at market prices)*

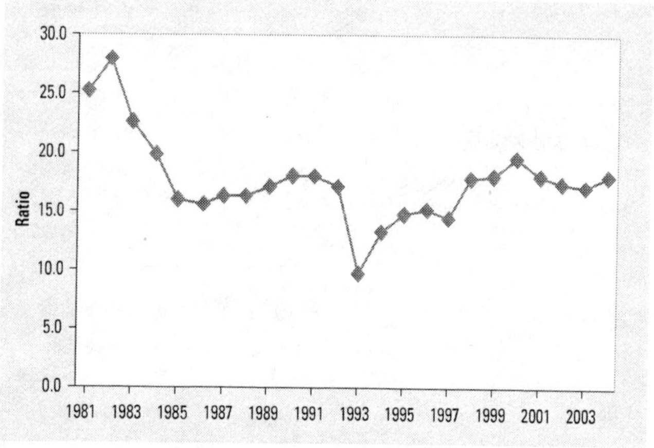

Source: Government statistics.

vi. Educational Quality

If, as was believed in the early independence years, the comparative advantage of Barbados lay in its relatively abundant factor (cheap labour), then improvements in worker welfare would erode that advantage, unless this was accompanied by improved worker productivity, which compensated for the increased compensation to the workforce. To achieve this improved worker productivity, investments in education, skills, health, and production of workforce are necessary inputs. One way of seeing the effect of this is in the changing composition of the educational level of the workforce. Data for the period 1981–1999 are shown in Table II-18. These reveal that, whereas in 1981, 47 percent of the workforce had only a primary level of education, by 1999 the ratio was more than halved (at 20 percent). For females, the share was even less at just fewer than 18 percent. This decline is reflected over the period in the improved

Table II-18. Educational Attainment:
Labour Force by Highest Level of Education Attained, Selected Years
(percent)

	Year				
Level	**1981**	**1986**	**1991**	**1996**	**1999**
Primary	46.8	37.6	28.5	20.8 (19.2)	20.4 (17.7)
Secondary	48.8	55.6	63.5	63.8 (65.2)	63.3 (65.5)
University	4.0	5.9	7.3	10.8 (12.0)	12.9 (14.0)
Technical	0.4	0.9	0.7	4.1	2.5 (1.8)
Other	0.1	0.0	0.0	1.4	0.9 (0.6)
Total (%)	100	100	100	100	100
Total (thousands)	112.4	116.9	129.6	135.4	136.6

Sources: Calculated from Caribbean Labour Force Statistics (ILO) and Barbados Statistical Service data.
Note: Female percentages in parentheses.

share for secondary education (which rose from just under one-half to nearly two-thirds of the total workforce) and university-trained workers whose ratio trebled from 4 percent of the workforce to 13 percent. In all these instances, females outperformed males. Over the same period, the total workforce had increased by 21 percent. The data in the table also reveal that most of these achievements were concentrated in a decade and a half (1981–1996).

This solid picture is reinforced by the data in Table II-19, which show that the share of government current expenditure on education out of total government current expenditure has risen substantially since 1960–61. Whereas in that fiscal year this category of expenditure ranked third, since 1970–71 it has ranked at the top. This achievement took place in the context of a rising share of government current expenditure as a percentage of GDP; this doubled between 1960–61 and 2000–01.

Table II-19. Central Government Current Expenditure on Education

Year	% of Total Current Expenditure (Rank)	Total Current Expenditure as % of GDP
1960/61	18 (3)	17
1970/71	23 (1)	29
1980/81	24 (1)	26
1990/91	23 (1)	32
2000/2001	23 (1)	35
2002/2003	22 (1)	31
2003/2004*	22 (1)	32

Source: Central Bank of Barbados.

Note: Numbers in parentheses show the ranking of education in the share of central government current expenditure by function (general services, defence, health, social security/welfare, housing, other social services, economic services and debt charges).

* Estimate.

vii. Labour Force Unemployment

As noted earlier, the workforce grew by 20 percent between 1981 and 1999. Since the early 1990s, the unemployment rate has been more than halved, declining from a peak of 23 percent in 1992 to 9.8 percent in 2004. Although more women remain unemployed than men, there was also a substantial decline in the unemployed numbers of the former—from a peak rate of 27.6 percent in 1993 to 10.6 percent in 2004 (see Table II-20). When examined by sub-periods we find that

Table II-20. Unemployment Rate *(percent of labour force)*

1991	17.3	(21.9)
1992	23.0	(26.1)
1993	24.3	(27.6)
1994	21.9	(26.4)
1995	19.7	(23.0)
1996	15.6	(18.9)
1997	14.7	(17.8)
1998	12.3	(16.4)
1999	10.4	(13.3)
2000	9.4	(11.4)
2001	9.9	(11.9)
2002	10.3	(12.1)
2003	10.7	(12.6)
2004	9.8	(10.6)

Sources: ILO (2004) and Government of Barbados statistics.

Note: Female unemployment in parentheses.

over the recession years (1991-93), unemployment grew substantially, with the rate increasing by over 40 percent. Thereafter it steadily declined, reaching a low of 9.4 percent in 2000. Again the economic slowdown of 2001–02 resulted in a rise in the rate, albeit substantially less than that which occurred in the previous recession.

viii. Macroeconomic, Fiscal, and Debt Performance Ranking

All work in the area of competitiveness stresses the importance of sound macroeconomic performance outcomes, and this holds true for Barbados. Macroeconomic policies influence many factors that relate directly to its competitiveness: costs, prices, output, demand, credit, interest rates and exchange-rate. In a recent study, Sahay (2004) has ranked 14 CARICOM economies in terms of their fiscal and debt performance for the period 1990–2003. Macroeconomic performance is ranked on the basis of the following six indicators:

1. total debt in 2003;
2. absolute change in debt between 1990–97 and 1998–2003;
3. overall fiscal balance in 2003;
4. absolute change in fiscal balance for the periods listed at (2) above;
5. CPI inflation in 2003; and
6. absolute change in GDP growth for the periods listed at (2) above.

Fiscal and debt performance uses the above six indicators and

7. primary balance in 2003
8. absolute change in primary balance for the periods listed at (2) above.

The results are shown in Table II-21. For both indicators, Barbados is ranked at 5. The first three positions are held by the same countries for both indicators, but the fourth position has been held by countries Barbados has outperformed in one of the two indicators, so they do not outperform Barbados in terms of the mean of the two rankings.

ix. Services Sector—Satellite Accounts

Two features of the services sector pose special problems for Barbados. One is that by its very nature, improving productivity in the services sector can never be achieved at the same rate as for the goods sector, because of the highly labour-intensive and personal nature of services supply. Second, the services sector is difficult to measure adequately for even routine national accounts purposes. This has led to efforts to produce special "satellite accounts" based on UN methodology for the sector. The World Travel and Tourism Council (WTTC)

Table II-21. Caribbean Rankings on Macroeconomic, Fiscal, and Debt Performance

Relative Ranking on Macroeconomic Performance[1]		Relative Ranking on Fiscal and Debt Performance[2]	
Trinidad and Tobago	(1)	The Bahamas	(1)
The Bahamas	(2)	Trinidad and Tobago	(2)
Dominican Republic	(3)	Dominican Republic	(3)
Suriname	(4)	St. Lucia	(4)
Barbados	(5)	Barbados	(5)
St. Vincent and the Grenadines	(6)	Suriname	(6)
Belize	(7)	St. Vincent and the Grenadines	(7)
Antigua and Barbuda	(8)	Guyana	(8)
St. Lucia	(9)	Antigua and Barbuda	(9)
Guyana	(10)	Jamaica	(10)
Grenada	(11)	Grenada	(11)
Dominica	(12)	Belize	(12)
Jamaica	(13)	Dominica	(13)
St. Kitts and Nevis	(14)	St. Kitts and Nevis	(14)

Sources: Sahay (2004), IMF.

[1] Calculated on the basis of six indicators: 1) total debt in 2003; 2) absolute change in debt 1990–97 compared to 1998–2003 as a ratio of absolute change in real GDP growth for 1990–97 to 1998–2003; 3) overall fiscal balance; 4) absolute change in overall fiscal balance 1990–1997 to 1998–2003; 5) CIP inflation 2003; 6) absolute change in GDP between 1990–97 and 1998–2003. Each indicator carries equal weight and the aggregate scores are normalized in the range 1–100 with the best performer receiving the highest score.

[2] Calculated on the basis of eight indicators. These are the six indicators listed above plus 7) the primary fiscal balance in 2003; and 8) absolute change in the primary fiscal balance from 1990–97 to 1998–2003. The other methodologies used also apply to this measure.

has recently completed satellite tourism and travel accounts for Barbados with projections. Some of these data are shown in Table II-22 along with comparisons of the Bahamas, Jamaica, Trinidad and Tobago and the Wider Caribbean.

For 2004, the travel and tourism industry is estimated to generate over US$1.6 billion of economic activity (total demand), which represents about 16 percent of GDP (or value

Table II-22. Travel and Tourism Satellite Accounts Comparison, 2004

Country/ Region	Total Demand (US million and % real growth)	Industry (% GDP)	Economy-Wide (% GDP)	Industry Jobs (% total jobs)	Economy-Wide Jobs (% total jobs)	Capital Investment (% of total)	Capital Investment (% real growth)
Barbados	1,621 (10.7)	15.8	52.2	20	58	65	2.4
Bahamas	1,613 (9.3)	18.6	56.0	26	70	65	3.5
Jamaica	1,301 (12.0)	11.8	36.0	11	32	32	2.1
Trinidad & Tobago	1,814 (7.5)	2.3	10.8	3	10.4	18	4.0
Wider Caribbean[1]	40,309 (10.0)	3.8	10.4	3	8.1	9	7.1

Source: WTTC/Oxford Economic Forecasting, Barbados Report (2004).

[1] This includes the 23 Caribbean countries listed as members of the WTTC.

Table II-23. Tourism Projections, 2004–2014

Items	Barbados: Growth Rate, 2004–2014	Barbados: Share of GDP in 2014	Caribbean Growth Rate	World Growth Rate
Total Rent	4.2	—	—	4.5
Travel and Tourism GDP	4.6	18.3	4.4	3.3
Direct and Indirect GDP	4.4	59.3	4.1	3.7
Jobs (Direct)	3.6	23.1	N.A.	1.7
Jobs (Direct and Indirect)	3.4	66.7	2.8	1.9
Capital Investment	3.7	66.2	N.A.	N.A.

Source: WTTC/Oxford Forecasting, Barbados Report (2004).

added of US$420 million) and 20 percent of jobs on a direct basis. Based on the satellite accounting methodology, which captures both direct and indirect effects, the sector accounts for 52 percent of GDP (a value added of US$1.4 billion), and 58 percent of total employment. Capital investment in the sector is estimated at about two-thirds of total investment in Barbados. Real growth in total demand for 2004 is estimated at 10.7 percent and for value added (GDP) the growth rate is estimated at 16 percent.

Projections for the period 2004–14 are shown in Table II-23. The estimated growth rates for Barbados, considering the relative maturity of the industry, are striking. These exceed in all available categories the performances of both the Caribbean as a region and the world as a whole, with the Caribbean also outperforming the world. These forecasts show an increased role for travel and tourism in the economy, particularly in terms of total demand, value added, investment and job creation.

x. Agriculture

FAO estimates of TFP, efficiency change and technological change in the agricultural sector of Barbados for the periods 1961–81 and 1981–2000 (see Table II-24) allow for comparisons

Table II-24. TFP, Efficiency Change, and Technological Change in Agriculture

	TFP Change		Efficiency Change		Technological Change	
Country/Region	1961/81	1981/2000	1961/81	1981/2000	1961/81	1981/2000
Barbados	2.9	0.9	0.3	−1.8	2.6	2.7
Jamaica	0.6	1.6	0.3	−0.8	0.2	2.4
Trinidad & Tobago	−1.6	0.5	−0.7	−1.2	0.9	1.7
LAC	−1.2	0.4	0.1	−0.1	−1.3	0.5
Developing Countries	−2.6	1.7	0.0	−0.4	2.6	2.0

Source: FAO (2004).

to be drawn with other CARICOM countries and regions. These calculations are based on the quantity of net agricultural production in constant (1989–91) international dollars divided by the quantity of inputs of land, labour, fertilizer, livestock and physical capital, applying data envelopment analysis (DEA) to estimate a Malmquist (1953) index. No data or input prices are required.

As we noted, the agricultural sector has been in long-term decline with shrinking production and export of sugar, severe threats of preference erosion, and the loss of market access for a crop whose production costs exceed five times the current world market price for raw sugar. The TFP and efficiency indicator show a worsening situation in the more recent period, which is consistent with our data. However, the technological change factor remains remarkably strong in comparison to the other countries/regions cited, a fact that appears to be counterintuitive.

Group 3: Other Indicators

Another set of indicators are ***broad assessments of social development and the performance of the social sector***. Earlier, descriptive data were given for a number of social outcomes, but here attention is drawn to broad assessments of the level of social development and Barbados' comparative standing.

Data on basic ***health indicators*** are shown in Table II-25. Barbados has met the Alma Ata targets of "Health for All by the Year 2000". There have been dramatic improvements in all the basic health indicators.

The Green Paper on Social Development (Thomas 2002) also makes this favourable assessment of the ***educational system***:

> Education facilities and opportunities from early childhood to the tertiary level, including TVET, Special Education, and

Table II-25. Basic Health Indicators for Barbados

Indicators	
Life Expectancy at Birth (2000)	76.8
Maternal Mortality (thousand births) (1999)	0.3
Infant Mortality (live births) (1999)	7.0
Newborns with LBW (2,500g) (%) (1990/98)	10
Calories Available (Kcal/pc/day) (1998)	2,978
HIV/AIDS (per million) (1997)	498
Contraceptive Prevalence (%) (1991–98)	55
Doctors Per 10,000 Pop. (1999)	13.7
Nurses Per 10,000 Pop. (1999)	51.2
Dentists Per 10,000 Pop. (1999)	1.9
Hospital Beds Per 1,000 Pop. (1996)	7.6
National Health Expenditure as % of GDP	6.7
Per Capita National Expenditure on Health (US$)	421
Public Financing Share (%)	62
Private Financing Share (%)	38
Population with Access to Services (%) (1997–99)	
Drinking Water	97.9
Sewerage and Excreta Disposal	99.4
Population with Access to Essential Drugs	100.0

Source: Cited in Thomas (2002).

Adult and Continuing Education, are excellent for a developing country. Public education is tuition free (at the point of delivery) and has been made compulsory for children up to age 16. There is, therefore, universal access at the primary and secondary levels. Educational access in the tertiary level is provided through government subsidies/loans for tuition to all that have attained a certain educational standard. (*ibid.*, page 15)

Safety-net programs in Barbados are summarized in Table II-26.

Table II-26. Safety Net Programs in Barbados

Target Group Program	Barbados
Children	
School Feeding	x
Travel to School	x
Uniforms, Books, Assistance	x
Low-Income Families	
Social Assistance (Cash)	x
Benefits in Kind	x
Housing	x
Unemployment	
Unemployment Benefit	x
Youth Training	x
Public Works	x
Small Business Development	x
Elderly	
Pension (Non-contributory)	x
NIS Pension (Contributory)	x
In-Kind Assistance	x
Homes for the Aged	x
Disabled	
NIS	x
Social Assistance	x
Residential Care	x

Source: Cited in Thomas (2002).

The same Green Paper identifies distinguishing features of ***the social welfare regime*** in Barbados as:

(1) The remarkably high level of social provisioning and one of the most complete social protection systems in the region.
(2) The role of state activism in promoting this.
(3) The support of the private, business, community and external development partners in this process.
(4) The location of the drive in favour of social development primarily in internal factors with external factors (obligations, commitments, targets) playing a strong complementary role.

The Green Paper also identifies the following areas of social provisioning and their institutional domains and makes the following assessment (see Table II-27).

Table II-27. Institutional Domains and Social Provisioning

Area	State	Market	Community	Family/Household
Education	High	Low +	Low	High
Health	High	Medium +	Low	Low
Pension	High	Medium +	Low	Low
Safety Nets	High	Low +	Low +	Medium +
Public Assistance	High	Low	Low +	Medium
Low-Income Housing	High	Low	Low	Low

Source: Thomas (2002).

Note: + means tending to increase.

From the table it can be observed that the level of state provisioning is considered to be high in all areas. Government is the most important institutional domain for both the formulation and implementation of social policies. The state's roles cover not only resource transfers and direct provisioning, but the regulation of social services delivery as well. This regulation takes many forms, including: 1) the determination of which services should be provided; 2) their level; and, 3) the manner of their delivery. In general therefore, these other indicators support the conclusion that there is a favourable social environment within which Barbados can successfully pursue measures designed to improve its national competitiveness.

D. Microeconomic Considerations

Competitiveness concerns cover national, sectoral, as well as enterprise issues, and, in this section of the chapter, problems posed at the enterprise/microeconomic level are considered. Separate studies on tourism, agriculture and the labour market are included in this book and we have therefore chosen three other areas of microeconomic concerns. The first relates to how foreign investors perceive the investment climate in Barbados; the second addresses issues affecting firms that may be classed as small and medium-sized enterprises (SMEs); and the third concentrates on information technology and telecommunications and an assessment of the e-readiness environment for enterprise development. We have been guided in this selection by discussions/interviews with stakeholders many of whom have stressed that the vision of the Government of Barbados (GOB) is that Barbados is to be a "centre of excellence for information technology and telecommunication in the Caribbean". Everyone expressed the view that this perspective is necessary if Barbados is to remain a competitive player in the international marketplace.

The Investment Climate in Barbados

At the firm level, it is difficult to overstate the importance of what is usually termed as the investment climate or business outlook in the country. This is a critical consideration at the micro level of firm decision as to whether to invest in new businesses or to expand operations. Although there is some variation in its usage, the standard view of the investment climate is that it comprises six key elements, namely:

- macroeconomic environment and outlook;
- the degree of political/social stability;
- the regulatory framework;
- support institutions for business;
- social and economic infrastructure; and
- the physical infrastructure.

The macroeconomic environment refers to such items as exchange-rate behaviour, inflation, public indebtedness and the state of the fiscal accounts. Political and social stability speaks to the issues of governance and regime credibility. The regulatory framework includes all laws and regulations that affect the business environment, their enforcement in a transparent and equitable manner, and the absence of corruption and/or discretionary exercise of governmental authority. Support institutions for business refer to those that relate to the support of the regulatory environment in which firms operate as well as those that facilitate businesses whether in areas *external* to doing businesses (for example the availability of financing and lowering transactions costs for the entry and exit of firms) or *internal* to doing business (for example business networks, associations and publications). The social and economic infrastructure would include the labour market, the provision of basic services, and the provision of social security and other safety nets. The physical infrastructure includes the full gamut of telecommunications, road and sea transport, ports and facilities as well as power, water and environmental sanitation.

In Barbados, domestic investment accounts form the bulk of total investment, but in this section we focus on the investment climate for FDI. Apart from data availability, as we shall see, the reason for this is that FDI is usually expected to contribute more to the growth of the economy than domestic investment. This is so for a number of reasons, including expectations that it would generate greater technology transfer, expose the economy to best practices in management, lead to the evolution of a framework to facilitate export-oriented firms, and generate strong entrepreneurial drive, a vibrant business culture and the promotion of better business ethics. FDI firms are expected also to encourage the establishment of other firms, both local and foreign, in related activities leading to agglomerations, spillovers and locational advantages from which clusters form.

The sectoral categorization of firms is expected to influence the relative rating of components in their assessment of the investment climate of a country. Thus agricultural firms would have a different set of priorities from those of manufacturing or service-based firms, reflecting the different factors that shape their competitiveness. Investment climate is also largely a matter of perception, and how this is acquired is a matter, therefore, of some importance. In Barbados there are three broad options open to the foreign investor, namely 1) the activities of the investment promotion agencies, 2) "word-of-mouth" assessments from persons operating locally, including other firms, and 3) on-the-spot business reconnaissance visits. Or there can be 4) some combination of the foregoing. From the limited data available, it seems that, as in other places in the Caribbean, the investment promotion agencies are not the major source. This is surprising, given the amount of public resources usually devoted to these bodies.

Empirical data on foreign investors' perception of the investment climate in Barbados are sparse to non-existent. One reported attempt to assess this was done by the FIAS Division of the World Bank (November, 2004), which surveyed 159 firms in the Caribbean, and Barbados was included in the sample. Of the surveyed firms, 45 percent were from the US and 40 percent from the Caribbean and the remainder from elsewhere. The survey identified seven main rating factors, each comprised of a number of components. These were the policy and legal environment, the FDI framework, market access, labour, administrative procedures, taxation and custom and infrastructure. There was an eighth rating factor (quality of life) which is not reported on here for lack of data. The policy and legal environment covered such areas as political stability, exchange-rate stability, the operation of due process, contract enforcement, government efficiency and anti-monopoly practices. The FDI framework covered attitudes to FDI, incentives, facilitation, finance and venture capital financing. Market access related to market size and proximity. Labour referred to productivity, the level of training and skills, the quality of industrial relations and the overall flexibility of the labour market. Administrative procedures referred to the usual concerns about registration, licensing, foreign-exchange control and access to land and other natural resources. Taxation and customs covered not only tariff rates but the quality of tax administration, auditing procedures and customs clearance. Infrastructure covered all the main sub-sectors of telecommunications, power, shipping and ports, air, water supply, and roads. These are summarized in Schedule II-1.

The survey data revealed that foreign investors rated the quality of infrastructure the highest factor in the region. On the rating scale of 1 to 5, this was placed above 4, which was classed as of "major importance", with "critical importance" the maximum, at 5. Infrastructure was followed by labour market issues (2nd), the policy and legal environment (3rd), quality of life (4th), taxation and customs (5th), and FDI framework (6th), all of which had ratings above 3.5 with 3 classed as of "moderate importance". The remaining two, market access and government administrative procedures, were placed just below 3.5.

Schedule II-1. Investment Climate: Rating Factors

Rating Factor	Components
Policy and Legal Environment	Political stability/exchange-rate stability/security/fairness and clarity of legal process/contract enforcement/government efficiency/anti-monopoly practices
FDI Framework	Attitude to FDI/investment incentives/export incentives (EPZs)/facilitation and services/local finance/government and venture capital financing
Market Access	Market size/inputs availability/proximity to other operations
Labour Market Issues	Productivity/skilled labour cost/availability of skills/industrial relations/health/unskilled labour availability/unskilled labour cost/labour market flexibility
Government Administration Procedures	Business registration and licencing/foreign exchange restriction/access to natural resources/access to land
Taxation and Customs	Tax rates/customs clearance procedures/ import tariff/tax administration and auditing/QRs
Infrastructure Quality	Telecommunications/power/shipping and ports/air/water supply/roads

The gap between "performance" and the "importance rating" is an indicator of the need for improvement and a good pointer to policy recommendations. In effect it constitutes the elements of a diagnostic assessment. Comparing these ratings of importance with the actual performance of countries showed that there was considerable variation in the CARICOM region. Barbados, however, was found to be doing quite well in policy and legal environment, FDI framework, and infrastructure but not as well in taxation and customs, and market access. Barbados is perceived by foreign investors to have a very good policy and legal environment, especially in terms of political and macroeconomic stability, fairness and clarity in its laws and regulations, government efficiency, and security. This has augured well for its position as a tourist destination and conforms to the picture drawn earlier in this section.

In terms of the FDI framework, Barbados is perceived as having perhaps the "best" investment climate in the region, particularly in regard to its attitude to FDI, the special incentives it gives to investors, and the financing options opened to investors. Although all the regional economies are small and the majority of the firms surveyed did not export, market access was listed as an important perception factor. Barbados did not fare well in this category and investors were particularly concerned about local supplies of business inputs. For the labour market, the key components are the skills and productivity of the workforce.

Of note, Barbados' wage costs are high for all categories of labour (professional, skilled and unskilled). Labour productivity is important, therefore, to firms. However, as we saw earlier in the chapter, there has been a tendency towards declining labour productivity in recent times with wages growth exceeding that of productivity, thereby raising unit labour costs. The migration of skilled persons is a major contributor to this situation.

In terms of administrative procedures, investors are generally satisfied that entry and exit as well as continuing in business in Barbados are not cumbersome. Issues, however, do arise in regard to accessing land, which is to be expected in a country of such limited physical size. The area where Barbados performed worst is taxation and customs. Overall, the region is considered to be a very highly taxed one, which accounts for the considerable role that incentives legislation plays in attracting business. This, however, creates the perception of "favoured" and "not-favoured" companies, which has the potential for arbitrariness and discrimination. It has been reported that the issues of customs delays and weak administration are currently being addressed. On the other hand, firms operating in Barbados consider infrastructure to be of good quality. As we indicated above, this factor topped the list of priority requirements firms considered in assessing the investment climate. Over 70 percent of all surveyed firms considered all six components of the infrastructure rating to be the priority.

Finally, we should briefly note the results of the IADB analysis of the most serious obstacles to business development in the broader Latin America and Caribbean area. This analysis was based on the World Business Environment Survey (WBES) that covered 20 countries for the years 1999 and 2000 but that did not include Barbados. Those results show that in terms of the percentage of responding firms the major obstacles listed in descending order of importance are financing, taxes and regulation, policy instability, inflation, exchange-rate, crime, infrastructure, anti-competitive practices, corruption, organized crime and judicial systems.[8]

Small and Microenterprise Issues

There is no standard definition of what constitutes an SME, as it is a location—and even perhaps a sector-specific concept. In Barbados, several operational definitions are in use.[9]

---

[8] About one-third of the firms listed financing as the most serious obstacle. About one in six considered taxes and regulations to be the most serious problem and just below that came policy instability and, less frequently, inflation and the exchange-rate. The other factors had less than 10 percent of the respondents identifying them as the greatest obstacle. Corruption, organized crime and the judicial system were identified by less than 5 percent of the respondents as the greatest obstacle.

[9] The Barbados Investment and Development Corporation (BIDC) defines a small manufacturing enterprise as having any three of the following four criteria: sales of not more than US$250,000; investment of not more than US$50,000; factory space of 4,000 sq. ft. or less; employment of 25 persons or fewer; and not more than US$500,000

A common denominator in all the definitions is the number of employees—25 or fewer. In Barbados some SMEs are formally registered as legal organizations (e.g., as cooperatives or business incorporated enterprise) and also meet regulatory obligations under the Inland Revenue Department, social security legislation, and so on. The vast majority, however, operate informally, i.e., outside the regulatory framework, and this constitutes an overriding characteristic of the sector. In Barbados, these SMEs include a variety of forms: sole proprietors, service providers, small farmers and professionals (Ellis, 2001). Based on these criteria, we find that the SME sector is a major contributor to value added, employment, and the smooth functioning of the Barbadian economy. In the Industrial Census of 1994, it was found that two-thirds of all firms had fewer than 26 employees.

Structure/Characteristics

From our diagnostic assessment, several features characterize the SME sector in Barbados. Chiefly they are that:

- They are mainly composed of "own-account" activities with primarily one owner-operator and heavily based within the household unit. An estimated 96 percent of operations were sole proprietorship (Ellis, 2001).
- Firms frequently operate from the place of residence or an extension, or are housed nearby.
- Where needed, firms utilize mostly family labour, but they also, at times, employ persons outside the family.
- The firms represent a major source of livelihood for their owners, but they are also frequently complementary to some other activity in which the owners are engaged.
- In significant numbers, and depending on the sector, firms that are operated by women face additional problems because of the household and other caring roles women simultaneously perform. Women have been estimated at 41 percent of the sole proprietorships (Ellis, 2001) (see Table II-28).
- Firms utilize low-level technology and low-level skills, although with the spread of Government and NGO support institutions, they are in the process of upgrading both skills and technology.

---

in equity. The Barbados Institute of Management and Productivity defines a small enterprise as having the following two criteria: not more than US$1.0 million in annual sales, and not more than 25 employees. The Caribbean Development Bank defines it as having the following four criteria: less than 4,000 sq. ft. of manufacturing area; less than US$50,000 investment in equipment; less than US$125,000 annual sales; and fewer than 25 employees. In the Small Business Development Act, it is defined as: not more than US$500,000 in equity; not more than US$1.0 million in annual sales; and not more than 25 employees.

Table II-28. Industries by Types of Ownership

Industry	Male	Female	Total
Agriculture	787	776	1,563
Manufacturing	312	50	362
Construction	431	39	470
Distribution	1,163	1,150	2,313
Tourism	58	0	58
Transport & communication	139	75	214
Finance & business services	45	0	45
Personal services	50	9	59
General services	367	173	540
Not stated	70	27	97
Total	3,422	2,298	5,721

Source: Barbados Statistical Service Department: Informal Sector Survey 1997/98, Government of Barbados, p. 20.

- Most firms are heavily concentrated in the retail and services sector, but increasingly some are providing "professional services" as education and training advance in Barbados.
- Firms are generally focused on the domestic market, but some operations are turning to markets in CARICOM and, in some instances, elsewhere.
- As a result of the smallness of operations and limited domestic markets, most firms are described as operating at "steady-state" levels with limited potential for growth (Wenner and Chalmers, 2001).
- Lacking suitable collateral, the growth of firm operations is constrained because credit is difficult to access and when it is available, it is usually at very high rates of interest, which raise transaction costs.
- Small business entrepreneurs are inclined towards risk-aversion and avoidance in decision-making, but, at the same time, these operations are considered to be too risky by formal credit institutions, especially banks.

There are three further broad features, which our assessment has identified separately. One is that, to the extent the SME sector is predominantly informal in Barbados, it unavoidably remains on the periphery of the formal sector. This situation constrains the growth and expansion of SMEs. This is particularly noticeable in the case of the difficulties these firms face when seeking to access formal finance or to benefit from the advantages of the regulatory framework for business activity. Alongside this is a second feature of the SME sector, which is that it seems to have become, by force of circumstance, a sort of "breeding ground" or "incubator" for the development of firms considered to have growth potential. This consideration we believe has played a major role in favouring government and NGO support for the sector.

However, it does seem as if the most important consideration for government is the sector's potential for generating jobs in a situation where the major formal firms are unlikely to achieve this in adequate numbers (Ellis, 2001). This expectation stems from the highly labour-intensive methods of SMEs operations. In some parts of the region, it has been estimated that SMEs contribute between 16 and 40 percent of the jobs in the economy. The danger we draw from this assessment is that this perspective is very close to a "welfare-oriented" view of the SME sector, in which the firms are considered as operating as a form of "social safety net" rather than as a dynamic, pro-growth business incubator.

On the basis of the foregoing structure and characteristics of the SME sector, a number of broad constraints were identified in the assessment. These include: inadequate access to formal finance/credit/capital resources; limitations in the operations of SME support institutions and other business development services (BDS) run by the GOB and NGOs; weak networking and alliance building among firms in the sector; the lack of entrepreneurial/business skills; a dire need for more training and the upgrading of workforce skills, as well as technology adaptation and transfer; problems of adjusting to the demands of globalization and new external trading arrangements (CSME, FTAA, the Cotonou Agreement, and WTO); and the lack of adequate survey data on the sector with which to facilitate programmatic and policy reforms. These constraints will be examined in the following sub-section.

Operational Constraints in the SME Sector

Four areas of operational constraints have been identified, namely: finance; constraints identified as a result of sector assessments; those identified as a result of firm surveys and case studies; and constraints identified at business fora.

Finance

The importance of financial depth and stability to the financial environment of SMEs cannot be overemphasized. In Barbados, the microfinance aspect of the financial environment refers to the provision of a wide range of financial services to relatively low- income households that operate microenterprises. Services include deposit-taking, credit/loans, payment facilities, money transfer and insurance. Limited access to formal finance for the SME sector has been widely recognized as a critical constraint to the development of the sector. Thus this problem of access has been held responsible for preventing start-ups as well as stunting the growth, modernization and expansion possibilities of many existing operations (Wenner, 2001). Some specific adaptive microenterprise intermediaries have appeared to fill this gap. The verdict, however, seems to be that within the wider Caribbean these intermediaries are, as a general rule, "immature compared to other parts of the developing world, particularly South Asia and Latin America" (*Ibid.*, p. 1.).

The existing range of financial intermediaries and technical assistance agencies that service the SME sector in Barbados is considerable.[10] The diagnostic assessment has identified the following general characteristics of the supply and demand for microfinance:

- Formal institutions rarely lend to the SME sector. According to the IADB, only an estimated 3–5 percent of microenterprises have access to formal financing (cited in Wenner, 2001).
- Most of the financing provided is through own savings, transfers, borrowing from family and friends, and the specialized microfinance intermediaries referred to above, which are typically run by government, NGOs and credit unions.
- Most microentrepreneurs lack standard forms of collateral, a situation that limits the willingness to supply finance.
- When SMEs borrow in the informal sector, they face high repayment costs, which raise their transaction costs and jeopardize their businesses.
- Some of the existing microfinance intermediaries suffer from "lower staff productivity, higher delinquency, less profitability and lower rates of recovery" when compared to their counterparts in Latin America (*Ibid.*, p. 5, Table 3).
- Existing intermediaries generally depend heavily on government and donor funding rather than their own portfolio growth, which is slow.
- The cost of monitoring small loans is often very high, which makes the provision of those loans problematic.
- Information asymmetries abound and lead to adverse selection/moral hazard. The absence of information-sharing institutions such as credit bureaus is also notable.

---

[10] These include:

Debt Financing: Agricultural Development Fund, Barbados Youth Business Trust, Caribbean Financial Services Corporation, Industrial Credit Fund, Industrial Investment & Employment Fund, Livestock Development Fund, Pinelands Enterprises Micro Credit Programme, Rural Development Commission, The Barbados Agency for Micro-Enterprise Development Ltd., Urban Development Commission, commercial banks, and credit unions.

Equity Financing: Barbados Investment Fund, Caribbean Financial Services Corporation, Small Business Venture Capital Inc., Enterprise Growth Fund Limited, and The Innovation Fund.

Grants: Barbados Youth Business Trust, Barbados Investment and Development Corporation, Export Grant & Incentive Scheme, Cariforum Agribusiness Research and Training Fund (CARTF), and Competitive Enhancement Scheme.

Technical Assistance: Barbados Investment and Development Corporation, Barbados Small Business Development Centre, The Barbados Agency for Micro-Enterprise Development Ltd., Caribbean Technological Consultancy Services Network, and Youth Entrepreneurship Scheme.

Credit Guarantees: Credit Guarantee Scheme.

Export Credit Insurance: Export Credit Insurance Scheme.

Export Finance Guarantees: Export Finance Guarantee Scheme.

Other: Barbados Public Workers' Co-operative Credit Union, and Small Business Lending & Development Programme.

Certain reform challenges emerge from the diagnostic assessment, namely: 1) the need for stronger efforts to make SME lending a significant product line for the dominant commercial banks, 2) similarly, stronger efforts to develop the NGO-type funding intermediaries (as well as statutory funding) into more formal financial institutional arrangements with close linkages to the dominant commercial banking sector, 3) the need to forge direct ties between the development of financial intermediary status, with the provision of well-targeted technical assistance to improve entrepreneurial, and other business skills in the sector. This may well call for closer linkage between business development services and microfinancing in an effort both to cut costs and reduce risks and 4) the need for an apex microfinance agency to improve the performance of the retail suppliers by enhancing their ability to reach larger numbers.

Constraints Identified from SME Sector Assessments (ILO)

ILO (2001) assessed the situation facing women entrepreneurs in the Caribbean, and Barbados was included as a case country. The assessment documented the scale and scope of their activities as well as the problems and barriers they were facing. To the extent possible, it also provided comparisons with male entrepreneurs. Its main findings in regard to the characteristics of female entrepreneurs are as follows: they tended to be more cautious and to avoid risky ventures as compared to males, so that their operations were kept small and products diversified rather than specialized; their activities conformed to their household commitments and the business therefore needed to afford a balance between that and family responsibilities. As a result, they were less profit oriented; they showed a strong preference for the services sector; they showed great eagerness for self-improvement and skills acquisitions, certainly compared to their male counterparts; and they were on average less experienced in business than their male counterparts. In general, therefore, men accessed credit and investment capital easier than women did; and women with "academic" qualifications gravitated towards paid employment and did so at an early age, while women without these qualifications gravitated towards small businesses and they did so at an older age.

In relation to the barriers and constraints encountered by women in their business operations, the assessment observed that, apart from the general ones covered in the previous sub-section, women faced additional directly related gender ones, which reflect women's position in society. These include: *sociological ones* (the absence of an entrepreneurial culture; discrimination in raising finance/capital as they suffer greater scrutiny from lenders; conflicting pressures arising from their dual roles in the business and the home); *educational ones* (while no official educational barriers exist against women, there is a lack of readily available access to business training); and *marketing/financial ones* (special problems of accessing finance, especially for start-up operations, aggravated by the relatively small volume of their operations). It was also found that generally women enter businesses that utilize skills acquired from their female roles. Additionally, they do not seem to network among themselves to the same extent that men do.

Constraints Identified in Surveys and Follow-Up Case Studies

Lashley (2003) surveyed 146 enterprises in the manufacturing sector of Barbados, and conducted case studies. Forty-two of these firms (30 percent) employed fewer than five persons, 58 firms (40 percent) were small enterprises employing between 6 and 20 persons and 40 (30 percent) were categorized as medium or large employing more than 20 persons. The main characteristics of these firms, revealed by the survey were: little growth in profits, turnover or employment in recent years; competition mainly in the form of product quality (55 percent) [a small percent (14) competed via cost or price]; little networking among firms, little use of support schemes/arrangements available (membership of associations was low and where the number was encouraging, for example in membership of the Small Business Association, there was great inactivity); focus on the domestic market in regard to their customers, competitors and suppliers; in the case of firms that exported, a regional focus on the CARICOM market; and attitudes towards the formation of the CSME described as being "at best non-negative". In general the firms surveyed were found to be lacking in an international orientation, and displaying weak linkages both among themselves and between themselves and the dedicated support schemes, arrangements and organizations that existed.

Case studies have been undertaken to determine the factors that lie behind these characteristics, and the following key characteristics were observed:

1. There was limited use of support structures, owing principally to a "lack of knowledge" concerning them. This was accompanied by some distrust of these institutions, born of past negative experiences, suspicion over their autonomy from the government, skepticism over their relevance, and concerns about the "cost" of membership. These findings provide a strong comment on the effectiveness of the business development and support organization in existence at the time of the survey.
2. There was a lack of information about exporting and the perception was one of initial high transactions costs, which deterred an export orientation. This was particularly noticeable for exports to non-CARICOM areas.
3. In several instances, firms expressed concern over the competition they were facing.
4. As a rule, it was also found that: "management and production styles appear to be acting as a constraint to business development". Management was found to be too much "hands on" and oriented towards "pushing" workers to get the job done, on

the assumption that workers were not motivated. There was little effort to explore alternative production methods. Therefore while management blamed workers as being averse to change, the same could be said of management.

5. Small firms were imitative of the production styles of large firms, which did not bode well as they did not have the advantage of scale economies. As a rule, they did not seem to exploit the flexibility and adaptability of small operations.
6. Although the firms were not strongly export oriented, several were dependent on imported supplies and indeed expressed a preference for these over local supplies (which were considered to be costlier and of lesser quality when available).
7. Many expressed a lack of information and faced high transaction costs of both imported inputs (information on sources, paperwork, port charges and other fees and levies) and exports (potential markets, payment arrangements, financing of exports, and paperwork).
8. In terms of their day-to-day operations, the case-study firms listed the following problems: locating suitable employees; restricted ability to hire/fire in response to market changes, because of unionism; low worker productivity and resistance to innovation and change; high cost of non-wage benefits (sickness, leave, holidays, absenteeism, lateness); worker attitudes; worker motivation; cost of material/utilities input supplies; high taxes and business levies; and access to finance (although this did not emerge as a top priority).

Overall, the case studies identified five classes of issues that need addressing: 1) concerns over worker attitudes, and motivation, 2) dissatisfaction over high taxes, 3) limited networking among businesses despite the existence of a number of association and other bodies, 4) limited orientation towards exporting and 5) the lack of promotion/ knowledge/awareness of support schemes offered by Governments and the NGO community.

The last issue has been the subject of an IADB study: "Lessons Learnt from Business Development Services (BDS) Programs for SMEs in Latin America, 1995–2002". This reviewed the Bank's experience and arrived at four general conclusions, which seem to be relevant to the Barbados situation:

- There is a trade-off between the outreach of BDS institutions and its effectiveness. Resolving this constitutes a major challenge.
- Private agencies have a comparative advantage over public agencies.
- Over the medium term, sponsored institutions face major challenges of transforming themselves into sustainable ones.
- In the design of BDS institutions, a long time-line should be provided for, as their real task is to transform the markets they are intended to serve.

Constraints Identified at Business Fora

Finally, based on the analysis of reports of decisions/conclusions arrived at, at recent business fora, the following emerge as critical constraints to the expansion of the SME sector: 1) the need for more specific research/information on the impact of trade liberalization in areas of technical and process requirements, 2) the careful handling of the global adjustment process and the need therein for strong government/private-sector linkage, 3) support for local firms less than that given to international business corporations, 4) firms addressing internally some of the competitiveness factors but better data availability on best practices, benchmarking surveys (which, like best practices, help to improve business processes and firm functions), and global surveys are required, 5) operationally, problems in regard to their: level of technology, human resource development; operational procedures and systems; plant and equipment improvement, marketing, worker productivity and incentive schemes (for which assistance is being provided to the Barbados National Productivity Council), information, and quality management.

ICT and the E-Readiness Environment

As referred to earlier the vision of the GOB is to make Barbados "the centre of excellence for information technology and telecommunications in the Caribbean". It is felt that this is the only sure way for the country to remain competitive and be an international player. This vision seems to be widely shared among Barbadian firms. The government, for its part, has fuelled a number of ICT and ICT-related initiatives. Some of these are broadly based and aim at the overall improvement of education, training and the knowledge base of the society. Some are more specifically geared to areas that directly impact on firms, for example, telecoms liberalization; incentives and support for business re-engineering to facilitate the digitalization of activities; and legislation to improve the regulation and oversight of the production, distribution and use of computerized information. In addition, some initiatives are directed at the development of ICT-based firms.

A Green Paper on Telecommunications Sector Policy (2000) sets out the main lines of Government's approach to the task it has set itself. Two important cornerstones of that policy are regulation and liberalization. Thus, in the area of regulatory reform, the stated aim is to protect consumers, encourage investment, promote efficiency and ensure quality service. Similarly, the aims of liberalization are to improve the efficiency of incumbents; promote the general responsiveness of the telecoms sector to customer demands in areas of pricing and product offerings; and widen employment and entrepreneurial opportunities in the sector.

In this sub-section the purpose of our diagnostic assessment is to gauge, at the micro-economic level, how enterprises view the progress that has been achieved towards these broad goals. The section firstly presents a summary of the telecommunications and connectivity indicators in Barbados, as well as indicators of the level of knowledge-based development achieved. Secondly we look at the results of a survey directed at obtaining businesses' views about Barbados' e-readiness. After that, we note recent observations from the government side about Barbados' e-readiness as well as refer to observations arising out of regional assessments of CARICOM's e-readiness.

Connectivity Indicators and Knowledge-Based Development

Not only is ICT a technology- and knowledge-intensive field of inquiry, but issues concerning it operate simultaneously at both the macro and micro levels. Its role in development depends not only on business (enterprise) adaptation to ICT but on the orientation of the broader society and culture to its uses. Our principal concern in this section, however, is with the microeconomic aspects, that is the enterprise's perspective, but the interconnection between micro and macro effects are not entirely separated in the presentation. Furthermore, e-commerce (that is on-line ordering and selling) and e-business do not refer simply to product purchase, e-mail and other similar communication platforms as is the perspective of most SMEs in Barbados. It incorporates as well ***all*** areas of information and services that can be provided via the Internet. This would include pre-purchase; market research, marketing and the widening of the customer base; process issues in the office (finance, and accounts management) and in production (automation, and inventory control); information gathering; human resource management; supply chain management; distribution and after-sales; and, other forms of business support. All these uses enable enterprises to reduce transactions costs by making for better time management and procedures along with improved marketing and services and to fully integrate business functions into ICT. They also facilitate the entry of firms based on ICT, for example call centres, software and supply services, and digital commerce. When these are taken into account, ICT would be seen as affecting the broader aspects of the organizational processes in enterprises, its entrepreneurial orientation, production systems, as well as training and improvement of workforce skills.

This combination of electronics, commerce and business is pertinent both to traditional areas of the Barbados economy, such as government or the social sectors (health and education) and the areas of the "new economy". The transition from website and e-mail office use to integration into business functions requires management and technical skills to do so, organizational changes to accompany it, and financing of the required investments. Before pursuing these issues, however, we present a snapshot view of the connectivity and knowledge-based level of development in Barbados in Table II-29. There we can see that compared to other developing countries, Barbados' situation in regard to the basic telecommunication and connectivity indicators is quite good. The number of telephone subscribers exceeds the population size. The connection rates for both land lines and cellular mobiles

Table II-29. Barbados Connectivity Indicators

Indicator	Statistic
Total telephone subscribers	336,000
Telephones per hundred inhabitants	124
Main telephone lines per hundred inhabitants	50
Cellular mobile subscribers per hundred inhabitants	74
Cellular mobile subscribers as percentage of total telephone lines	60
Internet users per hundred inhabitants	55
Internet hosts per ten thousand inhabitants	8
Personal computers per hundred inhabitants	13

are high. Internet users are 55 percent of the population, which is very high, and, PC availability is more than one in ten persons. However, compared to the developed world and some high-flying developing countries such as Singapore, Barbados' indicators still have some way to go overall.

Most of the improvement in Barbados has occurred in recent times. Thus, for example, cellular subscribers rose from 12,000 in 1999 to 200,000 in 2004. Main telephone lines did not increase as dramatically but, nevertheless, grew by nearly one-fifth between 1999 and 2004. Internet users at 55 per 100 had a penetration ratio more than several times higher than the LAC region and higher than Europe. Indeed, Barbados' indicators are well above those of upper middle-income countries and close to high-income ones.

The World Bank's knowledge economy index and knowledge index for Barbados also indicate the promising level of achievement and the strong strides that have been made over the past decade (see Table II-30). Thus, whereas in 1995, on a scale of 1–10, none of the indicators listed in the table below, with the exception of education (7.17), rated at 6, in the most recent year, five of the indicators were at 7 and only one at 6, (the economic incentive regime). That indicator had, however, nearly doubled in value during the interval. This assessment of improvements in the recent past is consistent with other information accessed for this report.

Table II-30. The Knowledge Economy Index and the Knowledge Index

	Index	1995	Most Recent Year
1	Knowledge Economy Index[1]	4.92	7.00
2	Knowledge Index[2]	5.52	7.33
3	Economic Incentive Regime	3.13	6.02
4	Education	7.17	7.77
5	Innovation	3.54	6.99
6	Information Infrastructure	5.83	7.23

Source: World Bank, Knowledge Assessment (2005).

[1] Average of 3,4,5,6.
[2] Average of 4,5,6.

E-Readiness Framework Analysis

There are different approaches towards determining how ready the business environment (and indeed the wider society) is for e-business. By e-readiness we refer to:

> the ability of businesses to extend easily into the Internet, their capacity to structure their activities to facilitate the digitalization of transactions, and the extent to which there is a framework for the seamless interconnection between public and private transactions.

We also refer to the extent to which the broader society and culture support these developments and the accompanying orientation of business activities.

There is a global networked e-readiness organization that has developed a standard framework that is very useful for diagnostic assessments of e-readiness in countries. The framework has five main indicators, namely: *infrastructure, policy environment, legal environment, human capital availability* and the *e-business environment.* The *infrastructure* covers such areas as connectivity, competition, access, reliability and the cost of ICT services. The *policy framework* addresses the issues of government and national prioritization, government and industry partnerships, and broader participation and access for all citizens—in other words, e-leadership in the broadest sense. The *legal framework* refers to policies to protect privacy, to guard against computer crimes and to put in place mechanisms for investigation, due process, and enforcement. *Human capital* speaks to the quality and effectiveness of the educational system, the culture of local creativity, information sharing in the society, and specific IT skills. Finally the *e-business framework* addresses concerns about the investment climate in relation to e-business. This depends on the extent of financial system support for e-transactions, transparency and predictability in laws and so forth. These framework items and components are summarized in Schedule II-2.

A survey commissioned by the National Council for Science and Technology (System Consultancy, 2003) to assess e-readiness in Barbados utilized this framework. The results of the survey are summarized in Schedule II-3.

In addition to the results in the schedule, it should be noted that 13 percent of firms had libraries equipped with Internet access, as against one-third for government departments and 20 percent for parastatal enterprises. Company websites were more popular, as 75 percent of the firms surveyed had websites. The website advantages were well recognized, and the main barrier was the high cost of establishing and maintaining/updating one. The survey supported the view that Internet usage in Barbados is on the increase. However, this usage was largely confined to young persons, as 71 percent of users are under 35, and among these, those with either vocational or university education were more likely to use the Internet.

Schedule II-2. Adaptation of the Framework: Design and Schedule

Framework Item	Components
Infrastructure Framework [Connectivity and Cost]	Availability of communication services, access centres and networked computers Effective competition Affordability and reliability of network access Cost of service Reliability of electrical supply Incubator facilities/IT parks
Policy Framework [E-Leadership and Participation]	Is e-readiness a national priority? Is there a national IT/e-commerce plan/strategy? Is there a lead agency? Is there promotion of e-government? Partnerships between industry and government to improve e-readiness Level of effort to promote access for all citizens
Legal Framework [Security and Privacy]	Legal framework with regard to e-commerce transaction Legal protections and progress in protecting intellectual property rights Extent of efforts to protect privacy Legal protection of networked information Legal framework to address and prosecute computer crimes, authorize digital signatures, and enable public key infrastructures
Human Capital Framework [E-Enabled Human Capital]	Quality of and participation levels in the education system Emphasis on efforts to create and support a knowledge-based society E-literacy campaigns Culture of local creativity and information sharing Skills and efficiency of the workforce Levels of IT training in education systems
E-Business Framework	Status of IT industry Transparency and predictability of regulatory implementation Openness of government, rule of law, and general business risk IT use in business Openness to foreign investors in ICT Ability of the financial system to support electronic transactions

Source: Adapted from E-Readiness Framework Design.

The diagnostic suggests therefore, that there is still some distance to go to make Barbados a world class ICT country. Nevertheless, great improvements have been made and the country's present situation is good for a developing country. If, however, ICT is to contribute

Schedule II-3. E-Readiness Framework Analysis

Framework Item	Responses	Suggestions
Infrastructure Framework [Connectivity and Cost]	Moderate levels of Internet accessibility and use of high speed connections. Rate structure considered too high.	Faster Internet connection speeds and increased bandwidth. Reduction in rates. Improvement in technology. Open the sectors to competition.
Policy Framework [E-Leadership and Participation]	***Overall*** rating of Government = 2.3 Making the Internet more accessible = 2.8 Creating partnerships with the private sector = 2.3 Having a defined strategy/policy = 2.2 Automation of governmental processes = 1.8	Reduce telecommunication rates. Create more public access facilities. Expand existing educational programmes. Provide incentives. Make greater effort at public sector–private sector–civil society links through joint ventures/seminars. Improve infrastructure.
Legal Framework [Security and Privacy]	***Overall*** rating of legal protection and level of security for e-transactions and intellectual property rights = 2.4 For protection of intellectual property rights = 2.9 Addressing computer crimes = 2.5 Protecting privacy = 2.3 Prosecuting computer crimes = 1.9 Information dissemination = 1.9	More public awareness campaigns. Periodic audit checks. Stricter enforcement. Legislative updating. More enforcement through better trained personnel.
Human Capital [E-Enabled Human Capital]	Moderately high educated workforce. Significant levels of training provided by firms (three quarters of firms committed to offering training). The barriers identified by respondents were: lack of IT training/knowledge; resistance to change; bad management attitudes and practices	More training. Greater public awareness.
E-Business Framework [Enabling Seamless E-Commerce]	***Overall*** rating of 3.1. Stability of political system = 4.2 Ability to support e-commerce = 3.6 Competition among ISPs = 3.0 Strength of the economy = 3.1 Competition among communication providers = 1.8	Break up existing monopoly in telecommunications.

Source: Adapted from System Technology (SCL) Report 2003.
Note: Rating Scale: 1 = very poor; 2 = poor; 3 = fair; 4 = very good; 5 = excellent.

to improved competitiveness, the problems in the sector will have to be addressed along the lines indicated above. There is also the issue of building a proper database for measuring ICT usage/indicators/performance as the Statistical Services Division cannot continue to leave this to occasional surveys conducted elsewhere, if the goal of making Barbados "a centre of excellence" in ICT is to be achieved. Greater usage of ICT will be also largely market-driven in Barbados as seems to be the case elsewhere (UNCTAD 2005). It is anticipated that the need to be competitive as market pressures unfold will impel firms/enterprises to consider the profitability of taking the next step in ICT usage, and, with their customers and suppliers, become more Internet-dependent. They will be left with little choice but to adapt or perish.

Other Observations

From discussions with persons connected to both the SME and ICT sectors, the impression has been gathered that for most SMEs the Internet is used primarily as a vehicle for e-mail, occasional information searches and a website. This picture is, on the whole, consistent with the survey data examined above. In a recent newspaper report, (*Barbados Advocate*, December 13, 2004) this view was endorsed in the statement: "e-commerce is yet to be embraced by local business as a way that would make a significant difference to the business environment."

We can say, therefore, that, while some sections of the environment are strong, the overall picture suggests that the "digital divide" still persists. In a speech reported in the newspaper item cited above, the Minister of Commerce, Consumer Affairs and Business Development highlighted a number of obstacles in the area of e-commerce, all of which accord with those derived from the survey discussed above. These included: insufficient telecoms bandwidth; high cost of Internet connections; high financial services fees; high setup costs for websites; high prices for on-line advertising; and the failure of firms to grasp the nature and amount of the benefits from e-commerce. The last observation has to be juxtaposed to the survey result, which has shown that those firms actually using the Internet are convinced that it helps their profit line. Legislation is one major area in which strong improvements are being seen. At the moment, legislation recently passed or coming on board include an Electronics Transaction Act, which makes provision for the legal recognition of business transactions done electronically; a Data Protection Act; a Computer Misuse Act; and a Policy Framework for Freedom of Information Act.

Cross-regional studies (see Singh, 2001 and Kirkman, 2002) support this general observation, as well as the earlier one that the "digital divide" survives in CARICOM. An assessment of best practices status in CARICOM 2001 cited Barbados for doing well in three areas: legal support for e-commerce transactions; the institutional framework for fostering development of ICT; and, local creativity. The Barbados Edu Tech 7-year programme has been designed to transform the education framework by upgrading facilities, curricula, and methods of teaching, and to facilitate the growth of a knowledge community. It has been highly commended by most observers. This program, with the support of IADB and Caribbean Development Bank funding, has the objective:

> not simply to place computers in schools, but to change the culture of the classroom to bring about an increase in the number of students contributing to the sustainable social and economic development of Barbados; and to develop students that are highly skilled and readily re-trainable in a technologically rich and rapidly changing environment (Braithwaite, 2004).

In conclusion ***certain policy priorities*** follow from the above analysis in regard to ICT and SMEs:

- First, the need to ensure affordable (low-cost) accessibility to the Internet.
- Second, continued legal and supervisory/regulatory efforts to build trust in e-business.
- Third, the development of skills to pioneer the leap from e-mail/website/office use to the integration of ICT into all business functions.
- Fourth, firms accessing the requisite financing to install ICT.
- Fifth, the continued building of awareness among members of the public and at the micro and firm levels as well. In this regard the Action Plan of the World Summit on the Information Society (WSIS), in which Barbados is a participant, offers useful guidance.

E. Conclusions and Recommendations

The diagnostic assessment has identified several important ***strengths*** in the Barbados situation, and some key ones are listed in Schedule II-4.

The country, nonetheless, faces formidable ***challenges*** as the diagnostic has revealed, and some of the key ones are highlighted in Schedule II-5.

Arising from the summary diagnostic, Schedule II-6 identifies the major areas for priority emphasis that are recommended. It should be stressed that it is tempting to draw up a long wish-list of issues needing to be addressed, and in this way seek to cover all bases. This was rejected as being an impractical way to approach the situation since all these possible areas cannot be addressed by one institution (the IADB), and in any case the absorptive capacity of the country would make this unfeasible.

Schedule II-4. Key Strengths Identified from the Diagnostic Assessment

1) Comparative stability of the social, cultural, and political environment.
2) The high regard and standing of Barbados in the region, hemisphere, and broader global economy, which is based on substantial past achievements. Its performance with such indicators as the HDI, governance, rule-of-law, transparency, accountability, democratic elections, scholarship and learning provides objective reinforcement of this reputation and standing.
3) The country's long tradition of economic and social planning, along with responsible state activism on development issues, and the broad social-political consensus within the country in favour of this approach to social, economic and political engineering.
4) The Social Partners model of industrial relations, productivity and competitiveness management as expressed in the four Protocols which they have institutionalized since 1993.
5) The high quality of its human resources and the exemplary outcomes it has had in its health, education, social protection and welfare, and ICT indicators.
6) The high quality and reputation of its leadership, which has resulted in its playing a disproportionately important role in regional, hemispheric, and SIDS arenas.
7) Its long (mature) experience in developing the services sector, an experience that started well before its leading role of services in economic activity came to be so widely appreciated.
8) In CARICOM and the broader Caribbean and SIDS groupings, its comparative success in macroeconomic management and the pursuit of diversification policies and programs since political independence.
9) A very small underground economy (estimated at less than 1 percent of GDP) and the seemingly weak influence of organized crime and the narcotics trade, which distinguishes it from several of its CARICOM neighbours.

Schedule II-5. Key Challenges Identified from the Diagnostic Assessment

1) How to manage a small economy in the face of the rapid and deep transformation of the global political economy, the emergence of a new global division of labour, and far-reaching changes in the intergovernmental framework for relations between nations.
2) How small firms in a small country will be able to cope with these globalisation pressures and increased competition.
3) General problems of making SMEs more effective.
   - Problems of the high cost, slow connectivity, weak integration of ICT into firm operations at the highest possible level
   - Problems of microfinance
   - Problems of training and skills upgrade of workforce
4) The compulsory requirement of a country with limited resources (human, financial, institutional, and natural) to adapt not only to economic globalization but to the transformation of the global regulatory and institutional architecture governing trade, finance, capital movements, technology transfer, human resources, enterprise structure and operations, and national policy in areas such as competition, rights of establishment, and investment.
5) Specific challenges arising from soon-to-be concluded external negotiations on several fronts: WTO, FTAA and EU-ACP.
6) The rapid advance of the CARICOM-CSME arrangements, which are projected to come into operation in 2006.
7) The small size/openness/vulnerability of the economy, as indicated in the data below:

Table II-31. Barbados: Openness and Vulnerability Indicators

	Composite Vulnerability Index (1998)		
Openness (2003)	**Index**	**Rank**	**Degree of Vulnerability**
108	5.78	38/110	High

Sources: Table I and Commonwealth Secretariat (1998).

8) The threat of preference erosion. The value of preference received by Barbados is shown below.

Table II-32. Barbados: Value of Preferences
(million US$)

Year	EU/ACP	USA/CBERA
1990/91	18.5	N.A.
1992/93	21.4	N.A.
1994/95	15.2	N.A.
1996/97	23.2	N.A.
1998/99	21.3	0.4
2000/01	15.5	0.4
2002/03	14.1[1]	0.7

Source: FAO (2004).

[1] Year 2002.

Schedule II-5 *(continued)*

9) Institutional overload. The following two assessments illustrate this.

A. Identified Institutional Constraints/Deficiencies (Green Paper)

- Slow rate of implementation of agreed recommendations
- Lack of timely monitoring and evaluation of reform measures
- Allegations of political/partisan interventions
- Inadequate formalization of civil society structures and participation
- The need for local government structures and constitutional reform
- Fragmentation and lack of coordination among various organizations

B. Institutional Constraints/Deficiencies (Vignoles and Jessen 2004)

"For a small country like Barbados, maintaining a large public sector is unrealistic. All ministries and agencies engaged in trade policymaking have to work under significant human resource and budgetary constraints. Maximizing the efficiency of these limited resources is therefore crucial, particularly in the current context of multiple simultaneous and technically complicated trade negotiations and significant new obligations assumed in the WTO and the CSME." (Ibid., page 41)

1) Specific sectoral concerns in the following key sectors: tourism, agriculture and infrastructure.
2) The short-term macroeconomic outlook, particularly the debt vulnerability discussed in the Report.
3) Weak areas of data and information requirements [several of the competitiveness indicators, for example, are not routinely measured and data on productivity, the REER, and even the national accounts have significant gaps and lags in their availability]
4) Pressures on the Social Partners model of managing industrial relations and productivity issues
5) A dramatic expansion in the number and range of intergovernmental conventions and agreements in the area of development to which Barbados as a signatory is obligated. In the UN system alone there are, for example, obligations in regard to: security of persons, democratic participation, minimum livelihoods, productive employment, labour standards, social service provision, social integration, accountable institutions and civil society, the MDG, and environmental standards.
6) Constraints in ICT and the impediments to enterprise development.
7) Greater effectiveness of business support organizations.
8) The tension created by the impact of globalisation on culture and behaviour in a small society.
9) The growing importance of geopolitical and security issues linked to terrorism, narcotics trading, prostitution, and human trafficking.

To these challenges, we should add the "internal" and "external" pressures on the economy/society identified in the Barbados Green Paper on Social Policy (Thomas 2002):

Table II-33. Major Pressures on Barbados' Social Welfare System

Source	Types of Pressure
Internal	Demographic changes. Health status and recent developments, e.g., HIV/AIDS, teenage pregnancies; obesity. Unemployment and underemployment. Poverty and other deprivational deficits. Gender and family issues. Youth in crisis. Crime and justice. Marginalization. Concerns over key educational indicators, e.g., drop-out rates, school quality and performance. Pension benefits. The elderly. Informalisation of safety nets. Budgetary pressures. Political will and the election cycle. Ideological pressures for and against state leadership in welfare provisioning. Incipient middle-class withdrawal from state to private provisioning. Allegations of disincentives effects, moral hazard, and free-riding behaviours.
External	
A. Inter-governmental	Increased role of international obligations, standards, and norms.
B. Globalisation	Economic uncertainty. Transformation of labour markets and work process. Pressures on competitiveness and innovation. Reduced concessional flows and increased reliance on private FDI. Loss of preferential market access. Harmonisation of costs of social protection to global firms. Growing number of international conventions and agreements, e.g., human rights, child rights, women, ILO labour conventions, population policy, migration and remittances.

Source: Thomas (2002).

Schedule II-6. Suggested Priority Interventions

1. Export promotion. Given the critical importance of the sector an approach to export promotion that benefits from the lessons learned from past experiences should be indicated. This might entail a re-conceptualization of the approach to the development of the services sector.
2. Despite its successes, the Social Partners model still possesses crucial areas of weakness and risk, which should be identified and addressed. This would entail coverage of the general issues related to productivity indicators and measurements.
3. There is evidence of institutional "overload" brought on by the numerous pressures on the state and the private sector. Here two priority areas for consideration should be 1) trade policy design and implementation; 2) the development of the National Coalition of Service Providers.
4. The identification of potential "clusters"/agglomerates/economies/development of critical mass and related human resource development (HRD) and usage of ICT. A key cluster would be the bringing together of cutting-edge economic interests, talented analysts and professionals in a "think-tank" to deliberate on future global, hemispheric, regional, and local scenarios in order to identify ways in which Barbados can be an efficient and effective player as it continues to insert itself into the global economy.
5. A program for export-based small and medium enterprise development.
6. The development of intensive non-traditional agriculture.
7. Infrastructure development, as the primary responsibility of the government and foreign partners.
8. The macroeconomic situation, with particular reference to the evaluation of the capital-management model approach of UNCTAD.
9. Database, information strengthening, and a program of research on competitiveness/productivity and related concerns.

References

Angelelli, P., and Suaznábar, C., 2004. "Business Development Services: The IDB Experience." *Microenterprise Development Review*. IADB, January.

Applewhaite, Lolita, 2004. "Edutech in Barbados". In Sanatan, R. (ed.), *Bridges on the Digital Divide – Caribbean Initiatives for the Information Society*, Centre for International Services, The University of the West Indies, Cave Hill Campus, Barbados, December.

Archibald, X., and Greenidge, K., 2003. Debt and Sustainability in Barbados. Central Bank of Barbados. Barbados.

Asian Development Bank, 2003. Asian Development Outlook 2003: Section III, Competitiveness in Developing Asia.

Baier, Scott L., Gerald Dwyer Jr. and Robert Tamura, 2002. "How Important Are Capital and Total Factor Productivity for Economic Growth"? *Working Paper Series* 2002–2. Atlanta, Georgia: Federal Reserve Bank of Atlanta.

Barbados Chamber of Commerce and Industry, 2004. Chamber Report, Barbados.

______ 2004. Increasing the International Competitiveness of the Distributive Sectors and General Services in Barbados to Sustain Growth. Presentation to the Social Partnership Forum.

Barbados Investment and Development Corporation (BIDC), 2003. Finance for Small Business, Sources & Conditions, Barbados.

Barbados National Productivity Council, various years. Annual Report, Barbados.

Barbados Small Business Association, various years. Annual Report, Barbados.

Barbados Statistical Service, 1997/98. Informal Sector Survey. Bridgetown, Barbados.

Barro, A.R., 1993. "Some Implications of New Growth Theory for Economic Development". *Journal of International Development*, Vol. 5, No. 5, Sept–Oct, pp. 531–558.

Barro, R.J., 1999. "Notes on Growth Accounting". *Journal of Economic Growth*, Vol. 4, June, pp. 119–137.

______ 1997. Determinants of Economic Growth: A Cross-Country Empirical Study. Cambridge, Mass., MIT Press.

______ 1991. "Economic Growth in a Cross Section of Countries". *Quarterly Journal of Economics*, CVI, pp. 407–443.

Belgrave, A. and Craigwell, R., 1997. "The Impact of Government Expenditure on Economic Growth in Barbados: A Disaggregated Approach". In D. Worrell and R. Craigwell (eds.), *Macroeconomics and Finance in the Caribbean: Quantitative Analyses*. (Trinidad and Tobago, Caribbean Centre for Monetary Studies Technical Paper Series, Vol. 2), pp. 139–152.

Belgrave, A. and Ward, W., 1997. "Foreign Investment and the Barbadian Economy". *Working Papers*, vol II, Research Dept., Central Bank of Barbados, pp. 75–90.

Best, M., 2001. *The New Competitive Advantage*. Oxford: Oxford University Press.

BIDC Small Business Development Centre, 2003. Competitiveness within Barbados' Manufacturing Sector, Barbados.

BIDC Small Business Development Unit, various years. Report on the Annual Manufacturers Forum, Barbados.

Blackman, C., 1998. "The Barbados Model". *Caribbean Affairs*, Vol. 8, No. 1, pp. 61–68.

Berger, M., 2004. "Do Apex Models Make Sense for Microfinance"? *Microenterprise Development Review*. IADB, January.

Boamah, D., 2001. "Human Capital and Economic Growth in Barbados". *Paper presented to the 33rd Annual Conference of Monetary Studies*, Belize.

bridges.org, 2002. Comparison of E-Readiness Assessment Models and Tools. http://www.bridges.org/publication/128.

Briguglio, L., and Cordina, G., 2004. Competitiveness Strategies for Small States. Commonwealth Secretariat and University of Malta.

Britton, H., and Pollard, A., 2004. "Barbados – Community Technology Programme". In Sanatan, R. (ed.), *Bridges on the Digital Divide – Caribbean Initiatives for the Information Society*, Centre for International Services. The University of the West Indies, Cave Hill Campus, Barbados, December.

Buckley, Peter J., Christopher L. Pass, and Kate Prescott, 1988. "Measures of International Competitiveness: A Critical Survey". *Journal of Marketing Management* 4 (2): 175–200.

Carey, K., 1989. "Tourism Development in LDCs: Hotel Capacity Expansion with Reference to Barbados". *World Development*, Vol. 17, No. 1, January, pp. 59–67.

Chang, Ha-Joong, 2002. *Kicking Away the Ladder*. London: Anthem Press.

——— 1996. *The Political Economy of Industrial Policy*. London: Macmillan Press Ltd.

CITU, 2004. The Networked Readiness Index Rankings.

Conway, D., 1997. "Why Barbados Has Exported People: International Mobility as a Fundamental Force in the Creation of Small Island Society". In J.M. Carrion (ed.), *Ethnicity, Race and Nationality in the Caribbean* (Puerto Rico, Institute of Caribbean Studies), pp. 274–308.

Cox, W., 1982. "The Manufacturing Sector in the Economy of Barbados 1946–1980". In D. Worrell (ed.), *The Economy of Barbados 1946–1980* (Bridgetown, Central Bank of Barbados), pp. 47–80.

Craigwell, R., Downes, D. and Howard, M., 2001. "The Finance-Growth Nexus: A Multivariate VAR Analysis of a Small Open Economy". *Savings and Development*, XXV, No. 2, pp. 209–221.

Crampton, P., 2003. Competition as an Organising Principle for all Economic and Regulatory Policymaking, Outreach Unit, Competitiveness Division, OECD.

CTAG/CRNM/CARICOM, 2001. Improving Competitiveness for Caribbean Development. Final Report of the Caribbean Trade and Adjustment Group.

Cumberbatch, C.A.N., 1997. "A Model of Inflation in Barbados". In D. Worrell and R. Craigwell (eds.), *Macroeconomics and Finance in the Caribbean: Quantitative Analyses* (Trinidad and Tobago, Caribbean Centre for Monetary Studies, UWI), pp. 109–136.

Downes, A., 2005. Jamaica: Productivity and Competitiveness in the Jamaican Economy, IADB, Region 3, July.

______ 2004. Economic Growth in a Small Developing Country: The Case of Barbados. GDN/IDB/LACEA Project on Economic Growth in Latin America and the Caribbean.

______ 2002. "Productivity Measurement in Barbados: From the Enterprises to the National Level". *Presentation to the ILO/ECCB Workshop on Comptuing the KLIM Productivity Indicators*, St. Kitts, July.

______ 1998. "An Economic Analysis of Unemployment in Trinidad and Tobago". *IADB Working Paper* No. 381.

Downes, A.S., 1989. "Budgetary Theory and Policy in a Small Developing Country: The Cases of Barbados 1966–1988". *Bulletin for International Fiscal Documentation*, Vol. 43, No. 10, October, pp. 446–457.

______ 1985. "Inflation in Barbados: An Econometric Investigation". *Economic Development and Cultural Change*, Vol. 33, No. 3, April, pp. 521–532.

Downes, A.S. and V. Alleyne, 1998. "An Evaluation of Gainsharing Schemes in Barbados". *Economic Review* (Central Bank of Barbados), Vol. 25, No. 3, Dec., pp. 18–40.

Downes, A.S. and Carter R., 2000. An Analysis of Economic and Social Development in Barbados: A Model for Small Island Developing States (Port of Spain, Trinidad and Tobago, UNECLAC).

Downes, A.S., N. Mamingi and R.-M. Antoine, 2004. "Labour Market Regulation and Employment in the Caribbean". In J.J. Heckman and C. Pages (eds.), *Law and Employment: Lessons from Latin America and the Caribbean* (Chicago University Press), pp. 5517–51.

Downes, A.S., and L. Nurse, 2004. "Macroeconomic Management and Building Social Consensus: An Evaluation of the Barbados Protocols". *Journal of Eastern Caribbean Studies*, Vol. 29, No. 4, pp. 1–41.

Downes, Darrin A., 1996. "Incentives and Investment. A Review of the United Nations Publication, Incentives and Foreign Direct Investment". *Economic Review*, December, XXIII (3), pp. 47–50.

Downes, Darrin, and Craigwell, Roland, 2000. "A Review of A.H.J. Helmsing, Competitive Response, Innovation and Creating An Innovative Milieu: The Case of Manufacturing Industry in Bulawayo, Zimbabwe, and J. Tybout, Manufacturing Firms in Developing Countries. How Well They Do and Why". *Economic Review*, September, XXVII (2), pp. 38–42.

Durand, Martine, Jacques Simon, and Colin Webb, 1992. "OECD's Indicators of International Trade and Competitiveness". *OECD, Economic Department, Working Paper* No. 120. Paris.

Easterly, W., and Kraay. A., 2000. "Small States, Small Problems? Income, Growth and Volatility in Small States". *World Development*, Vol. 28, No. 11, November, pp. 2013–2027.

Eastmond, L., 2003. Statement Delivered by Senator, the Honourable Lynette Eastmond, Minister of Commerce, Consumer Affairs and Business Development to the World Summit on the Information Society. Geneva, December 12.

ECLAC, 2004. Toward an Information Society Measurement Instrument for Latin America and the Caribbean: Getting Started with Census, Household and Business Surveys. Preliminary Report. Santiago.

——— 2003. Export Promotion Policies in CARICOM. Port-of-Spain.

——— 2003. Caribbean Tourism, Trends, Policies and Impact 1985–2002.

——— 2003. The Quality of Insertion and Competitiveness in the Greater Caribbean: Applying ECLAC Instruments in Assessing Competitiveness. Port-of-Spain.

Economist Intelligence Unit, 2004. Barbados: Country Profile, 2004. London, United Kingdom.

Edwards, S., 1998. "Openness, Productivity and Growth! What Do We Really Know?" *Economic Journal* 108: 383–398.

Ellis, E., 2001. "Jobs, Gender and Small Enterprises: Country Paper on Barbados". In Ferdinand, C., (ed.), 2001. *Jobs, Gender and Small Enterprises in the Caribbean: Lessons from Barbados, Suriname and Trinidad and Tobago*. ILO, SEED Working Paper No. 19.

Ernst and Young, 2003. Caribbean Business Outlook Survey Results.

Fair Trading Commission Barbados, 2004. "Notes on Institutional Challenges in Promoting Competitiveness: The Barbados Experience". *Presentation to the Latin American Competitiveness Forum*, Second Annual Meeting, June.

Franklin, M., 2002. The Labour Force of the New Millennium, Barbados LMIS. Ministry of Labour, Barbados.

Goddard, Sir John, 2003. Barbados Social Partnership Protocols. Barbados.

Gonzales, P., 2002. CARICOM Report #1. Intal, IADB, Washington.

Government of Barbados, 2004. Report of the National Commission on Law & Order. Bridgetown, Barbados.

Greenidge, K., and Peter S., 1999. "Export-Output Causality in Barbados: A Cointegration Approach". *Central Bank of Barbados, Annual Review Seminar*. July.

Hall, R.E., and Jones, C., 1999. "Why Do Some Countries Produce So Much More Output Per Worker Than Others"? *Quarterly Journal of Economics*, pp. 83–116.

——— 1996. "The Productivity of Nations". *NBER Working Paper*, No. 5812.

Haynes, C., 1997. "Lessons from Barbados' Experience with the International Monetary Fund". In H. Codrington et al. (eds.), *Central Banking in Barbados: Reflections and Challenges* (Bridgetown, Central Bank of Barbados), pp. 83–110.

Henry, C., 2001. "Measuring Competitiveness in the Jamaica Economy". *Working Paper*, Bank of Jamaica.

Henry, L., 2003. The Digital Divide, Economic Growth and Potential Poverty Reduction: The Case of the English-Speaking Caribbean. CRNM Report.

Howard, M., 1989. Dependence and Development in Barbados 1945–1985 (Barbados, Carib Research and Publications).

IADB, 2004. Growth Productivity and Competitiveness in Latin America. Washington, D.C.

______ 2004. Toward Sustainable and Equitable Development. Washington, D.C.

______ 2004. Barbados: Country Focus Report. Bridgetown, Barbados.

______ 2004. Policy and Evaluation Committee, Strategy Document 2003. Competitiveness, Washington.

______ 2003. Competitiveness Strategy Document coordinated by RES and SDS. Washington, D.C.

______ 2001. *The Business of Growth*, Economic and Social Progress in Latin America, 2001 Report.

______ 1998. Poverty and Income Distribution in Barbados, 1996–97. Washington, D.C.

IMD International, 2004. World Competitiveness Yearbook, 2004.

IMF, various years. Article IV Consultations and Statistical Appendices, Washington.

International Telecommunications Union (ITU), 2004. Internet Indicators: Hosts, Users and Numbers of PCs. www.itu.int/ITU-D/ict/statistics, as consulted April 2005.

ITC: International Trade Centre publishes in the quarterly *International Trade Forum* a number of articles and policy briefs for use by members, which have proved useful. These include:

- Barclay, B., Putting It All Together, Issue 1/2003.
- Von Kirchbach, F., A Country's Competitive Advantage, Issue 1/2003.
- Williams, P., Measuring Performance, Issue 1/2003.

ITC, 2000. Export Performance of LDC's: Country Profiles, Geneva.

Jaggernauth, R., 2003. "Developing Business Incubation and Innovation in the Caribbean". *Presentation to the Pan-Commonwealth Caribbean Workshop on E-Commerce Competitiveness.* Port-of-Spain, Trinidad.

Jansson, Tor and Mark Wenner, 1997. "Financial Regulation and Its Significance for Microfinance in Latin America and the Caribbean". *Working Paper*. Microenterprise Unit. Inter-American Development Bank.

Jessen, A., and Vignoles, C., 2004. Barbados: Trade and Integration Sector Note. INT/ITD, IADB, Washington.

——— 2004. Trinidad and Tobago: Trade and Integration Sector Note. INT/ITD, IADB, Washington, D.C.

Kaufmann, D., Kraay, A., and Mastruzzi, M., 2003. Governance Matters III: Governance Indicators for 1996–2002. World Bank.

Kirkman, G.S., 2002. "Networked Readiness and Small Island Developing States". *Paper presented to the Conference on Small Island Economies in the Era of Globalization*, Centre for International Development, Harvard University.

Krugman, Paul, 2001. "Competitiveness Indices and Developing Countries: An Economic Evaluation of the Global Competitiveness Report". *World Development* 29 (9): 1501–1525.

——— 1996. "Making Sense of the Competitiveness Debate". *Oxford Review of Economic Policy* 12 (3): 17–25.

——— 1994. "Competitiveness: A Dangerous Obsession". *Foreign Affairs* 73 (2): 28–44.

Lall, Sanjaya, 2004. "Reinventing Industrial Strategy: The Role of Government Policy in Building Industrial Competitiveness". *G-24 Discussion Paper Series*. United Nations, April.

——— 2003. The Employment Impact of Globalization in Developing Countries. Oxford: Queen Elizabeth House, paper prepared for the ILO. Available at http://www2.qeh.ox.ac.uk/research/wpaction.html?jor_id=251.

——— 2001. *Competitiveness, Technology and Skills*. Cheltenham: Edward Elgar.

——— 1996. "Learning from the Asian Tigers". London: Macmillan.

——— 1992. "Technological Capabilities and Industrialization". *World Development* 20 (2): 165–186.

Lall, S., Alolahadejo, M., and Moreira, M., 2004. Latin America Industrial Competitiveness and the Challenges of Globalisation, IADB.

Lashley, J., 2003. "Small and Micro Business Issues in Barbados: Investigating the Contingent Environment". *Presentation to the SALISES Fourth Annual Conference*, Barbados, January.

Lewis, D., and Craigwell, R., 1998. "The Determinants of Growth in a Small Open Economy: Barbados". *Journal of Eastern Caribbean Studies*, Vol. 23, No. 2, June, pp. 1–29.

Lewis-Bynoe, Denny, et al., 2000. "The Impact of Trade Liberalisation on Specific Sector of the Barbados Economy and Consumers". *Economic Review*, June, XXVII (1), pp. 21–30.

Loehr, W., 2003. Labor Markets and Competitiveness. IDB Economic and Sector Study. RE3–97–003.

——— 1997. Labour Markets and Competitiveness in Barbados. Washington, October.

Looney, R.E., 1989. "Macroeconomic Consequences of the Size of Third World Nations: With Special Reference to the Caribbean". *World Development*, Vol. 17, No. 1, January, pp. 69–83.

Martia, R., and Sunley, P., 2001. "Deconstructing Clusters: Chaotic Concept or Policy Panacea"? *Paper presented to the Conference on Regionalising the Knowledge Economy.* London, November.

Mascoll, Clyde, 1985. "Wages, Productivity and Employment in Barbados 1949–82". *Economic Review*, December 1985, XII (3), pp. 10–23.

Microrate, 2000. Various Tables Reviewing Financial Performance of Microfinance Organizations in Latin America and the Caribbean. Washington, D.C.

Ministry of Economic Development, 2000. Telecommunications Sector Policy, Green Paper for the Government of Barbados.

Ministry of Tourism, 2001. Green Paper on the Sustainable Development of Tourism in Barbados: A Policy Framework, Barbados.

Moore, W. et al., 2004. "Estimates of Long Run Equilibrium Exchange-Rate in Three Caribbean Countries", *Economic Review*, Central Bank of Barbados, Vol. XXX, No. 3, December, pp. 28–38.

______ 2003. Exchange-Rate Misalignment in Selected Caribbean Countries. Central Bank of Barbados. Barbados.

Moore, Winston and Whitehall, Peter, 2000. "Financing the Small and Micro Business Sector in Barbados". *Economic Review*, December, XXVII (3), pp. 21–33.

Neary, J.P., 2003. "Competitive versus Comparative Advantage". *The World Economy*, 26 (4), pp. 457–470.

Outlon, N., 1997. "Total Factor Productivity Growth and the Role of Externalities". *National Institute of Economic Review*, October 1997, Issue 162, pp. 99–121.

Parris, Yvonne, 2002. "The State of Electronic Banking in Barbados". *Economic Review*, December, XXIX (3), pp. 17–22.

Pio, A., 1994. "New Growth Theory and Old Development Problems: How Recent Developments in Endogenous Growth Theory Apply to Developing Countries". *Development Policy Review*, Vol. 12, pp. 277–300.

Porter, Michael, 2003. "Building the Microeconomic Foundations of Prosperity: Findings from the Microeconomic Competitiveness Index". WEF, *Global Competitiveness Report 2002/2003.* New York: Oxford University Press for the World Economic Forum.

______ 1990. *The Competitive Advantage of Nations.* New York: Free Press.

Poyo, Jeff, Joan Parker and Abigail Golden-Vasquez, 1996. Microenterprise Development in Latin America and the Caribbean: An Overview and Review of the IDB's Experience. Microenterprise Unit, Inter-American Development Bank, Washington, D.C.

OTF Group Inc., 2004. Building the Competitive Advantages of Trinidad and Tobago: Business Environment Assessment Report.

Ruttan, V., 1998. "The New Growth Theory and Development Economics: A Survey". *Journal of Development Studies*, Vol. 35, No. 2, December, pp. 1–26.

Sahay, R., 2004. "Stabilization, Debt, and Fiscal Policy in the Caribbean". *Paper presented to the Central Bank of Trinidad and Tobago and IMF, High Level Seminar, Development Challenges Facing the Caribbean*, June 11–12.

Samuel, W., and Mounsey, A., 2002. "Indicators of Competitiveness in the ECCB". *Presentation to the XXXIV Annual Monetary Studies Conference*, Guyana.

Sanatan, R. (ed)., 2004. Bridges on the Digital Divide: Caribbean Initiatives for the Information Society, UWI, Barbados.

SCL Systems Consulting, 2003. Report: E-Readiness Assessment Study, Barbados.

Singh, A.D., 2001. A Rainbow Technology for a Rainbow People: E-Business Capacity Development for the CARICOM. Commonwealth Secretariat, London.

Stevens, C., 2004. Approaches for Export Services Diversification: Removing Market Access Barriers. *Paper presented to the Commonwealth Secretariat and Ministry of Trade and Industry. (Republic of Trinidad and Tobago) ITC Executive Forum on Small States in Transition – From Vulnerability to Competitiveness, Port-of-Spain.*

Stiglitz, Joseph, 2002. *Globalization and Its Discontents.* Penguin Books.

Stumpp, Suzanne, and Craigwell, Roland, 1999. "An Overview of Current Labour Market Programmes in Barbados". *Economic Review*, June, XXVI (1), pp. 17–34.

Temple, J., 1999. "The New Growth Evidence". *Journal of Economic Literature*, Vol. XXXVII, No 1, March, pp. 112–156.

Tewarie, Bhoendradatt, 1998. The Informal Sector, Micro, Small and Medium-Sized Enterprises and Job Creation in the Caribbean. University of the West Indies' Institute of Business, Port-of-Spain, Trinidad and Tobago.

UNCTAD, 2004. Competition, Competitiveness and Development. Geneva.

——— 2004. E-Commerce and Development Report, Geneva.

——— 2004. Model Law on Competition, Geneva.

——— TD/B/COM.3/58 and Corr.1, 2004. Policy Options for Strengthening SME Competitiveness, Geneva.

——— TD/B/COM.3/64, 2004. Report of the Commission on Enterprise, Business Facilitation and Development on Its 8th Session, Geneva.

——— TD(XI)/BP/5, 2004. Prospects for FDI Flows, Transnational Corporation Strategies and Promotion Policies: 2004–2007, Geneva.

——— TD/136, 2004. Strengthening Participation of Developing Countries in Dynamic New Sectors of World Trade: Trading Issues and Policies, Geneva.

——— TD/394, 2004. Partnership for Development: Information and Knowledge for Development, Geneva.

UNDP, 2004. Commission on the Private Sector and Development. Report to the UN Secretary-General, New York.

UNIDO, 2005. Capability Building for Catching Up, Industrial Development Report 2005, Vienna.

______ 2004. Industrialization, Environment and the Millennium Development Goals for Africa, Vienna: UNIDO.

Weisskopf, T., Bowles, S., and Gordon, D., 1983. "Hearts and Minds: A Social Model of US Productivity Growth". *Brookings Papers on Economic Activity*, 2.

Wenner, M., and Chalmers, G., 2001. "Microfinance Issues and Challenges in the Anglophone Caribbean". *IADB Working Paper*. Washington, D.C.

Wignaraja, Ganeshan, 1999. "Competitiveness in a Rapidly Globalizing Economy: Lesson of Experience. Action Programme on Productivity Improvement, Competitiveness and Quality Jobs in Developing Countries"—*Working Paper* PMD2. International Labour Organization.

Wint, A., 2003. Competitiveness in Small Developing Countries: Insights from the Caribbean. UWI, Kingston, Jamaica.

Wint, A., 2002. "Exchange-Rate Regime Choice: The Case of Barbados". In Wint, A., *Competitiveness in Small Developing Economies*. Ian Randle Publishers, Jamaica.

Wood, A., 1993. "Financial Development and Economic Growth in Barbados: Causal Evidence". *Savings and Development*, No. 4, XVII, pp. 379–389.

World Bank, 2005. Doing Business in 2005. Washington, D.C.

______ 2005. Knowledge Assessment Methodology. Washington, D.C. http://www.info.worldbank.org/etools/kam2005/weighted/scorecard_bs.asp

______ 2005. A Time to Choose: Caribbean Development in the 21st Century. Washington, D.C.

______ 2002. Macroeconomic Volatility, Household Vulnerability, and Institutional and Policy Responses in the Caribbean Countries. Washington, D.C.

______ 2002. MENA Region, MDF Papers. http://www.worldbank.org/mdf.
Papers include:
El Garimal, H., The Role of Social Funds for Development: Egypt's Experience
Johnson, G., Rethinking Education for the Information Age
Kettanu, S., Le Maroc Competitif: A Cluster Development Initiative in Morocco
Khemani, R., Fostering Competitiveness
Page, J., Productivity, Learning and Industrial Development
Porter, M., Building Competitive Advantage: Lessons from Other Countries
Shafik, N., Global Competitiveness and the Changing Relationship between the Public-Private Sectors in the MENA Region
Stiglitz, J., An Agenda for Development for the Twenty-First Century
Van Eeghen, W., Education and Economic Growth

World Bank, Report No. 15301CRG, 1996. Prospects for Services Export from the English-Speaking Caribbean.

______ Report No. 1281LAC, 1994. Caribbean Region: Coping with Changes in the External Environment.

World Bank (FIAS), 2005. Investment Climate Indicators. http://www.fias.net/investment_climate.html

World Economic Forum, 2004. Global Competitiveness Report, Geneva.

——— Global Information Technology Report 2003–2004. Oxford University Press, New York.

World Summit on the Information Society, 2003. Plan of Action. Document WSIS-03/Geneva/DOC/5-E. 12 December 2003. www.itu.int/wsis/documents/doc_multi-en-1161/1160.asp.

World Travel and Tourism Council, 2004. Barbados: Travel Tourism Forging Ahead, London.

Worrell, DeLisle, 1995. A Down-to-Earth Look at Competitiveness: A Review of David Dollar and Edward N. Wolff, Competitiveness, Convergence and International Specialisation, MIT Press, 1993". *Economic Review*, December, XXII (3), pp. 13–14.

Worrell, DeLisle, Boamah, Daniel, and Campbell, Trevor, 1996. "The Price Competitiveness of Barbados' Exports". *Economic Review*, June, XXIII (1), pp. 12–32.

Worrell, DeLisle, Codrington, H., Craigwell, R., and Greenidge, K., 2003. "Economic Resilience with an Exchange-Rate Regime: The Barbados Experience 1985–2000", *IMF Working Paper*, WP/03/168.

Worrell, DeLisle, Marshall, D., and Smith, N., 2000. "The Political Economy of Exchange-Rate Policy in the Caribbean". *IADB Research Network Working Paper* No. R-401.

WTO, 2002. Trade Policy Review. Geneva.

Yue, Chia Slow, n.d. Critical Elements in Competitiveness Strategies of Countries of East Asia, Singapore. Draft Notes for presentation at the Third Asia Development Forum, Asia's Future Economy, Plenary Session I, New Directions for Business in Asia's Future Economy.

CHAPTER III

Reforming the Labour Market

Andrew S. Downes

A. Introduction: Labour as a Factor in Competitiveness

This study examines the operation of the Barbados labour market in the context of international competitiveness. It extends the work undertaken by Loehr (1997) by updating the performance of the labour market since 1995 and specifying policies that can enhance the efficiency and effectiveness of the labour market. One of the main concerns confronting economic managers in Barbados relates to how the economic systems in the country can be improved to enhance the competitiveness of Barbadian goods and services in the international market. (See Thomas, Chapter II of this volume.) As a small developing country, Barbados has to rely on the export market to propel economic growth and development. With the removal of preferential treatment in traditional markets, greater emphasis has been placed on boosting the competitiveness of exports and identifying new avenues of economic activity that can be pursued on a competitive basis in the international market. (See Jessen and Vignoles, Chapter IV of this volume.) While several policy measures can be used to enhance competitiveness—exchange-rate, new technology, production integration—some focus has been placed on labour-market policies.

One commonly used measure of international (price) competitiveness is the real unit labour cost (RULC), which is the ratio of real wages to labour productivity. If the RULC of a country's products (goods and services) falls relative to that of its main competitors, then that country's products are said to be more price-competitive than those of its competitors. Although the RULC only measures one dimension of the competitiveness equa-

The writer thanks the Inter-American Development Bank (IADB) for the opportunity to undertake this study, with special thanks to Dr. Desmond Thomas for facilitating the process. The study has benefited tremendously from the valuable information provided by the Barbados Statistical Service and the key informants identified in Appendix 3. Thanks also to Doris Downes for assistance in typing, editing and research and to Gustavo Marquez, Reynold Simmons, Ronald Ramkissoon, Courtney Blackman, Clive Thomas and Delisle Worrell for their comments on the first draft of this study at a conference organized by the IADB. Liliana Rojas-Suárez provided very useful suggestions and comments on the final version.

tion, it highlights the role that a dynamic, flexible and efficient labour market plays in the economic growth and competitiveness process. The need to increase labour productivity faster than increases in real wages becomes a critical element in the economic management of a country.

An understanding of the factors affecting the relative movement of real wages and labour productivity therefore helps to situate the role of the labour market in the competitiveness equation. Several institutional factors contribute to the ability of the labour market to fulfil its role in promoting economic growth and the socio-economic welfare of the population of a country. For example, labour unions, employer associations, labour legislation, educational and training institutions, public administrative systems and conflict-resolution arrangements are some of the elements that affect the functioning of the labour market.

In the next section, an analysis of the supply side of the labour market is undertaken. The focus will be on the changing nature and determinants of labour-market participation in Barbados. The third section examines the characteristics of labour demand (that is, employment) and the factors affecting such demand over the past decade. Issues of unemployment and underemployment are then examined in the fourth section. The critical role that labour costs (wages, salaries and other compensation elements) play in the labour market is analysed. This analysis is linked to productivity and international price competitiveness.

The role of labour market regulations and institutions—labour unions, employer associations and government departments—is examined. Barbados has been able to develop a Social Partnership involving the Government and representatives of workers and employers since 1993. This Social Partnership has agreed to the implementation of a number of Protocols that have allowed workers and employers to contribute to economic and industrial relations policy-making in Barbados. (See Downes and Nurse, 2004 for a full discussion.) In addition to the Protocols, these institutions have also implemented a number of projects and programs that are aimed at improving the functioning of the labour market. Existing and proposed legislative measures will also be examined to determine the extent to which they increase labour adjustment costs and reduce labour-market flexibility.

Finally, recommendations are made to improve the functioning of the labour market and hence its ability to contribute to improved international competitiveness and adaptation to technological and other changes.

B. Evaluating the Labour Supply

The Changing Face of Labour in Barbados

An analysis of the supply side of the labour market involves an examination of the forces giving rise to the changing nature of the labour force, the participation of persons in the market and the quality of the persons entering labour-market activity. Between 1995 and

Table III-1. Labour Force, 1995–2004

	Total	Male		Female	
Year	Thousands	Thousands	%	Thousands	%
1995	136.8	69.1	50.5	67.6	49.5
1996	135.4	69.0	50.9	66.5	49.1
1997	135.8	69.8	51.4	66.0	48.1
1998	136.3	70.3	51.6	66.0	48.4
1999	136.6	71.1	52.0	65.5	47.9
2000	138.4	71.9	51.9	66.5	48.0
2001	145.2	74.9	51.5	70.3	48.4
2002	143.4	74.1	51.7	69.2	48.3
2003	145.5	74.6	51.3	70.9	48.7
2004	146.3	75.0	51.3	71.3	48.7
Growth Rate (%)	0.8	1.0	—	0.6	—

Sources: Barbados Statistical Service (BSS), Labour Force Sample Survey Report, 1994–1999, 1996–2001; Central Bank of Barbados, Annual Statistical Digest, 2005.

2004, the total labour force increased from 136,800 to 146,300 persons, that is, an average annual growth rate of 0.8 percent. During that period, the male labour force grew at a rate of 1 percent per annum, while the female growth rate was 0.6 percent per annum. The higher male labour force growth rate resulted in an increase in the proportion of males in the labour force. (See Table III-1.) During the same period, the adult population increased from 200,800 to 210,600 persons, representing an average annual growth rate of approximately 0.5 percent. With the labour-force growth rate being higher than the adult population growth rate, there is an increasing tightness in the labour market which, has implications for immigration, hours of work, wages and the retirement age.

Upward Trend in Labour-Force Participation

The labour-force participation rate (that is, the percentage of labour force out of the adult population) continued to exhibit a general upward trend during the 1995–2004 period. The overall participation rate rose from 68.2 percent in 1995 to 69.2 percent in 2004, with the female rate increasing at a slightly faster pace than the male rate. (See Table III-2.) There was a slight decline in the participation rates during the 2001–02 recession and probably reflected a net 'discouraged worker' effect associated with the increase in unemployment and the inability to obtain a job after a reasonable period of search.

The increase in the female participation rate has been noticeable over the past three decades. Several factors have been identified to explain this trend, namely, improved educational and training opportunities for females, which boost their competitiveness in the labour market, the expansion of activities in selected areas of the economy (for example, information services, distribution, banking and finance), the increased use of modern household production technology, which releases time from household production activities, and the need for self-actualization and financial independence.

Table III-2. Labour-Force Participation Rates by Sex, 1995–2004
(percent)

Year	Male	Female	Total
1995	74.5	62.7	68.2
1996	74.3	81.6	67.4
1997	73.6	62.1	67.5
1998	74.0	62.0	67.7
1999	74.7	61.4	67.7
2000	74.8	62.7	68.4
2001	75.9	63.8	69.5
2002	74.8	62.7	68.5
2003	75.1	64.0	69.2
2004	75.3	64.2	69.5

Source: Barbados Statistical Service, Continuous Labour Force Sample Survey Report, 1994–1999, 1996–2001; Central Bank of Barbados: Annual Statistical Digest, 2005.

An examination of the relationship between the real–wage-rate index and both the labour force and the labour-force participation rates over the period 1995 to 2003 suggests a positive and statistically significant result. The Pearson correlation coefficient between the real wage index and the total labour force was 0.852, while the coefficient between the real wage index and the overall labour-force participation rate was 0.745. Both of these coefficients are statistically significant at the 5-percent level and point to an upward sloping labour-supply curve.

Recent econometric research undertaken by Downes and Browne (2004) using a probit analysis of labour-force participation in 2003 produced the following results for the overall labour-force participation:

(i) The age variable was quadratic and statistically significant, indicating that the probability of labour-force participation increases in the early years of life and falls in the later years.
(ii) The higher the dependency ratio, the lower the probability of participation.
(iii) The higher the remittances that a household receives from abroad, the lower the probability of participation.
(iv) The greater the number of children in the household, the higher the probability of participation.
(v) The more educated an individual becomes, the higher the probability of participation in the labour market.

There are, however, some variations from these overall labour-force participation results when male and female participation rates are examined. In the case of male labour-force participation, age, dependency ratio, remittances and number of children yield the same results as the overall labour force. However, the probit analysis indicated that the larger the

Table III-3. Labour Force by Industry Group
(percent)

	1995			1998			2001		
Industry	B	M	F	B	M	F	B	M	F
No Work Experience	3.14	1.88	4.44	1.29	0.69	1.94	0.62	0.40	0.85
Sugar	1.82	2.31	1.33	1.01	1.25	0.75	0.69	0.66	0.71
Other Agriculture and Fishing	2.77	3.04	2.37	3.32	3.90	2.69	3.30	3.87	2.70
Manufacturing	10.59	9.12	12.13	8.74	7.81	9.71	7.16	7.08	7.39
Electricity, Gas, Water	0.80	1.30	0.15	1.29	1.95	0.59	1.45	1.73	0.99
Construction and Quarrying	8.92	16.64	0.74	10.76	19.66	1.19	11.43	20.56	1.71
Wholesale and Retail Trade	15.27	13.75	16.71	14.94	12.69	17.34	14.87	12.28	17.63
Tourism	10.67	8.97	12.43	11.48	9.34	13.75	10.74	8.28	13.22
Transport and Communications	4.30	6.22	2.22	3.97	5.58	2.39	4.27	5.61	2.84
Finance, Insurance, Business Services	6.14	3.47	8.87	6.21	4.04	8.37	7.78	5.47	10.24
General Services	17.69	14.90	20.41	16.89	13.95	20.02	18.11	16.55	19.77
Government Services	17.98	18.08	17.89	18.99	18.13	20.02	19.00	16.82	21.30
Not Stated	0	0	0.88	1.01	0.97	1.19	0.62	0.53	0.70
Total	100.0	100.0	100.0	100.0	100.0	100.0	100.0	100.0	100.0

Source: Barbados Statistical Service, Continuous Labour Force Sample Survey Report, 1994–1999 and 1996–2001.

Note: B – Both; M – Male; F – Female.

household size, the lower the probability of male participation, while technical/vocational education was the only significant education variable influencing the probability of male participation.

For female labour-force participation, it was found that being single or widowed increased the probability of participation, while the larger the number of children in the household, the lower the probability of participation. Greater female participation in the labour force, however, is more likely in cases of larger household sizes, greater dependency ratios and higher educational attainment (especially at the secondary and university levels).

An analysis of the labour force by industrial attachment indicates that the services sectors, especially general services, government services, tourism and wholesale/retail trade accounted for over 70 percent of the attachment. (See Table III-3.) The manufacturing and construction/quarrying sectors accounted for approximately 20 percent of the labour force attachment over the 1995–2001 period.

Towards a More High-Quality Work Force

An examination of the educational attachment of the labour force indicates that over 60 percent of the force had attained at least secondary-level education over the 1995–2001 period.

Table III-4. Labour Force by Educational Attainment, 1995, 1998, 2001 *(percent)*

	1995			1998			2001		
Highest Level of Education	**B**	**M**	**F**	**B**	**M**	**F**	**B**	**M**	**F**
None	0	0	0	0.07	0.14	0.15	0.07	0.13	0
Primary	21.45	23.6	19.28	20.56	21.81	19.28	16.66	18.18	15.05
Secondary	66.78	64.3	69.51	63.56	62.65	64.87	59.57	60.00	59.00
University	9.48	8.15	10.90	11.39	10.62	12.41	20.38	17.11	23.86
Technical/Vocational	2.06	3.77	0.29	3.68	4.33	2.84	2.41	3.61	1.14
Other	0.07	0.14	0	0.14	0	0.15	0.21	0.13	0.28
Not Stated	0.15	—	0	8.60	0.69	0.29	0.67	0.80	0.57
Total	100.0	100.0	100.0	100.0	100.0	100.0	100.0	100.0	100.0

Source: Barbados Statistical Service, Continuous Labour Force Sample Survey Report, 1994–1999 and 1996–2001.

Note: B – Both; M – Male; F – Female.

The percentage of the labour force that had attained university-level education increased significantly from 9.5 percent in 1995 to 20.4 percent in 2001, with females outnumbering males in this area. (See Table III-4.) The relatively high level of educational attainment in Barbados is due largely to the enforcement of compulsory school attendance up to the age of 16+ years.

Although enrolment rates at the primary and secondary levels are very high, with the institution of universal education at these levels, there is some concern about the low degree of certification among labour-market participants. It is estimated from the population censuses that approximately 63 percent of the adult population had no certification in 1990, while in 2000 the figure stood at 57 percent. This problem is more severe among the older cohorts of the labour force, 50 years and older in 1990, who may not have benefited from 'free' secondary-level education since the mid-1960s. (See Figure III-1.)

Figure III-1. Adult Population Passing No Examinations, by Age Group, 1990, 2000

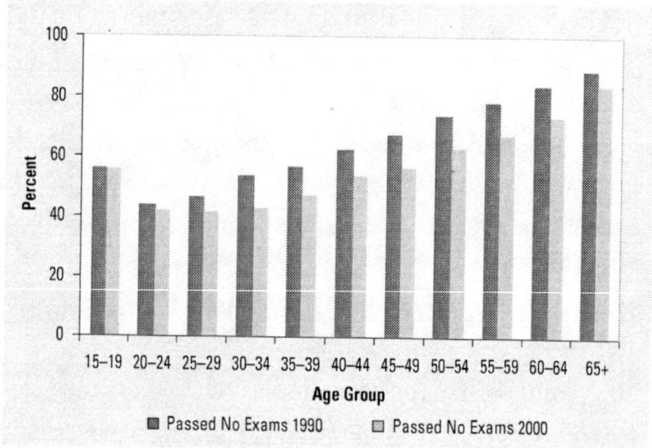

The quality of the labour force has been enhanced by post-secondary institutional and on-the-job training. Although recent graduates from the secondary-school system have a better background in technical and vocational subjects, most of the human capital enhancement of the labour force has been undertaken through on-the-job training and through several training institutions. Ashton et al. (2001) and B.E.C. (2002) indicate that companies in Barbados engage in a high degree of on-the-job training especially for clerical, technical and vocational workers.

Institutional training is conducted by several governmental agencies: the Barbados Vocational Training Board (BVTB), the Technical and Vocational Education and Training (TVET) Council, the Samuel Jackman Prescod Polytechnic (SJPP) and the Barbados Community College (BCC), along with the Barbados Institute of Management and Productivity (BIMAP), the School of Continuing Studies of the University of the West Indies (UWI) and several community groups, non-governmental organisations, trade unions and private institutions.

Technical and vocational training has been an important aspect of human resources development in Barbados. The BVTB, for example, has developed vocational programs for persons who need to acquire entry-level skills in order to enter the labour market, to upgrade their existing skills or to retrain for new occupations. The BVTB operates a number of programs for both unemployed and employed persons: an apprenticeship program, a skills-training program, an evening program, an in-plant program and a program for the retraining of retrenched workers. The apprenticeship program currently has 11 schemes with the electrical installation and automotive engineering schemes being the most heavily subscribed (250 persons in 2002–03 with 93 percent being male). The main areas of activity in the skills-training program are masonry, computer applications, carpentry, plumbing, tractor operations, needlecraft and tiling. In 2002–03, 1,594 persons were registered in the program with 66 percent being male. Females tend to dominate the computer applications program. The evening program covers a range of activities: masonry, tiling and decorative finishes, plumbing, dressmaking, upholstery and small business management.

But Problems Remain

Although the Board seeks to provide training for persons who would be competitive in the local labour market, there are still problems associated with the provision of these training programs. These problems include:

(i) insufficient funding;
(ii) the lack of access to current manpower planning information;
(iii) the inability of employers to provide information on future plans;
(iv) keeping up with changes in technology (e.g., the automotive program);
(v) insufficient space to mount programs; and
(vi) the indifferent attitude of several participants in the programs.

While the Board has been able to address some of these matters, for example through the inclusion of 'soft skills' such as deportment, conflict management and punctuality in the programs, the work of the Board is still hampered by a lack of resources. Research work undertaken by the Board suggests that employers are generally satisfied with the apprenticeship scheme and the impact of the technical training on the apprentices (see Annual Report, 2002, p 24). Concern was, however, expressed about the poor attitudes of the apprentices. A tracer study of the graduates of the skills training program for 2000 produced the following results:

(i) 80 percent of the 204 respondents completed their respective courses;
(ii) 71 percent found work within one year of training;
(iii) 43 percent found work in the area in which they trained;
(iv) 64 percent of males and 45 percent of females found employment within three months of completing their training; and
(v) 29 percent remained unemployed.

These results suggest that there are still deficiencies in the training-employment relationship that need to be resolved.

BIMAP provides short- and long-term training in various areas of management. Participation in short-term programs increased from 1,496 in 1998 to 1,820 in 2004 with the main focal areas being marketing and customer service, supervisory management and information technology (especially certification as MCP, MCSA and MCSE). The long-term training program includes certificates, diplomas and degrees. The MSc and MBA programs in various areas of management are offered in collaboration with the University of Surrey. The majority of students in the certificate and diploma programs have been registered in supervisory/administrative management, accounting and finance, human resource management, marketing and especially information technology. Over the 1998–2004 period, there was an average annual registration of about 1,440 persons in these programs. The available data suggest that most of the participants in the training programs work in the services sector. There has been a shift from company-sponsored training to individually-funded training as individuals, especially females, focus on career development and human capital formation.

In cases of technical and vocational training as well as managerial training, key informants emphasize the need to promote on-the-job training in order to close the 'knowing-doing' gap which exists in the labour market. In addition, the 'soft skills' should be incorporated into the various training programs. Educational and training institutions are gradually incorporating such 'soft skills' in their programs as institutions become important providers of training in Barbados. (See Table III-5.)

Table III-5. Population 15 Years and Over by Nature of Training, 1980, 1990, 2000

	1980		1990		2000	
Type of Training	Number	%	Number	%	Number	%
Institutional	11786	38.6	23695	52.4	40013	54.9
Non-Institutional[1]	18166	59.4	20086	44.4	26926	37.0
Not Stated	612	2.0	1445	3.2	5936	8.1
Total	30564	100.0	45226	100.0	72875	100.0

Source: Population Census of Barbados, 1980, 1990, 2000.

[1] Includes on-the-job, private study and other forms.

The Samuel Jackman Prescod Polytechnic (SJPP), which is the main provider of certified technical and vocational education in Barbados, has seen its enrolment increase from 1,200 in 1970–71 to about 3,000 in 2003–04. SJPP accounts for 27 percent of the total enrolment in tertiary-level institutions in Barbados with male students being dominant in automotive, electrical/electronic and mechanical engineering, building trades and agriculture and female students recording high enrolment in the commercial and human ecology programs. Program enrolment at the SJPP partly reflects the structural changes taking place in the economy with a decline in the agricultural and, to a limited extent, the manufacturing sectors and the rise of new service such as information technology and personal-care services (Downes, 2004).

Pros and Cons of Human Capital Formation in Barbados

An index of human capital formation in Barbados developed by Boamah (1995) and extended by the author indicates a significant increase in the human capital base of the country. There are, however, shortages and skill deficiencies that can reduce the effectiveness of the labour market in promoting international competitiveness through labour productivity growth. Work-permit data indicate that the main occupational categories granted such permits in recent years have been senior officials and managers, professionals, technicians and associate professionals. Labour shortages have, therefore, been in the skilled category, although there have been periodic shortages in the semi-skilled category (for example, masons and carpenters). Several initiatives have been introduced to boost the quality of the labour force. First, the Government has implemented an Education Sector Enhancement Program (EDUTECH) to improve the teaching methods in the school system and also to enhance the information technology skills of school leavers. Secondly, a Barbados National Diploma of Secondary Education (BNDSE) has been established. This certification would provide secondary school leavers with independent indicators of their school achievement and would provide employers with information on their skills and competencies in both academic and non-academic achievements in the school system. The present system provides very few labour-market signals of potential employees' labour productivity and makes screening/sorting in the labour market a highly subjective exercise. Finally, the TVET Council has introduced National Vocational Qualifications (NVQs) which would shift the qualification system from 'education' and 'experience' to 'competence' and 'practical work'. As a competency-based qualification, NVQs would pave the way for the adoption of regional certification to support the existing Caribbean Examination Council's system of examination and hence promote the greater regional mobility of labour in the context of the CARICOM Single Market and Economy (CSME).

Although there are problems associated with the output of the school system, it still provides the basic foundation upon which the trainability of the labour force can be based. There are a range of institutions providing various types of training in order to enhance the quality of the labour force, which is needed for a highly competitive economic environment. While employees may have the technical skills, employers and trainers still express concern about the attitude of employees to work (that is, deportment, punctuality, respect, concern for quality and timeliness and response to customers/clients). The development of new certification arrangements and the use of psychometric testing would provide employers with better information on the skills, competencies and personality of workers and therefore promote better job fits.

C. Employment: Reflecting Socio-economic Change

Shifting from Agriculture

Employment creation has been an important goal of economic policy-making in Barbados over the years. Between 1995 and 2004 the number of persons employed increased from 109,900 to 132,100, that is, an average annual growth rate of 2.1 percent. The rate of female employment growth was 2.2 percent per annum while the rate for males was 2.0 percent. (See Table III-6.) The ratio of male to female employment also declined from 1.11 in 1995 to 1.07 in 2004.

Table III-6. Employment in Barbados by Sex for Selected Years

	Number of Persons Employed (thousands)			Percent	
Year	Total	Male	Female	Male	Female
1995	109.9	57.7	52.1	52.5	47.4
1998	119.6	64.4	55.2	53.8	46.1
2001	130.9	68.9	61.9	52.6	47.2
2004[P]	132.1	68.3	63.8	51.7	48.3

Source: Barbados Economic and Social Report, 2004.

[P] - provisional.

Over the past three decades, Barbados has witnessed a secular decline in both the absolute and the relative number of persons employed in the agricultural sector. Over the 1995–2003 period, the sector employed about 5,400 persons per annum, that is, about 5 percent of the employed labour force. The manufacturing sector also witnessed a decline in employment over the period: from 11,700 in 1995 to 7,600 in 2004. (See Table III-7.) A decline is also seen in the number employed in IDC-assisted manufacturing and service companies—from 15,240 in 1995 to 13,674 in 2004.

Government, general services, distribution/commerce, tourism and, to some extent, construction/quarrying were the main absorbers of labour in Barbados. Government has been the single largest employer of labour, with the share of government employment in total employment remaining relatively consistent at about 21 percent over the period. Government employment grew by 2.1 percent per annum, which is slightly higher than the overall employment growth rate. General services grew at an average annual rate of 4.7 percent over the 1995–2004 period.

The sectoral distribution of the employed labour force therefore reflects the general shift of economic activity from agriculture and manufacturing towards the services sector, which employed over 70 percent of the total number of persons employed during the 1995–2004 period. Females outnumbered males in four of the services: wholesale and retail trade, financial services, government services and general services. Several of these females are employed as clerical and service/shop workers. In recent years, the number of employed professional females has been greater than that of males and reflects the growing trend of women seeking to enhance their human capital and enter the labour market. Indeed, data on graduates from the Cave Hill Campus of the University of the West Indies (UWI) indicate that the ratio of female to male graduates was 2.02 to 1 for first degrees in 2001.

Table III-7. Sectoral Distribution of Employment for Selected Years *(thousands)*

Sector	1995	1998	2001	2004[P]
Sugar, Other Agriculture and Fishing	5.1	5.2	5.4	4.4
Construction and Quarrying	8.8	12.5	14.2	13.4
Manufacturing	11.7	10.7	9.2	7.6
Electricity, Gas and Water	1.0	1.3	1.9	1.8
Wholesale and Retail	16.6	18.2	19.1	19.6
Tourism	11.9	13.8	13.7	12.2
Transport and Communications	5.1	5.1	5.7	5.2
Financial Services	7.6	7.5	10.4	10.8
General Services	19.3	19.9	22.9	28.9
Government	22.9	24.5	26.2	27.5
Total	109.9	119.6	128.8	132.0

Source: Barbados Economic and Social Report, 2004.

[P] - provisional.

The Private and Public Sectors

Although the government is the single largest employer of labour (over 20 percent), private-sector companies account for over 60 percent of the total number of persons employed, while the self-employed account for about 13 percent of total employment. There has been a gradual increase in female employment in the Government over the past decade so that female employees now outnumber males. The Government recently regularised the employment status of casual workers so that they can qualify for better pensions and gratuities from the Government. There are now only temporary or permanent workers in the government services.

Informal Sector

There are very few estimates of employment in the informal sector in Barbados. Although there has been an increase in the employed labour force classified as "employer" or "self-employed", that is, from 9,600 in 1996 to 12,700 in 2001, these categories included persons working in the 'formal labour market' (for example, lawyers, doctors, consultants, accountants). One study of the informal sector undertaken by the Barbados Statistical Service in 1997–98 indicated that:

(i) the number of informal-sector business operations constituted 40.4 percent of the average number of 'employers' and 'own-account' or 'self-employed' workers;

(ii) the number of informal-sector employees was 5.9 percent of the average number of persons employed;

(iii) of the estimated 6,904 persons employed in the informal sector, 61.4 percent are males and 38.6 percent females;

(iv) the concentration of the sector was in distribution, agriculture and, to a lesser extent, general services and construction;

(v) few of the operators had university education (1.1 percent) or technical/vocational education (less than 1 percent). Most of the operators had primary- or secondary-level education;

(vi) production units were very small and operated either singularly or by family members. Labour-intensive technologies were used in these units;

(vii) approximately 62 percent of the persons employed were between the ages of 30 and 59 years, while 12 percent were aged 20–29 years. This feature would suggest that work experience was important in the sector; and

(viii) most of the employees were either self-taught or had no training and usually worked for 4–12 hours per day.

Educational Levels

A noticeable feature in the labour market is the number of persons with university-level education, which rose from 11,900 (10.8 percent) in 1995 to 28,300 (21.7 percent) in 2001. The number of employed females with university education increased from 6,900 (6.3 percent of the employed) in 1995 to 15,900 (12.1 percent of the employed) in 2001. The corresponding figures for males were 5,100 (4.6 percent) in 1995 and 12,300 (9.4 percent) in 2001. The ratio of females to males with university education in 2001 was 1.29 to 1 which was lower than the ratio of female to male graduates from the UWI.

The number of persons giving their highest level of education as technical/vocational, however, declined over the period, from 8,000 in 1996 to 3,200 in 2001. This employment trend may reflect either the declining employment opportunities in these areas or the fact that some individuals seek to improve their educational attainment (that is, pursue a university education) in order to provide better signals in the labour market.

Accounting for Employment Growth

Econometric research on employment determination points to the critical role that output expansion, more so than wage-rate changes, plays in expanding employment in Barbados. (See Boamah (1985), Coppin (1994a, 1994b, 1995) and Downes, Mamingi and Antoine (2004).) Labour-market regulations, which have not changed significantly for several years (for example, national insurance, severance payment), do not seem to have had a significant impact on employment growth in Barbados (Downes et al., 2004).

These results suggest that economic growth is critical to employment growth in Barbados. Union bargaining tends to reflect the 'right to manage' model, whereby labour unions and employers negotiate wage/salary levels and other conditions of service, while employers determine the level of employment given the wage/salary levels.

Providing employment opportunities in non-Barbadian labour markets, especially Canada and the USA, has been a policy focus of the Government. Barbadian workers have been placed in such programs as the Canadian Farm Labour Program, Canadian Hotel Program, Canadian Domestic Program, USA Cruise Ship Program and the US H2b Hotel Program. Between 1995 and 2004, there was a steady decline in the number of persons (mainly males) using these programs. In 1995, 662 persons were placed in jobs under these short contractual arrangements, while in 2004, only 517 persons were so employed.

The demand side of the Barbadian labour market shows a shift from low- and semi-skilled employment to skilled employment, especially in the services sector. There is a growing 'feminization' of the labour market with increased female labour-market participation and improvement in human capital as evidenced by the higher proportion of university-educated and professional employed females. There is a large percentage of females still employed in the traditional clerical and service occupations. Government has not only been the single largest employer of labour in the country (a fact that has fiscal implications), but its share in total employment increased over the study period. Informal-sector employment is relatively small. Output growth has been identified as the main determinant of employment growth in Barbados. External employment programs, which in the past provided an avenue for the employment of low- and semi-skilled persons, have declined over the years. The Government does not have active employment programs (crash programs) as in other Caribbean countries, although poverty alleviation programs in the rural and urban areas have employment effects.

D. Unemployment

Statistical Features

The unemployed in Barbados are defined as those persons in the labour force who are available and looking for work but who are unable to find any form of work during a three-month period immediately preceding the date of enumeration. Such a definition yields higher unemployment rates in Barbados than in countries that employ the widely used definition based on 'one week preceding the date of enumeration'. (See Loehr, 1997, Annex A.)

The total number of unemployed persons fell from 26,900 in 1995 to 14,200 in 2004, with the corresponding unemployment rates being 19.6 percent in 1995 and 9.8 percent in 2004. The unemployment rate declined to 9.4 percent in 2000, before it increased in 2001 with the onset of a recession in the economy. The unemployment rate for females has always been higher than that for males. Over the 1995–2004 period, the male unemployment rate declined from 16.2 percent to 9.0 percent, while the female unemployment rate fell from 23.2 percent to 10.6 percent. (See Table III-8.)

Like many other developing countries, Barbados has a 'youth unemployment' problem. Although the school-leaving age is 16+ years, the unemployment rate among the 15–19-years age group was 52.9 percent in 1995 and among the 20–24 years age group, it was 31.1 percent. In 2001, the corresponding rates were 30.4 percent for the 15–19-years age group and 19.7 for the 20–24-years age group. These rates are significantly higher than the national rates. Not surprisingly, among the youth, females have suffered higher rates of unemployment than males. In 2001, the unemployment rates for males 15–19 and 20–24 years of age were 25 and 18.2 percent, respectively, while for females, the corresponding rates were 36.7 and 21.3 percent respectively. With the increase in female employment, there has been a narrowing of the differential between the male and female unemployment rates. In 1995, the differential in the 15–19 years age group was 12.6 percentage points, while in 2001, it was 11.7 percentage points. For 1995 and 2001, the differentials for the 20–24 years of age groups were 9.9 and 3 percentage points, respectively.

Table III-8. Unemployment in Barbados, 1995–2004

Year	Number Unemployed (thousands)			Unemployment Rate (%)		
	Total	Male	Female	Total	Male	Female
1995	26.9	11.2	15.7	19.7	16.5	22.7
1996	21.5	8.5	13.0	15.6	12.4	18.9
1997	20.0	8.0	12.0	14.5	11.3	17.8
1998	16.9	6.0	10.9	12.3	8.4	16.4
1999	14.6	5.7	5.9	10.4	7.5	13.3
2000	12.4	5.1	7.3	9.3	7.4	11.4
2001	13.0	7.3	5.7	9.9	8.0	11.9
2002	14.8	6.4	8.4	10.3	8.7	12.1
2003	16.0	7.2	8.8	11.0	8.6	12.6
2004[P]	14.2	6.7	7.5	9.8	9.0	10.6

Source: Central Bank of Barbados, Annual Statistical Digest, 2005.

[P] - provisional.

Given that over 55 percent of the adult population had no form of certification in 2000, it is expected that a high proportion of the unemployed would have no certification in spite of acquiring a secondary-level education. Unemployment rates among university and technical/vocational education graduates are very low. (See Table III-9.)

The high level of youth unemployment, coupled with a high incidence of workers without certification, suggests a 'mismatch' problem associated with a dysfunctional educational system. Employers and their representatives indicate that it is difficult to recruit workers with the appropriate work ethic and attitude, job experience and technical skills. Although training institutions have started to include "attitudinal skills" in their programs, key informants interviewed for this study still express some degree of concern about the attitude of young entrants into the labour market.

Table III-9. Unemployment by Educational Attainment, Both Sexes (*thousands*)

Highest Level of Education	1995			1998			2001		
	B	M	F	B	M	F	B	M	F
None	0.0	0.0	0.0	0.0	0.0	0.0	0.0	0.0	0.0
Primary	5.3	2.5	2.8	3.0	1.2	1.8	1.9	0.8	1.0
Secondary	20.0	8.0	12.8	12.5	4.0	8.5	10.6	4.4	6.2
University	1.0	0.5	0.5	0.7	0.3	0.4	1.3	0.5	0.8
Technical/Vocational	0	0.4	0.2	0.5	0.3	0.1	0.3	0.2	0.1
Other	—	—	—	0.1	0.0	0.1	0.0	0.0	0.0
Not Stated	—	—	—	0.1	0.1	0.0	0.1	0.0	0.1
Total	26.3	11.4	15.5	16.8	5.9	10.9	14.3	6.0	8.3

Source: Barbados Statistical Service, Continuous Labour Force Sample Survey, 1994–1999 and 1996–2001.

An examination of unemployed by last occupation indicates that approximately 30 percent were in elementary occupations, which require little or no human capital formation. Unemployment was also high among service/shop workers and, to a lesser extent, among craft and related workers.

Severance Payments and Unemployment Insurance

Barbados is the only country in the Caribbean with an unemployment insurance scheme. That scheme was established in July 1981. The number of claims received rose from 8,830 in 1995 to 14,956 in 2003, while the number of claims allowed increased from 7,601 in 1995 to 12,437 in 2003. A sectoral analysis of the unemployment claims indicates that the wholesale and retail trade, manufacturing, construction/installation and hotel/restaurant/tourism sectors were the main ones affected by the temporary unemployment of workers. The main occupational categories that were susceptible to unemployment and hence the claim for an unemployment benefit were service workers, clerical workers, production workers and unskilled/casual/general workers. These tend to be females between the ages of 25 and 44 years. The increase in claims, coupled with the decline in the number of unemployed and the unemployment rate, suggests that the unemployment spells of those covered by the scheme are relatively short. Unemployment benefit is "payable for each day of unemployment, excluding Sundays, as long as unemployment continues, subject to a maximum of 26 weeks in any continuous period of unemployment, or for an aggregate of 26 weeks in the 52 weeks immediately preceding the commencement of the current week of unemployment". Data on the number of unemployment benefit recipients by number of days indicate that, on average, 56 percent of the recipients received the benefit for a period of up to 78 days (approximately 3 months). (See Table III-10.)

Table III-10. Unemployment Benefit Recipients for Selected Years by Number of Days Paid

	1998		2000		2002	
Days Paid	**# Recipients**	**Percent**	**# Recipients**	**Percent**	**# Recipients**	**Percent**
1–12	1245	13.1	1390	14.1	2874	28.3
13–42	2039	21.5	2246	22.8	1842	18.2
43–78	1797	19.0	2202	22.3	1039	10.3
79–108	1214	12.8	1402	14.2	602	5.9
109–138	1281	13.5	1226	12.5	480	4.7
139–155	1412	14.9	1110	11.3	276	2.7
156	490	5.2	27	2.8	3032	29.9

Source: National Insurance Board, Unemployment Report, 2000, 2002.

Table III-11. Employees Severed, by Sex Distribution, 1995–2002

	Males Severed		Females Severed		
Year	Number	Percent	Number	Percent	Total
1995	355	57.4	263	42.5	618
1996	1009	53.6	872	46.3	1881
1997	429	50.1	427	49.8	856
1998	375	48.0	406	51.9	781
1999	660	42.7	885	57.2	1545
2000	415	33.8	812	66.2	1227
2001	380	40.7	553	59.2	933
2002	147	32.3	308	67.6	455

Source: National Insurance Board, Severance Payment Report, various issues.

The Severance Payment Scheme was introduced in 1973 to compensate workers for involuntary and permanent job loss occasioned by the closure, relocation or sales reduction of a company. The Scheme covers private-sector employees only, as tenured Government employees are excluded.

Over the 1995–2002 period, there was a high degree of fluctuation in the number of employees severed with the range being 618 in 1995 to 1,881 in 1996. During the 1995–96 and 2001–02 periods, more males than females were severed. (See Table III-11.)

Reorganization and closure of businesses were identified as the main reasons for severing workers. The main sectors affected by job loss were commerce, retail trade, manufacturing and, to a lesser extent, hotels and construction. Clerical, sales, and service and production workers were mainly affected. Low levels of severance occur among professional, administrative, managerial and skilled persons. This pattern of severance follows the standard 'pecking order' approach with frontline service and production workers being the first group to be severed, followed by supervisory and then managerial staff, when a business reorganizes.

The process of severing workers usually follows the 'inverse seniority' rule with junior workers with short lengths of service (many of whom tend to be young) being among the first to be severed. The data suggest that the highest degree of severance occurred among the young and junior categories of workers. Between 1995 and 2002, approximately 58 percent of those severed were under 40 years of age. The severance payment arrangements were changed in 1991 to make the severance of older and relatively long serving employees less costly. Between 1995 and 2002, on average, 60 percent of those severed had been employed for less than 10 years. (See Table III-12.)

There has been an ongoing concern with the issue of 'double-dipping' whereby a severed worker can claim both severance pay and unemployment insurance up to 26 weeks after separation. Although there are no statistics on the extent of this phenomenon, it might not

Table III-12. Employees Severed, by Years of Service, Selected Years

Years of Service	1996		1998		2000		2002	
	Number	Percent	Number	Percent	Number	Percent	Number	Percent
Under 5	482	25.6	247	31.6	374	30.5	677	43.2
5–10	673	35.8	215	27.5	448	36.5	414	26.4
11–15	285	15.1	89	11.4	138	11.2	193	12.3
16–20	202	10.7	114	14.6	128	10.4	146	9.3
21–25	142	7.5	54	6.9	70	5.7	75	4.8
26–30	54	2.9	42	5.4	47	3.8	61	3.9
31 and over	43	2.3	20	2.6	22	1.8	—	—
Total	1881	100	781	100	1227	100	1566	100

Source: National Insurance Board, Severance Report (various issues).

be a severe problem, given the relatively small number of persons who are severed. There is, however, a need to rationalize the unemployment benefit and severance payment schemes to reduce the overall costs of job separation. This process can include adjusting the qualifying requirements for the two schemes, reducing the amount of benefits in one scheme relative to another or reducing the contributions paid by the parties into the respective funds. The final result would be dependent on the rapidity with which an individual can reasonably be expected to find a new job and the extent of adjustment costs paid by employers.

The relatively high unemployment rates in Barbados stem not only from the way that unemployment is measured but also from structural features in the form of mismatch, job queuing and movements in business activity. There is a formal social safety net to assist the unemployed in Barbados (that is, unemployment insurance and severance payment scheme), but the provisions in these schemes apply only to those who qualify. Several of the unemployed are young dependents who share in household resources in a form of a family or household safety net. Others engage in informal-sector activities until jobs in the formal sector arise. The key to unemployment reduction is to expand productive activity in the economy on a long-term and sustainable basis (that is, economic growth) coupled with human resource development.

E. Wages, Productivity, and Competitiveness

Two variables through which the labour market affects the degree of international competitiveness are changes in wages and labour productivity. With a fixed-exchange-rate with its main trading partner, the USA, Barbados has to ensure that real wage increases do not outstrip increases in (labour) productivity.

Barbados has established a Social Partnership involving the Government, the private sector and the labour unions. This Partnership seeks to maintain a balance between wages,

Table III-13. Wages, Prices, and Labour Productivity, 1995–2003

Year	Nominal Wage Index (1995=100)	Retail Price Index (1995=100)	Real Wage Index (1995=100)	Labour Productivity Index (1995=100)
1995	100.0	100.0	100.0	100.0
1996	103.0	102.4	100.6	99.2
1997	109.2	110.3	99.0	102.2
1998	113.6	108.9	104.3	105.3
1999	118.2	110.9	106.6	103.5
2000	122.7	113.3	108.3	103.3
2001	127.0	116.3	109.2	95.6
2002	130.8	116.3	112.5	96.9
2003	134.7	118.3	113.9	98.4

Sources: Calculated from data in Barbados Economic and Social Report, 2003; and Central Bank of Barbados, Annual Statistical Digest, 2004.

Note: The nominal wage index is calculated using data from the Annual Statistical Digest and average salary increases granted by the Government and private sector.

prices and productivity, inter alia. This understanding is expressed in the form of Protocols which have been in existence since 1993: Protocol 1 (1993–95), Protocol 2 (1995–97), Protocol 3 (1998–2000), Protocol 4 (2000–04) and Protocol 5 (2005–07). These Protocols have given non-governmental entities a 'voice' in economic decision-making. (See Downes and Nurse, 2004 for a full discussion).

Between 1995 and 2003, nominal wage rates increased at a rate of 3.8 percent per annum, while the average annual inflation rate was 2.1 percent. Overall, real wages increased by 1.7 percent per annum over the 1995–2003 period. Using the ratio of real GDP at factor cost to the number of persons employed as an indicator of labour productivity, the available data indicate that labour productivity fluctuated over the period 1995–2003 with a general negative trend. (See Table III-13.)

Overall, real wage increases were higher than estimated changes in labour productivity. (See Figure III-2.). There is the possibility that labour productivity growth may be underestimated since the base year for measuring real GDP has not changed since 1974.

Figure III-2. Trend in Real Wages and Labour Productivity, 1995–2002

Sectoral Wages and Salaries

In the public service, there was a slight increase in real wages/salaries, as nominal wage/salary increases were above the rate of inflation over the period. (See Table III-14.) Over the years, public officers have been granted 'across-the-board' increases which have narrowed the range between the top and bottom salaries. It is estimated that the ratio of the top (S1) to bottom (Z38) salary is currently 5.5 to 1, which is a reduction from a ratio of 15 to 1 in 1960. It is generally thought that whilst lower ranks of the public service are competitive with the private sector, the upper ranks are not. Despite the security of tenure that public officers enjoy in established posts, attracting individuals to the civil service, especially in senior professional and administrative posts, appears to be difficult. This can have a long-term negative impact on the productivity of the economy as public service productivity can be slowed down.

Over the 1995–96 to 2004–05 period, wages and salaries accounted for a decreasing share of government current expenditure from 41.2 percent to 33.0 percent (provisional). (See Table III-15.) There was a significant

Table III-14. Public Service Wage/Salary Increases, 1995–2003
(percent)

Year	Wage/Salary Increases	Retail Price Index Increase	Real Wage Increase
1995	3.0	1.9	1.1
1996	3.0	2.4	0.6
1997	6.3	7.7	−1.4
1998	3.0	−1.3	4.3
1999	4.2	1.6	2.6
2000	3.0	2.4	0.6
2001	3.0	2.8	0.2
2002	3.0	0.2	2.8
2003	2.0	1.5	0.5

Source: IMF. Barbados Statistical Appendix (various issues).

Table III-15. Wages and Salaries in Central Government, 1995–96 through 2004–05

Year	Wages and Salaries (Bds$ millions)	Share of Current Expenditure (%)	Growth of Wages /Salaries (%)	Government Employment (thousands)
1995/6	435.7	41.2	6.0	22.9
1996/7	462.9	40.8	6.2	23.9
1997/8	503.5	40.1	8.8	25.2
1998/9	530.6	39.8	5.4	25.0
1999/2000	579.9	41.2	9.3	26.9
2000/1	601.5	39.7	3.7	25.0
2001/2	606.5	38.3	0.8	26.7
2002/3	641.9	38.4	5.8	27.7
2003/4	571.2	32.7	−11.0	27.9
2004/5[P]	601.2	33.0	5.3	27.5

Source: Central Bank of Barbados, *Annual Statistical Digest*, 2005, p. 153.

Note: Government employment is based on the calendar year.

[P] - provisional.

Table III-16. Employment and Earnings by Industrial Group, Quarter Ending September 2003

Industrial Group	Total Employees			Average Weekly Earnings (Bds $)		
	All Employees	Wage Earners	Salaried Employees	All Employees	Wage Earners	Salaried Employees
Agriculture	2,089	1,723	366	417.35	328.08	838.14
Mining and Quarrying	468	308	160	816.20	737.48	968.21
Electricity, Gas, Water	10,614	7,441	3,174	494.08	383.32	730.32
Construction	1,926	1,220	706	834.09	565.94	1,297.17
Wholesale and Retail Trade	5,448	4,486	962	511.93	441.58	839.95
Hotels and Restaurants[1]	26,763	17,834	8,929	426.06	324.57	628.76
Transport and Communications	8,650	2,902	5,748	598.03	434.08	680.81
Financial Services/Real Estate	15,752	6,655	9,096	538.23	333.14	688.28
Gov't Services/Other Services	32,950	12,092	20,858	643.79	447.28	757.74
Total/Overall	104,658	54,660	49,998	546.15	385.35	721.95

[1] Average Weekly Earnings for Hotels and Restaurants and Other Services are as follows:

	All Employees	Wage Earners	Salaried Employees
Hotels and Restaurants	386.36	330.64	674.46
Other Services	496.25	278.92	619.28

Source: Barbados Statistical Service, Occupational Wage Survey, September 2003.

growth in the wages and salaries bill during the 1995–96 to 1999–2000 period as government employment expanded from 22,900 persons in 1995 to 26,900 persons in 2000. While there was a slowing down in the growth of the wages and salaries bill during the recession of 2001–02, there was some reversal in this situation as further employment in the government services expanded to 27,500 persons in 2004.

Data from a recent occupational wage survey indicate that 52 percent of employed persons were wage earners, while 48 percent were salaried employees during the third quarter of 2003. (See Table III-16). The average weekly earnings of both wage earners and salaried employees were highest in mining and quarrying, electricity, gas and water and construction, and lowest in agriculture, manufacturing and distribution, hotels and restaurants. The ratio of highest to lowest average weekly earnings was 2 for all employees, 2.27 for wage earners and 2.06 for salaried employees. These ratios are much lower than that which obtains in the central government where the ratio is 5.5.

Productivity and the Social Partnership

Estimates for average labour productivity at the sectoral level (defined as real sectoral GDP divided by the number of persons employed in the sector) indicate that the highest levels

Table III-17. Labour Productivity by Sector, 1995–2003
(Bds$ thousands)

Sector	1995	1996	1997	1998	1999	2000	2001	2002	2003
Agriculture and Fishing	10.4	9.6	10.2	10.4	11.3	12.7	10.3	10.2	8.5
Manufacturing	7.3	8.5	8.2	8.5	8.6	8.7	8.8	9.0	9.0
Electricity, Gas and Water	30.4	28.8	23.5	29.0	19.8	19.8	20.6	20.9	15.7
Construction, Mining, Quarrying	6.1	6.2	6.1	6.0	6.5	6.1	5.5	6.1	6.7
Wholesale and Retail Trade	9.7	11.1	11.9	11.2	10.9	10.1	9.6	9.4	9.7
Tourism	11.0	10.8	11.0	10.4	11.7	11.1	10.8	10.1	11.0
Transport and Communications	13.7	15.9	16.1	15.4	18.2	16.5	14.7	17.2	17.0
Finan., Bus. Services, Gen. Services	5.5	4.8	5.3	6.0	5.4	4.8	4.9	4.9	4.8
Government	5.1	5.0	5.1	5.1	4.9	5.5	5.1	4.9	4.9
Total	7.7	7.6	7.9	8.1	8.0	8.0	7.5	7.5	7.6

Source: Central Bank of Barbados, Statistical Digest (various issues).

were obtained in electricity, gas and water, tourism and transportation and communications. The lowest levels were in government services, financial and business services and construction, mining and quarrying. (See Table III-17.) Although there are measurement problems associated with the calculation of labour productivity (especially in the services sector), the data suggest that labour productivity is high in 'capital intensive' sectors and low in 'labour intensive' services sectors. All of the sectors exhibited a decline in labour productivity over the 1995–2003 period with the exception of the manufacturing and transportation and communication sectors, both of which exhibited some increase in productivity primarily owing to labour shedding.

An important aspect of Protocols 1 to 4 was the design and use of productivity or performance-based payment schemes in both the private and public sectors. Protocol 1 (1993–1995) included a provision whereby there was a freeze on basic nominal wages and salaries with provision for the payment of profit-sharing and productivity bonus. Protocol 2 (1995–97) and subsequent Protocols called for greater wage restraint in the negotiation process, with provision for bonus payments based on productivity and other measures of organizational performance. Studies by Downes and Alleyne (1998) and Bannister (2004) indicate that productivity-based payment schemes have not been as prevalent as one would have expected with the establishment of a National Productivity Board (now Council) in 1993. The Council has undertaken an educational and training program to promote the design and use of such schemes, but companies have not proceeded with the implementation process. Several reasons have been cited by the key informants for the lack of implementation:

(i) the high informational requirements of the schemes;
(ii) improvement in the economy which reduces the necessity to resort to such schemes;
(iii) the need to keep certain types of information confidential;
(iv) the lack of tax incentives for such schemes;
(v) the absence of submission by unions; and
(vi) the lack of enthusiasm by management of companies.

Empirical studies of the available schemes however indicate that such schemes have a positive impact on cooperation with others (teamwork), commitment to the organisation, labour-management relations, productivity, profitability and competitiveness. The data also indicate that such schemes were prevalent during periods of recession in the economy (1990–92 and 2001–02), a fact that reflects the origin of gain-sharing schemes.

Productivity and Competitiveness

Using the ratio of real wages to labour productivity as a measure of competitiveness, one can observe that, at the aggregate level, real unit labour costs (RULC) showed an upward trend over the period 1995–2003, suggesting a possible loss in competitiveness. (See Table III-18.)

The increase in RULC has slowed down since 2002. Another indicator of competitiveness, the real effective exchange rate (REER) supports the general result emerging from the use of the RULC. The REER showed an appreciating trend up to 2000 and a depreciating trend thereafter (Figure III-3).

The depreciating trend in the REER is partly due to the decline in the US dollar (to which the Barbadian dollar is tied) against major international currencies over the past four years. The improvement in international competitiveness of Barbadian exports depends on greater increases

Table III-18. Indicators of Competitiveness, 1995–2003

Year	Real Unit Labour Cost (1995=100)	Change in RULC (%)	Changes in the Real Effective Exchange Rate (%)
1995	100.0	−1.7	−1.0
1996	101.4	1.4	0.0
1997	96.9	−4.4	5.1
1998	99.1	2.3	−1.1
1999	103.0	3.9	4.1
2000	104.8	1.7	6.0
2001	114.2	9.0	−1.3
2002	116.1	1.7	−5.3
2003	115.8	0.3	−9.4

Sources: Table III-13; IMF, Staff Reports for Barbados (various issues).

Note: The real unit labour cost (RULC) is calculated from data in Table III-13. The real effective exchange rate (REER) is an index of relative prices adjusted for nominal exchange rate movements. Minus signs indicate depreciation in the exchange rate or improved competitiveness.

in labour productivity than in real wages. Labour productivity growth depends, inter alia, on investment in human and physical capital, the adoption of new technology, plant organization and adroit management system. Little research has been undertaken on the factors influencing labour productivity in Barbados.

Figure III-3. Change in RULC and REER, 1995–2002

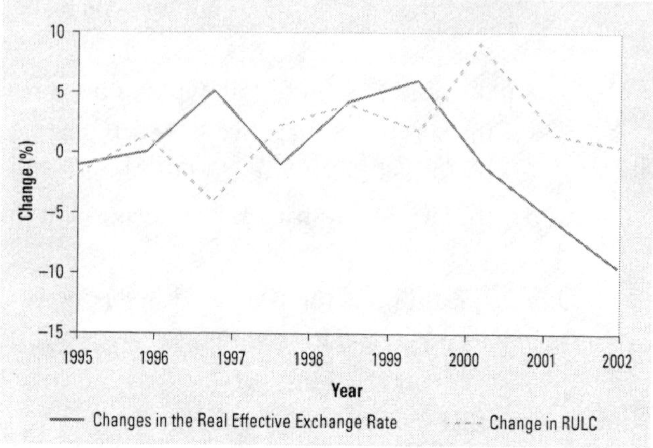

Wage Rates and Productivity: A Comparative Analysis

The extent to which Barbados has lost or gained competitiveness via labour market behaviour and outcomes can be discovered through a comparative analysis of wage rates and labour productivity. Recent data on labour productivity in four Caribbean countries (Barbados, Jamaica, St. Lucia and Trinidad and Tobago), using a common methodology, indicate that over the period 1985–2001, labour productivity in Barbados was higher than in Jamaica and St. Lucia. (See Table III-19.)

However labour productivity in Trinidad and Tobago was higher than that in Barbados. As indicated earlier, there has been a general decline in labour productivity in Barbados, while in Trinidad and Tobago, there was a general decline between 1985 and 1993, and a rise

Table III-19. Value Added Per Person Employed (*US$1990*)

Year	Barbados	Jamaica	St. Lucia	Trinidad and Tobago
1985	28223		11324	29186
1986	28393	9577	12752	28465
1987	26630	9829	12669	28315
1988	26761	9680	14026	26871
1989	26881	10446	14855	26841
1990	25627	11094	15125	27231
1991	26049	11259	14786	26084
1992	25464	11825	15516	25013
1993	25979	12108	14975	24336
1994	25856	12110	15324	24801
1995	25386	11765	15032	25251
1996	24685	11946	14937	25717
1997	25308	11965	14893	25073
1998	25546	11635	14926	25125
1999	25657	11684	14341	26550
2000	25736	11916	13725	27692
2001	24644	12054		28530

Source: ILO (2000), *Establishing Labour Productivity Indicators for the Caribbean* (Port-of-Spain, Trinidad and Tobago).

between 1994 and 2001. (See Figure III-4.)

Figure III-4. Value Added Per Person Employed in Barbados, Jamaica, St. Lucia, and Trinidad & Tobago

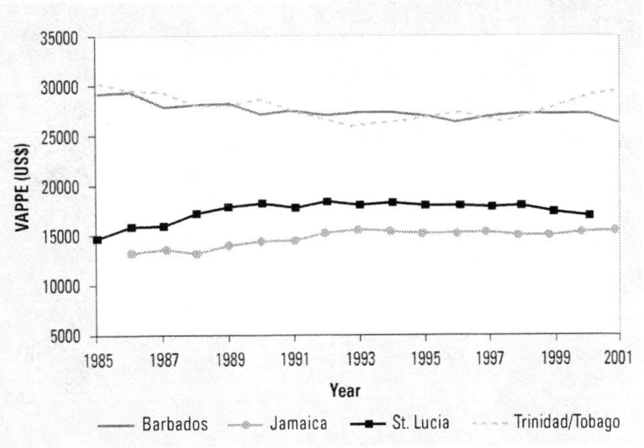

A comparison of unit labour costs across Barbados, Jamaica and Trinidad and Tobago indicates that unit labour costs in Barbados were lower than those in Trinidad and Tobago between 1985 and 1994 and higher thereafter. Indeed, unit labour cost has been increasing in Barbados relative to Trinidad and Tobago. (See Table III-20.) These results indicate that while Barbados is relatively more competitive than Jamaica, it is less competitive than Trinidad and Tobago. This result, reinforced by a recent study on comparative real effective exchange-rates in Barbados, Jamaica, and Trinidad and Tobago, indicates that Trinidad and Tobago is the most competitive economy in the region (Moore, Skeete and Greenidge, 2004).

Available data on weekly wages in the hotel industry and the retail, manufacturing and construction sectors in selected Caribbean countries indicate that, in 2001, wages in the hotel industry in Antigua and Barbuda and in Barbados were comparable for various posts. Jamaican workers received relatively lower wages while in the Bahamas, hotel workers received relatively higher wages. (See Table III-21.)

In the construction sector, the Bahamas offers the highest wages per hour for various posts, whereas there is some degree of similarity

Table III-20. Unit Labour Cost in Selected Caribbean Countries

Year	Barbados	Jamaica	Trinidad and Tobago
1985	0.20		0.38
1986	0.13	0.21	0.27
1987		0.24	0.27
1988		0.27	0.26
1989		0.30	0.24
1990		0.28	0.25
1991	0.17	0.22	0.26
1992	0.17	0.19	0.28
1993	0.19	0.25	0.24
1994	0.19	0.25	0.22
1995	0.25	0.32	0.22
1996	0.28	0.37	0.22
1997	0.31	0.43	0.21
1998	0.29	0.47	
1999	0.32	0.48	0.23
2000	0.34	0.47	
2001	0.37	0.47	0.23

Source: ILO (2000), *Establishing Labour Productivity Indicators for the Caribbean* (Port-of-Spain, Trinidad and Tobago).

Table III-21. Weekly Wages Data for Selected Categories of Workers in the Hotel Industry, 2001
(Bds $)

Category	Antigua	Bahamas	Barbados	Dominica	Jamaica
Baker	251.49	563.64	289.23	135.28–180.10	
Bartender	233.02	565.50	302.62	126.03–164.78	73.44–163.48
Bell Captain	218.64	324.84	292.28		
Bus Person	211.34	264.00	266.10	65.88–143.36	
Butcher		563.34	289.23		
Dishwasher	209.15	417.00	263.04	107.82–112.90	
Front Desk Clerk	239.08	569.00	289.22		217.02–294.96
Headwaiter	266.67	443.50	302.62		
Laundry Worker	209.15	488.50	269.14	71.74–143.36	73.44–149.85
Night Auditor	239.08	571.16	331.39	102.48–156.66	
Pantry Worker		497.34	269.14	107.82–112.90	
Receptionist	251.49	531.16	289.22	122.98–225.46	78.26–258.36
Security Guard	231.05	450.00	268.62	116.18–231.32	
Security Supervisor	240.54				
Waiter/Waitress	211.34	190.00	289.22	96.63–150.79	73.44–149.85
Wine Steward	211.34	376.34	289.22	107.82–112.90	

Source: Barbados Employers' Confederation, *Labour Digest 2001*.
Note: Bds$2 = US$1.

for various posts in Antigua, Barbados, Dominica, Jamaica and Trinidad and Tobago. In the manufacturing sector, the Bahamas and Barbados offer relatively high wages, while in the retail sector, there is some degree of 'wage convergence' for selected posts. (See Table III-22.) These data do not take into consideration non-wage elements that can increase labour costs and hence lead to a decline in relative competitiveness. The labour-market mobility afforded by the CSME can have the effect of bringing about some degree of 'wage and non-wage convergence' while providing access to a wider pool of skilled resources to enhance overall productivity.

In general, the data on wages and labour productivity for selected Caribbean countries suggest that Barbados is not very competitive in the international market. With declining labour productivity and increasing wage rates, unit labour cost has increased over time. Concerns by employers with respect to the attitude of workers towards work further complicate the situation.

F. Labour-Market Regulation

Labour-market regulation can be broadly defined as the range of economic, social and judicial measures and mechanisms involved in the determination of labour-market behaviour and outcomes. They emerge from both the legislative machinery of the state and the collective

Table III-22. Hourly Wages within the Retail, Manufacturing, and Construction Sectors in Select Caribbean Countries, 2001
(Bds $)

	Antigua	Bahamas	Barbados	Dominica	Jamaica	Trinidad
Construction						
Truck Driver	16.23	19.00	11.25–12.55	4.72–6.07	3.46–10.58	5.31
Labourer	7.36	14.00	8.05	2.91–3.66	1.81–4.86	2.73–4.92
Carpenter	10.59	19.00	9.95–10.66	4.72–6.07	4.24–10.01	4.97
Mason	10.45	16.00	12.55	4.72–6.07	4.24–10.01	4.97
Machine Operator	10.57	18.00	10.70–15.86	3.90–4.43	5.72–12.39	2.91
Electrician	17.78	44.00	9.22–12.75	4.72–6.07	4.27–11.85	6.99
Painter	11.19	16.00	12.50–13.30	4.72–6.07	0.61–0.84	3.64–9.77
Foreman	29.37	30.00		10.32–11.13	3.46–16.70	4.96–11.06
Manufacturing						
Lab Technician		17.30	15.35		2.70–18.99	7.08–8.66
Plant Electrician	9.96	20.48	20.31	3.75–8.29	4.18–12.62	7.73
Welder/Fabricator	12.05	21.04	12.90	3.75–8.29	3.50–12.62	8.44–9.25
Product Supervisor	8.52	37.02	25.11	3.88–6.74	2.07–29.26	6.38–8.16
Receptionist	7.59	18.76	10.62	4.98	2.29–5.16	5.18–6.16
General Worker	6.01	12.20	9.33	4.05–4.52	1.52–10.03	3.82–5.12
Payroll Clerk (A/C clerk)	4.38	22.12	12.93	4.08–7.02	3.76–17.60	10.41
Retail						
Cashier	5.80	8.00	5.48–7.53	3.97–6.06	3.34–13.42	3.91–5.41
Van Driver	9.33		8.08–9.10	4.62–9.81	2.29–10.79	4.65
Clerk	8.30	6.70	6.18	3.77	4.60–6.62	2.56–3.99
Porter	6.21	7.00	6.53–8.13	3.07–5.24	2.30–8.49	7.38
Forklift Driver	6.42	12.00	10.30–11.85	2.93–5.00	3.55–10.87	8.20
Messenger	5.48	10.00	6.70–8.13	3.84–4.39	2.29–7.53	5.30–5.69
Security Guard	14.70	10.00–12.00	5.93	3.86–8.72	3.49–13.13	2.33–3.33

Source: Barbados Employers' Confederation, *Labour Digest 2001*.

bargaining process between labour unions and employers. (See Downes, 2002.) These measures and mechanisms can result in some degree of labour-market rigidity or inflexibility and increase the non-wage labour costs. The regulations have been developed to protect the rights of both workers and employers. From a labour economics perspective, the regulations give rise to labour adjustment costs (that is, the costs associated with the hiring and firing of workers) and make the labour input in the production process a quasi-fixed factor.

There are several laws that directly govern the operation of labour matters in Barbados. (See Appendix 1.) In addition, Barbados is a member of the International Labour Organisation (ILO), hence it has ratified a number of conventions. Some of these have been subsequently incorporated into the labour laws of the country. Probably, the most prominent of the labour laws that impact on labour costs are:

(i) national insurance and social security;
(ii) holiday with pay;
(iii) severance payment; and
(iv) shops.

National Insurance and Social Security

The National Insurance and Social Security Scheme provides a range of benefits, which include: old age, disability, death/funeral, sickness, maternity, work injury, unemployment and survivors. The Scheme collects contributions from employed and self-employed persons based on a percentage of their maximum insurable earnings. While the maximum insurable earnings did not increase during the 1995–2004 period, the contribution rates for employed persons (16–65 years) increased by 1.5 percentage points, from 17.75 to 19.25 percent. For self-employed persons, the increase was 3.5 percentage points. (See Table III-23.) The contribution rate for employees (16–65 years) increased from 8 percent in 1995 to 9 percent in 2004 (1 percentage point), and, for employers, it rose from 9.75 percent in 1995 to 10.25 percent in 2004 (0.5 percentage point). For self-employed persons, the contribution rate increased by 3.5 percentage points.

Further changes in the national insurance contribution rates have been introduced by the Government to cover the period 2005–06. (See Table III-24.) These changes would mean that the overall contribution rate for employed persons (15–65 years) would increase by 3.5 percentage points with a rise in the national insurance contribution rate of 5.5 percentage points and a reduction in the severance payments and unemployment insurance rates of 2 percentage points. This adjustment suggests that the Government plans to maintain a certain level of employment in the country so that the call on the unemployment insurance and severance payment funds would not be excessive. Furthermore, there has been a slight shift in the payment of national insurance contributions towards the employee and a significant increase in the contribution rate for self-employed persons. The maximum insurable earnings were increased from Bds$3100 to Bds$3190 per month from January 1, 2005.

These changes in the contribution rates and the maximum insurable earnings would increase non-wage labour costs. For example, assuming that a person's monthly salary is equal to the maximum insurable earnings, then in 1995 the employee would have paid Bds $248 and the employer, Bds $302.25. In 2004, the payments would have been Bds $279 for employees and Bds $317.75 for employers, while in 2006 the payments would be Bds $319 for employees and Bds $358.88 for employers. No changes are planned for the contribution rates for the training fund, employment injury and non-contributory components of the overall national insurance.

Table III-23. National Insurance Contributions for Selected Years
(percentage of maximum insurable earnings)

	1995			2003			2004		
	Employee	Employer	Total	Employee	Employer	Total	Employee	Employer	Total
Employed Persons 16–65 Years									
National Insurance	4.00	4.00	8.00	5.25	5.25	10.50	5.75	5.75	11.50
Non-contributory	2.00	2.00	4.00	2.00	2.00	4.00	2.00	2.00	4.00
Employment Injury	—	0.75	0.75	—	0.75	0.75	—	0.75	0.75
Unemployment	1.50	1.50	3.00	0.75	0.75	1.50	0.75	0.75	1.50
Severance Fund	—	1.00	1.00	—	0.50	0.50	—	0.50	0.50
Training Fund Levy	0.50	0.50	1.00	0.50	0.50	1.00	0.50	0.50	1.00
Total	8.00	9.75	17.75	8.50	9.75	18.25	9.00	10.25	19.25
Employed Persons Under 16 and 65 Years and Over									
Employment Injury	—	0.75	0.75	—	0.75	0.75	—	0.75	0.75
Training Fund	0.50	0.50	1.00	1.00	0.50	0.50	0.50	0.50	1.00
Total	0.50	1.25	1.75	1.75	0.50	1.25	0.50	1.25	1.75
Self-Employed Persons									
National Insurance	8.00	10.50	11.50						
Non-contributory	—	2.00	2.00						
Health Service Levy	2.00	—	—						
Training Levy	0.50	0.50	0.50						
Total	10.50	13.00	14.00						
Maximum Insurable Earnings									
Monthly (Bds$)			3100			3100			3100
Weekly (Bds$)			715			715			7.15

Table III-24. National Insurance Contributions, 2005 and 2006 (*percent*)

	2005 Total %	2005 Employee %	2005 Employer %	2006 Total %	2006 Employee %	2006 Employer %
Employed Persons 16–65 Years						
National Insurance	12.50	6.25	6.25	13.50	6.75	6.75
Non-contributory	4.00	2.00	2.00	4.00	2.00	2.00
Employment Injury	0.75	—	0.75	0.75	—	0.75
Unemployment	1.50	0.75	0.75	1.50	0.75	0.75
Severance Fund	0.50	—	0.50	0.50	—	0.50
Training Fund Levy	1.00	0.50	0.50	1.00	0.50	0.50
Total	20.25	9.50	10.75	21.25	10.00	11.25
Employed Persons Under 16 and 65 Years and Over						
Employment Injury	0.75	—	0.75	0.75	—	0.75
Training Fund Levy	1.00	0.50	0.50	1.00	0.50	0.50
Total	1.75	0.50	1.25	1.75	0.50	1.25
Self-Employed Persons						
National Insurance	12.50			13.50		
Non-contributory	2.00			2.00		
Training Fund Levy	0.50			0.50		
Total	15.00			16.00		

Source: PriceWaterhouseCoopers, *Tax Facts and Figures Barbados 20.*

Holiday with Pay

Data on holiday pay for selected Caribbean countries indicate that workers in Barbados are better off than those in several other countries. (See Table III-25.) For example, a worker in Barbados is entitled, by statute, to three weeks (15 working days) holiday with pay if he/she is employed for less than five years, and four weeks (20 days) if he/she is employed for more than five years. In Jamaica, the statutory requirement is two weeks regardless of the period of

Table III-25. Holiday with Pay Provision in Selected Caribbean Countries, October–November 2004

	Alternative Employment Periods		
Country	One Year	Less than One Year	Ten Years
Antigua and Barbuda	12	60	120
Barbados	15	15	20
Dominica	10	10	15
Grenada	10	15	15
Guyana	10	10	10
Jamaica	10	10	10
St. Lucia	10	10	15
St. Vincent	4–14	18	21
Trinidad and Tobago	10	10	10

Source: Barbados Employers' Confederation, BEC@WORK, Vol. 4, No. 6, December 2004, p. 3.

Note: The days represent statutory requirements only. Employees may obtain longer vacation with pay due to collective bargaining arrangements.

employment. In practice, workers receive longer periods of holiday with pay either through individual contractual arrangement or via the collective bargaining process.

During the holiday period, the employer incurs direct cost without a corresponding output if the worker is not temporarily replaced during the holiday period. If an additional worker is hired or existing workers work overtime to cover the work of the employee who is on holiday, then the employer incurs an additional cost. The longer the holiday period, the higher the incremental cost. It can be argued, however, that the holiday period allows the worker to recuperate from the stress in the workplace, thus avoiding fatigue. This recuperation enhances long-term labour productivity, which is rewarded by the payment during the holiday period. While holiday with pay may appear costly to the firm in the short run, it can bring long-term benefits especially in the case of long tenured workers.

Severance Payments

The Severance Payments scheme is a form of income protection that provides compensation to workers who are terminated by a company because of redundancy or national disaster or whose contract of employment is terminated after a period of lay-off or short time. All employers (except the Government) are required to contribute a percentage of their wage bill to a Severance Payments Fund. (See Tables III-23 and III-24.) Severance payment is paid by the employer to the employee who qualifies—that is, a person (16–65 years) who has been employed by the company continuously for two years (104 continuous weeks), and is contracted to work for no fewer than 21 hours per week.). Employers who pay employees according to the provisions of the Act are entitled to a rebate of 25 percent of the payment from the Severance Payment Fund (that is, they absorb 75 percent of the employee's severance payment). If the employer refuses to make such payment or he/she is unable to make the payment because of insolvency, then the Fund makes the payment to the employee. This payment is later recovered, if possible, from the employer.

From the employer's perspective, payments into the Fund represent a contingent payment, which is triggered when severance occurs. During periods of economic recession, the claims can be very high. For example, during the 1990–93 recession, there was a severe cash imbalance in the Fund, which required a financial injection from the Government and prompted a change in 1991 in the contribution rate, the rate of severance payment and the definition of 'basic pay' in terms of insurable earnings.

Since 1993, there has been a general decline in the level of unemployment, hence there has been no pressure to change the arrangements governing the scheme. Indeed, the contribution rate was reduced from 1 percent to 0.5 percent of insurable earnings in 2003. In 2002, an employer paying 1 percent of maximum insurable earnings (Bds $3100) would have contributed $31 to the Fund, while in 2003, the contribution would have been $15.50.

Although there was an increase in the maximum insurable earnings in 2005, the increased contribution to the Fund was very marginal (an additional 45 cents).

The provisions in the Severance Payments Act represent minimum payments. Employers are free to pay employees higher amounts than are required by statute. There is a view that in the context of mergers and acquisitions associated with the globalization process, firms should seek to pay highly skilled senior personnel much more than the statutory minimum (that is, a golden handshake/parachute). It has been suggested that the Fund be used to effect the re-training of severed/redundant employees. (See Downes and Antoine, 1994.)

The Shops Act

The other significant legislative change that took place in the labour market since 1995 was the amendments to the Shops Act in 1996. Several issues have been raised by employers with respect to some of the provisions of the Act and the impact of those provisions on operational efficiency and labour costs. The main amendments relate to:

(i) changing Sunday from being a 'closed' day to an ordinary working day except for Easter Sunday. This amendment has provided employers with some degree of operational (time) flexibility;

(ii) extending the concept of a 'shop' to include establishments that have hitherto been excluded from the provisions of the Act;

(iii) the provision whereby a shop assistant cannot be made to work on his/her day of religious worship without his/her consent and also the provision of penalties for breaching this regulation;

(iv) the provision for a five-day work week for shop assistants with a rest period of at least 2 days, one of which should be a day observed as the day of religious worship. The two-day rest period would not apply where a shop assistant agrees to work overtime. The employers feel that the concept of 'overtime' should be clearly defined.

The Social Partners have been discussing the implications of the amendments with a view to increasing their operational efficiency without disadvantaging the shop assistants. The statutory minimum remuneration payable to shop assistants was changed in 1997 and 2004. (See Table III-26.) The dual rate for persons under and over 18 years was removed in 2004, thus increasing the minimum rates of payment for those under 18 years more than for those above 18. Although the minimum rates have been calculated to be marginally sufficient to meet minimum living standards, most employees earn more than the statutory minimum rates. Household domestics are the only other category of workers subject to minimum wage legislation.

Labour-Market Indices

The range of legislative measures has been developed into indices by Rama (1995), Marquez and Pages (1998) and Heckman and Pages (2000). The data for the mid- to late 1990s suggest that the degree of labour-market rigidity in Barbados, as defined by the Rama index, was the highest in the CARICOM region, while the degree of employment protection in Barbados was relatively low as defined by the Marquez-Pages index. (See Table III-27.)

Heckman and Pages (2004) have examined legislative provisions relating to the termination of indefinite contracts (advance notice and compensation if the worker quits) and indemnities for dismissal (compensation for dismissal due to economic reasons) across a number of Latin American and Caribbean countries for 1999. (See Table III-28.) The data for a selection of countries indicate that Barbados compares favourably in these areas of labour-market regulation.

Table III-26. Statutory Minimum Remuneration Payable to Shop Assistants, 1997, 2004 *(Bds $)*

Item	From June 12, 1997	From December 20, 2004
Weekly payable rate	158.00[1] 170.00[2]	200.00
Daily payable rate for persons not employed on a weekly basis	31.60[1] 34.00[2]	40.00
Hourly payable rate for non-weekly and non-hourly paid workers	3.95[1] 4.25[2]	5.00
Overtime rate of wages payable for ordinary working days	5.93[1] 6.38[2]	7.50 per hour or part thereof
Overtime rate of wages for public holidays	7.90[1] 8.50[2]	10.00 per hour or part thereof

[1] For persons under 18 years of age.
[2] For persons 18 years and over.

Table III-27. Labour-Market Indices for Selected Caribbean Countries

Country	Rama's Labour Rigidity Index	Marquez-Pages Employment Protection Index
Antigua/Barbuda	0.390	—
Bahamas	0.580	2
Barbados	0.182	8
Belize	0.223	5
Grenada	0.328	—
Guyana	0.415	—
Haiti	0.393	16
Jamaica	0.278	12
St. Kitts/Nevis	0.476	4
St. Lucia	0.306	—
St. Vincent	0.251	—
Suriname	0.283	15
Trinidad and Tobago	0.354	17

Note: Rama's (1995) index includes ILO conventions ratified, annual leave with pay, maternity leave, social security contributions, government, minimum wage, severance pay, unionization. The Marquez-Pages (1998) index includes definition of just cause for dismissal, tenure-related severance payment, probationary period, severance at 20 years and reinstatement. The higher the value of the Rama index, the higher the degree of labour-market rigidity. A similar result obtains for the Marquez-Pages index.

Table III-28. Labour Legislation Features in Selected Caribbean and Latin American Countries, 1999

Country	Advance Notice	Compensation if worker quits	Compensation for Dismissal due to Economic reasons	Upper limit to compensation for dismissal
Bahamas	Half to one month	0	Negotiable	No
Barbados	Negotiable (in practice, one month)	0	0.41 W·N if N ≥ 2	3.75 monthly salaries
Belize	Half to one month	1/6 W·N if N > 10	1/4 W·N if N > 5	Max 42 weeks
Costa Rica	One month	0	W·N	8 monthly salaries
Dominican Republic	Half to one month	0	0.67 W·N if N = 1 to 4 0.74 W·N if N > 5	No
Guyana	Half month	0	1/4 W·N if N = 1 to 5 1/2 W·N if N = 5 to 10	12 monthly salaries
Jamaica	Two to twelve weeks	0	1/3 W·N if N = 2 to 5 1/2 W·N if N > 5	No
Panama	One month	1/4 W·N	3/4 W·N if N <10 7.5W + 1/4 W·N if N ≥ 10	No
Suriname	Quarter to six months	0	Negotiable	No
Trinidad and Tobago	Two months	0	1/3 W·N if N = 1 to 4 1/2 if N > 5	No

Source: Heckman and Pages (2004), Table A1.

Note: W – monthly wages; N – years of tenure.

New Legislation

In recent years, there has been a significant degree of consultation and discussion relating to new pieces of labour legislation:

(i) the Employment Rights Bill (fourth draft January 2001);
(ii) the Safety and Health at Work Act (passed in 2005); and
(iii) the Sexual Harassment Bill.

There has also been discussion on trade union recognition, HIV/AIDS, minimum wages, severance payments and provisions in the Shops (Amendment) Act. These consultations and discussions involving the Social Partners (Government, labour unions and employers) have been ongoing for some period as aspects of the changes have implications for both workers and employers. For example, the provisions in the Safety and Health Act can increase costs to employers while providing protection for workers.

The Employment Rights Bill provides for a statement of particulars on the nature of the employment contract from employers along with an itemised pay statement, statutory minimum amount of notice of termination, a certificate of termination, the right not to be dismissed unfairly and the establishment of an employment rights tribunal. The Bill seeks to be anti-discriminatory as it provides for equal opportunities for all categories of workers.

The definition of sexual harassment and the liability on the company are issues associated with the Sexual Harassment Bill.

Collective Bargaining

The range of labour laws usually provides for statutory minimum levels of the various entitlements to workers. Workers are able to obtain significant benefits through the collective bargaining process. It is estimated that 30 percent of the labour force is unionized. Available data indicate that there has been an increase in the degree of unionization of the labour force since 1995. Total trade union membership as a percentage of the labour force increased from approximately 24 percent in 1995 to 31 percent in 2002.

There has also been a significant rise in the new membership of the main trade union, the Barbados Workers Union (BWU). (See Table III-29.) The increase in new BWU membership has been as a result of a membership drive in the financial services, information services (especially call centres) and general business services sectors. The shift in union membership has followed the general pattern of labour employment in Barbados, namely a decline in agricultural and traditional manufacturing membership relative to 'new manufacturing' and services sector membership.

The other unions and staff associations largely cover public-sector employees (the National Union of Public Workers, the Barbados Union of Teachers, the Barbados Secondary Teachers Union and associations for nurses, police, firemen and school principals). These entities form the Congress of Trade Unions and Staff Associations of Barbados (CTUSAB). The Barbados Employers' Confed-

Table III-29. Unionisation in Barbados, 1995–2004

Year	Unionisation (%)[1]	BWU New Membership
1995	23.9	2406
1996	25.8	2442
1997	24.1	5397
1998	25.3	4311
1999	25.5	3689
2000	27.5	3501
2001	29.1	2911
2002	30.7	4096
2003	30.4	2563
2004	n.a.	2709

Sources: Ministry of Labour, Digest of Statistics (various issues); Barbados Workers Union.

Note: Unionisation is defined as estimated trade union membership as a percentage of the labour force.

n.a. – not available.

eration negotiates with the labour unions on behalf of private-sector employers. In those areas of the labour market not covered by unionization, remuneration and employment are based on the principles of the internal labour market, whereby the pricing and allocation of labour are determined by administrative rules and procedures. In some cases, the elements of the unionized labour market are used in the internal labour market.

The collective bargaining process in Barbados is based on the principle of voluntarism whereby trade unions and employers regulate their own relations without interference from public authorities. The voluntary system of industrial relations is premised on the 'freedom of contract' and the 'freedom of association' and is based on the principles of free collective bargaining and legal abstention in industrial relations. (See Goolsarran, 2002, pp 3–4). Collective bargaining agreements are not binding in a court of law, hence there is a self-policing mechanism to ensure that parties to the agreements fulfil their obligations. Through the collective bargaining process workers have been able to obtain additional benefits from the employment contract in the form of allowances and other fringe payments. These include allowances for uniform, overtime, hazard, acting and responsibility, car, travelling, laundry, transportation, gas, hazard. These benefits, together with statutory payments such as national insurance payments, constitute non-wage labour costs. The structure of allowances for an entity in the manufacturing sector is given in Appendix 2.

Although a Protocol arrangement has existed since 1993, there has been an increase in work stoppages and industrial disputes since 1993, especially in the public sector. (See Table III-30.) The man days lost due to such work stoppages constitute a loss in production and hence an economic cost. Several of these disputes and stoppages have been due to unsatisfactory working conditions, dismissals and bargaining rights. Also, the rapid changes in the local business environment that have resulted in lay-offs owing to mergers, acquisitions and the re-organization of companies in order to meet the demands of a highly competitive environment may have heightened both the degree of unionization and industrial disputes/work stoppages.

Table III-30. Number of Man Days Lost Due to Work Stoppages[1]

Year	Private Sector	Public Sector	Total
1993	190	10	200
1994	343	0	343
1995	799	8	807
1996	2299	22	2321
1997	1995	392*	2387*
1998	2724	1567	4291
1999	203	2434	2637
2000	110	977	1087
2001	1396	3414	4810
2002	1058	1088	2146
2003	1538	1539	3077
2004	127	3344	3471

Sources: Barbados Employers' Confederation, *Labour Digest 2001* and *Annual Reports 2001* and *2002*.

[1] Man day is equivalent to an 8-hour work day.

* Excludes data on the Sanitation Service Authority work stoppage in the public sector.

A Need for Reform?

As indicated in this section, the existence of both statutory and non-statutory regulations has increased the costs of labour services which can impact on the international competitiveness of Barbadian goods and services. Key informants interviewed for this study have expressed the view that aspects of the labour market require some reform in order to make the market efficient and flexible. The changes identified by these informants include:

(i) the use of unemployment insurance and severance payments funds for the training and retraining of workers;
(ii) the provision of a greater degree of labour market information to facilitate the match between the supply of and demand for labour as well as the training of workers;
(iii) a reduction in the number of public holidays;
(iv) adequate financing of education and training;
(v) the institution of more flexible working hours in keeping with a '24–7' culture and with links to the international community with its different time zones;
(vi) the strengthening of the administrative agencies of the labour market to facilitate the settlement of disputes, to shorten the period of job search, to provide timely labour-market information in order to enforce regulations and monitor workplace practices, and to hasten the introduction of new labour legislation;
(vii) the introduction of a national minimum wage to protect workers against exploitation by foreign investors;
(viii) the strengthening of public-sector reform in order to reduce the degree of 'red tape' and transaction costs;
(ix) the institution of a social safety net and other safeguards to protect the rights and interests of workers and employers; and
(x) the institution of standards for professionals who need to enter the international labour market (e.g., the export of professional services).

These suggestions indicate the need for a thorough examination of labour regulations and practices in Barbados as new international events and requirements impinge on the economy and hence the labour market. While changes in the national insurance scheme have slightly reduced the costs of labour to employers, several of the provisions in the proposed legislation are likely to increase the costs of doing business including the costs of labour. In addition, several factors that affect the efficient operations of the labour market have not been incorporated into the legislative measures.

G. Labour Market Reform Initiatives

Reform: Why and How?

The specification of labour-reform measures must start with an understanding of why labour market regulations were initially introduced and what adverse effects such regulations have on labour-market behaviour and outcomes. In addition, changes in the economic and social environments necessitate labour-market reform. An analysis of these effects and changes permits a clearer understanding of the type of labour-market reforms that are needed. A cost-benefit analysis of labour-market reforms becomes essential as such reforms can affect several stakeholders in the market. (See Pages, 2004.)

Tzannatos (1995) has identified several reasons why the government should intervene in the labour market by means of a set of regulations. These reasons include:

(i) to achieve a necessary wider social objective (e.g., workplace health and safety, decent work, no child labour);
(ii) to provide for social insurance and guard against risks (e.g., old age pension, unemployment insurance, severance);
(iii) to protect the rights of individuals and parties (e.g., anti–discrimination measures);
(iv) to resolve a missing market problem due to incomplete information (e.g., job search measures); and
(v) to promote greater employment (e.g., active employment programs).

In effect, the main areas subject to regulatory control in the labour market include: labour rights and standards, conflict resolution, intermediation and information, direct wage and benefit interventions, job security and social insurance and assistance. (See Tzannatos, 1995). In addition to legislative changes, non-legislative practices and procedures also require reform.

Research work undertaken by Downes (1999) and Downes, Mamingi and Antoine (2004) suggests that existing labour laws do not have a significant effect on employment since few changes have taken place over the years. However, the regulations do seem to have some positive impact on working conditions. A survey undertaken on labour-market flexibility in 1998 indicated that the most beneficial protection to workers was offered by national insurance benefits, severance payments, occupational health and safety, holiday with pay and security of tenure. (See Downes, 1999.) Employers, on the other hand, would like to see changes in the following labour-market regulations and behaviours:

(i) severance payments—reduction in payments to the Fund and employees;
(ii) Shops Act—change in working conditions;
(iii) National Insurance Scheme—reduction in payments;
(iv) a reduction in the number of sick leave days; and
(v) the implementation of a more flexible work week.

Several of these measures were supported by key informants who were interviewed for this study. (See Appendix III-3).

Some of these suggestions have been implemented by the Government since 1995, for example, the reduction in the contribution rate for severance. However, the pace of labour-market reform has been slow in Barbados. A review of labour legislation over the period 1995–2004 indicates that there have only been minor changes to existing labour laws—amendments to the Shops Act and to the Public Service (Restoration of Emoluments) Act, the introduction of the National Productivity Council Act and the TVET Council Regulations, and the issue of orders. The Safety and Health at Work Act was passed in 2005 after a long gestation. Some of the main pieces of labour legislation are still under review and discussion: the Employment Rights Bill, the Sexual Harassment Bill, the Shops Act and Trade Union Recognition.

Since successful reform involves consensus among the stakeholders—or, in the case of Barbados, the Social Partners—changes in labour-market regulations will take some time. Loehr (1997) made a number of recommendations relating to changes in the Severance Payments Scheme, but these have not been acted upon. (See also Downes and Antoine, 1994.) As indicated in the previous section, the key informants have identified several areas in the labour market that need to be examined in an effort to enhance Barbados' competitiveness.

Some Current Initiatives

There are some current initiatives that can affect the labour market both directly and indirectly.

First, as part of its public-sector reform program, the Government has piloted a new Performance Review and Development System (PRDS) in a number of departments and ministries. The PRDS has been designed to improve work planning in the public service, link individual work performance to key tasks and results, undertake the appraisal of work performance and improve work practices in the various agencies. In addition, there are plans to develop a productivity-based payment scheme for the public sector. These measures should enhance employee efficiency and effectiveness thus reducing the level of costs associated with undertaking transactions with government agencies.

Increasing public-sector productivity is critical to the overall competitiveness of the country since international transactions involve the intermediate role of a government agency (e.g., Customs, VAT office, Foreign Trade, Central Bank). There is therefore a direct link between labour reform and public-sector reform—a link embodied not in labour legislation but in labour practices. The trade union movement is supportive of such changes, but needs to be more involved in the design, implementation, monitoring and evaluation of the process. There is also concern with the issues of supersession and the physical working environment in the public sector.

Second, the Social Partners have introduced a number of initiatives to promote national awareness of the need to improve productivity and enhance competitiveness in order to increase socio-economic welfare in the long run. These initiatives include the May Day Declaration 2004, which seeks to incorporate the following elements:

(i) upholding the principles of decent work—the provision of productive jobs at acceptable earnings levels in conditions of freedom, equity, security and human dignity and in keeping with the core labour standards. These standards include the prohibition of forced labour and child labour, freedom of association and the right to organize and bargain collectively, equal remuneration for men and women for work of equal value, and non-discrimination in employment;
(ii) the use of the voluntaristic model of social dialogue to influence the development process. Non-governmental groups (civil society) would be incorporated into the consultation process;
(iii) the development of work and business opportunities for persons living with disabilities;
(iv) the protection of the intellectual property of cultural workers as Barbados seeks to develop its cultural industries;
(v) upholding the principle of non-discrimination (respect and dignity) in the labour market in the context of the CSME.

The National Initiative for Service Excellence (NISE) program seeks to "build consensus and generate a powerful national drive towards excellence in the delivery of Barbados' products, but with particular emphasis on the services sector upon which the economy has come to rely heavily". Strategies, programs and projects will be developed to enable workers not only to be productive but also to offer world-class customer service. In this way, Barbados would enhance its competitive advantage in selected service areas.

Third, the Barbados National Productivity Council is reviewing its efforts to promote the use of productivity and performance-based payment schemes. It is currently developing designs for the public service and the hotel sector. Since Barbados maintains a fixed-exchange-rate regime with its main trading partner, the USA, international competitiveness would have to focus on increasing productivity in all sectors of the economy.

Fourth, one of the concerns of the key informants was the lack of adequate information on labour-market trends and needs. The Ministry of Labour has a Manpower Research and Studies Unit (MRSU), which undertakes periodic studies of labour-market trends and practices. Barbados is part of the Caribbean Labour Market Information System (CLMIS) project, which seeks to provide information on labour-market trends in the region. Progress has not been as rapid as labour-market stakeholders would like in the provision of labour-market information, hence there is a need to intensify work in this area.

Fifth, various institutions in the labour market—labour unions, the employer association and training and educational institutions—have been offering skill training for workers. These courses and programs are designed to enhance the employability and productivity of workers in the workplace. There are skill shortages in tourism and the agricultural sectors. For example, there is a shortage of highly qualified and experienced food and beverage personnel in the hotel sector. In the tourism sector, as in other sectors, supervisory management is weak and needs to be enhanced to improve productivity in the workplace. Several training institutions have been offering courses in supervisory management. The Barbados Workers' Union Labour College and the National Union of Public Workers Academy, for example, offer courses in productivity, change management, negotiations, industrial relations and supervisory management. The Barbados Employers' Confederation (BEC) also offers a range of seminars and courses on industrial relations, supervisory management and human resources management.

The Future of Reform

Labour-market reform in a small developing country such as Barbados should focus on the need to create a dynamic labour market that can foster productivity and promote flexibility and organisational agility while providing effective social safety nets to guard against vulnerability and deprivation. Labour-market flexibility consists of several elements: functional/technical (multi-skilling, multi-tasking, re-training, job rotation), numerical (outsourcing, contract worker, self-employed workers), financial (incentive bonuses, productivity-based pay), temporal (staggered work, overtime, flexitime, job sharing) and locational (telework, homework, relocation—in the context of the CSME).

An analysis of the Barbados labour market over the period 1995 to 2004 indicates slow progress with the legislative aspect of labour-market reform, with legislative measures still under discussion. There have been several initiatives in the non-legislative aspects of reform especially with respect to training and skill development, building social dialogue and establishing a labour-market information system. In this regard, some of the recommendations made by Loehr (1997) have been followed up. There is still a need to further the reform process by:

(i) completing the legislative process with respect to the draft Bills once the Social Partners are satisfied with the provisions;
(ii) promoting the use of simple productivity/performance-based payment schemes;
(iii) establishing labour standards and accreditation systems to permit the free mobility of labour with the CSME and to allow professionals to compete for contracts in international markets;
(iv) intensifying training and development in occupational areas which are in short supply—managerial and supervisory personnel in key economic sectors and in new areas such as information technology—by using the training levy more creatively. There is a case for increasing the levy;
(v) rationalizing the social safety net system with respect to the severance payment and unemployment insurance scheme to allow re-training and quick re-entry to the labour market;
(vi) building labour-market information systems that are known and easily accessible to existing and potential labour-market participants.

For these measures to effect the labour-market reform needed, there is a need to strengthen the Ministry of Labour in the areas of data collection, training and development, job placement and labour administration, promote the consultation process so that all stakeholders can contribute to labour-market reform, strengthen private-sector agencies to contribute meaningfully to labour-market policies through the supply of labour data, establish advisory groups (think-tanks) to discuss proposed labour-market measures and provide adequate technical and administrative support to monitor and evaluate labour-market policies.

H. Recommendations

The review of the performance of the Barbados labour market over the period 1995 to 2004 points to a number of recommendations, which can enhance the efficiency and effectiveness of the market. Some of these recommendations reinforce some of those made by Loehr (1997). It is recommended that:

(i) the training levy contribution rate be increased and the funds be earmarked for training in supervisory management and new skills in the technical and vocational areas (e.g., information technology, electronics). Some funds should be allocated to improving the facilities and equipment used in various training programs.

(ii) the labour-market information system (LMIS) should be greatly improved to provide information on the labour market to existing and potential participants. There is need for information on job vacancies, employer needs, new labour-market trends, etc. Regular surveys should be undertaken by the MRSU of the Ministry of Labour. Information should be available in both electronic and hard-copy format.

(iii) professionals offering their services to the export market should be encouraged to adopt international standards and to remain up-to-date. In addition, senior management seminars should be mounted on a regular basis to keep managers abreast of the latest developments in the business and labour environments. Some companies have linked the training of senior managers to the performance evaluation and pay of those managers. The Human Resource Management Association of Barbados (HRMAB) has a key role to play in this process.

(iv) the severance payment and unemployment insurance payment schemes should be re-examined together to avoid cases of double dipping and to provide for the re-training/skilling of severed/unemployed workers. This would lower the effective cost of labour and permit quick re-employment.

(v) the Barbados National Productivity Council should redouble its efforts to promote performance-based payment schemes in Barbadian firms. These schemes should be kept simple and comprehensible. Tax incentives for such schemes should be introduced and probably linked to pension schemes. It should also promote new work organizational arrangements such as job rotation, multi-skilling/tasking, flexitime, etc., in collaboration with the trade union movement.

(vi) the existing and proposed labour legislation should be comprehensively reviewed by the Social Partners in an effort to promote labour-market flexibility while providing adequate protection for workers. A labour-market review committee should be established to undertake this review of the legal, economic, environmental and social aspects of the labour market.

(vii) measures to promote investment and economic growth are needed to create new employment opportunities. Although there is a growth in self-employment, enterprise development at all levels should be encouraged through fiscal and monetary incentives.

(viii) there is a need to strengthen the administrative machinery of the government (for example, more trained staff and speedier decision-making) to facilitate the more timely passing of legislative measures, enforcement and monitoring of provisions in the various labour laws and the resolution of labour disputes.

(ix) the Social Partnership needs to be strengthened so that its impact is felt much more at the firm and sectoral levels. Such enhanced dialogue would reduce workplace conflict, industrial disputes and work stoppages. These stoppages add to production costs and erode competitiveness. With the increase in unionization, there is a dire need to promote industrial dialogue and harmony.

(x) in the context of the CSME, there is a need to promote greater understanding of the regional labour market. Programs should be put in place to educate labour-market participants about the implications of the CSME for labour-market relations in Barbados.

Appendix 1

Labour Legislation in Barbados

Title of Act	Chapter (Cap)
Labour Department	23
Occupational Training	42
National Insurance and Social Security	47
Better Security	160
Accidents and Occupational Diseases (Notification)	338
Domestic Employees (Hours of Duty)	344
Employment Exchanges	345
Employment of Women (Maternity Leave)	345A
Employment (Miscellaneous Provisions)	346
Factories	347
Holiday with Pay	348
Labour Clauses (Public Contracts)	349
Protection of Wages	351
Public Holidays	352
Radiation Protection	353A
Recruiting of Workers	354
Severance Payments	355
Shops	356A
Sugar Workers (Minimum Wage and Guaranteed Employment)	359
Trade Disputes (Arbitration and Enquiry)	360
Trade Unions	361
Wage Councils	362

Source: Barbados Employers' Confederation, *Labour Digest*, 1997.

APPENDIX 2

Structure of Allowances in a Manufacturing Enterprise 2001

1. Acting/Responsibility Allowance

Hourly Rated, Weekly Paid Employees

An employee required to act in a higher position in which no orientation is required shall be paid an Acting Allowance from the first day of acting. Where orientation is required, the acting allowance shall apply after twenty-one (21) days with effect from the first day of acting.

The allowance shall be the full difference between the worker's rate and that rate of the job in which the employee is acting. An employee who is required to act in a position not covered by this agreement shall be paid at the entrance level or the grade. Where the employee's present salary exceeds the entrance level, he shall be paid an amount of $100.00 per week. In either case, he shall be paid the allowances of the relevant grade.

Monthly Paid Employees

Acting allowance shall be the difference between the employee's present salary and the minimum of the grade in which he is acting. No employee shall in ordinary circumstances be required to serve in an acting capacity for more than six (6) months.

2. Call Out Allowance

Hourly Rated, Weekly Paid Employees

An employee is deemed to be "called out" if the employee has:

(i) completed eight (8) hours of work for the day, has made all preparations to leave the compound and then is requested to return to a job; or
(ii) completed eight (8) hours of work for the day, has reached their place of residence and is then requested to return to a job; or

(iii) completed their prescribed number of hours for the week and on the appointed day off is called from their place of residence and requested to attend.

On occasions as have been outlined above, the employee is entitled to be paid at double the basic rate with a guarantee of at least four (4) hours per occasion.

Monthly Paid Employees

An allowance of $350.00 will be paid to specific persons who by virtue of their levels of responsibility are required to be "called out" to work should the circumstances demand it.

3. Confined Space Allowance

A confined space is defined as a difficult working area where movement is somewhat restricted and entry to which is through a personal access port (manhole). Where employees are required to work in a confined space they shall be entitled to a lump sum payment of $108.70 per person per job.

4. Gasoline Allowance

Monthly Paid Employees

Employees who own and use vehicles for the purpose of getting to and from work can purchase gasoline from pumps located on the company's compound at $0.15 below the prevailing retail price.

5. Heat Allowance

Employees who are required to work in an area where the prevailing air temperature exceeds 50°C, and provided that it is safe to work, shall be paid a lump sum of $108.70 per job.

6. Laundry Allowance

Hourly Rated, Weekly Paid Employees

A Laundry Allowance of $22.50 per week shall be paid to employees covered by this agreement and who are issued with uniforms.

7. Mileage Allowance

Monthly Paid Employees

An employee who is required to use his vehicle on specially approved company business shall be entitled to a Mileage Allowance at the rate of $1.50 per km.

An employee who receives a Call Out Allowance and is required to attend work will be paid a mileage allowance at the rate of $1.50 per km.

8. Minimum Guarantee Allowance

Hourly Rated, Weekly Paid Employees

Full time employees who report to work but cannot work through no fault of their own, shall be guaranteed four (4) hours pay at the appropriate rate.

9. Overtime Meal Allowance

When an employee, already on duty, is required to remain on duty, without previous notice, for at least four (4) hours beyond the end of his previous rostered duty, he shall be entitled to receive a Meal Allowance of $20.00. A minimum of twenty (20) minutes will be permitted at the start of such additional duty as described above for the purpose of taking a meal.

10. Transportation Allowance

Hourly Rated, Weekly Paid Employees

Employees called upon to work after completing their tour of duty or called out to work before the scheduled commencement of their tour of duty shall be entitled to a transportation allowance of $1.50 per kilometre for the distance from home to work.

11. Uniforms Allowance

The maid shall be provided with four (4) changes of uniform annually. Uniforms shall be issued to other employees whose job functions warrant the issue of uniforms. The provision shall be four (4) uniforms per annum with allowance for normal wear and tear.

Source: BEC, *Labour Digest*, 2001.

Appendix 3

Key Informants Survey

Name	Institution/Organisation
Ian Carrington Richard Nunez Derek Lowe	National Insurance Scheme (NIS)
Rudy Gibbons	Barbados Institute of Management and Productivity (BIMAP)
Shirley Farnum Mark Franklin Antonio Thompson Erica Watson	Ministry of Labour
Trevor King	Technical and Vocational Education and Training (TVET) Council
Raphael Cave Cassandra Delauney	Barbados Vocational Training Board (BVTB)
John Pilgrim Anthony Sobers Ryan Straughn	Barbados National Productivity Council (BNPC)
Harry Husbands	Barbados Employers' Confederation (BEC)
Sir Roy Trotman Robert Morris Veronica Griffith Ulric Sealey Vere Rock Keith Seale	Barbados Workers' Union (BWU)
Ann Marie Lorde Derek Alleyne	National Union of Public Workers (NUPW)
James Paul	Barbados Agricultural Society (BAS)
Sue Springer	Barbados Hotel and Tourism Association (BHTA)
Ruall Harris	Barbados Chamber of Commerce and Industry (BCCI)
Grenville Phillips	Barbados Coalition of Service Industries (BCSI)
Ronald Fitt	Ministry of the Civil Service
Stuart Layne	Barbados Tourism Authority (BTA)
Yvette Browne	Human Resources Management Association of Barbados (HRMAB)

References

Ashton D. et al. (2001). *Training and Development in Barbados 2000* (Centre for Labour Market Studies, University of Leicester), August.

Bannister A. (2004). An Analysis of the Impact of Performance-Based Incentive Plans on Organisational Performance in Barbados (Prepared for the Barbados National Productivity Council), October.

Barbados Employers' Confederation (2002). *Annual Report.*

Barbados Statistical Service (1997/98). *Informal Sector Survey* (Bridgetown, Barbados).

Boamah D. (1985). Wage Formation, Employment and Output in Barbados, *Social and Economic Studies*, vol. 34, no. 4, December, pp. 199–217.

Boamah D. (1995). "An Approach Towards the Measurement of Human Capital in Barbados" (Bridgetown, Central Bank of Barbados).

Coppin A. (1994). Sectoral Labour Employment in a Caribbean Community: The Case of Barbados, *Review of Black Political Economy*, vol. 23, Sept., 49–66.

Coppin A. (1994). The Demand for Labour in Caribbean Community MDCs, *Review of Black Political Economy*, Fall, vol. 23, no. 2, pp. 39–56.

Coppin A. (1995). Female Participation in Barbados Labour Market: A Post-Independence Perspective, *Economic Review* (Central Bank of Barbados), vol. 22, no. 1, pp. 15–23.

Downes A.S. (1999). Labour Market Flexibility in Barbados: A Survey Report, in W. Momm (ed): *Labour Issues in the Context of Economic Integration and Free Trade: A Caribbean Perspective* (International Labour Organisation, Caribbean Office, Trinidad and Tobago), 201–215.

Downes A.S. (2002). Indices of Labour Market Regulation: Principles and Cases, *Indian Journal of Labour Economics*, vol. 45, no. 1, January–March 2002, pp. 117–126.

Downes A.S. (2004). The Contribution of the Samuel Jackman Prescod Polytechnic to the National Development of Barbados (Inaugural Samuel Jackman Prescod Polytechnic Lecture), September, 30 pages.

Downes A.S. and R. Antoine (1994). *The Portability and Financing of the Barbados Severance Payments Scheme.* Report prepared for the World Bank, December, 1994, 113 pages.

Downes A.S. and V. Alleyne (1998). An Evaluation of Gainsharing Schemes in Barbados, *Economic Review* (Central Bank of Barbados), vol. 25, no. 3, Dec., pp. 18–40.

Downes A.S. and V. Browne (2004). An Econometric Analysis of Aspects of Labour Market Behaviour in Barbados (Paper presented at the Barbados Statistical Service Annual Seminar), October.

Downes A.S., N. Mamingi and R.-M. Antoine (2004). Labour Market Regulation and Employment in the Caribbean. In J.J. Heckman and C. Pages (eds.): *Law and Employ-*

ment: Lessons from Latin America and the Caribbean (Chicago University Press), pp. 517–551.

Downes A.S. and L. Nurse (2004). Macroeconomic Management and Building Social Consensus: An Evaluation of the Barbados Protocols, *Journal of Eastern Caribbean Studies*, vol. 29, no. 4, pp. 1–41.

Goolsarran S.J. (2002). *Caribbean Labour Relations: An Overview*, Trinidad: ILO Office – Caribbean.

Guasch J.L. (1999). *Labour Market Reform and Job Creation: The Unfinished Agenda in Latin American and Caribbean Countries* (Washington, D.C., World Bank).

Heckman J.J. and C. Pages (2000). The Cost of Job Security Regulation: Evidence from Latin American Labour Markets, *Economica: The Journal of the Latin American and Caribbean Economic Association* 1(1): 109–154.

Loehr W. (1997). Labour Markets and Competitiveness in Barbados (Washington: IADB), October.

Marquez G. and C. Pages (1998). *Ties that Bind: Employment Protection and Labour Market Outcomes in Latin America* (Inter-American Development Bank, Mimeograph).

Moore W., R. Skeete and K. Greenidge (2004). Estimates of Long Run Equilibrium Exchange-Rate in Three Caribbean Counties, *Economic Review* (Central Bank of Barbados), vol. XXX, no. 3, Dec., pp. 28–38.

Pages C. (2004). A Cost-Benefit Approach to Labour Market Reform, *Economic Review* (Federal Reserve Bank of Atlanta), vol. 89, no. 2, April, pp. 67–85.

Rama M. (1995). Do Labour Market Policies and Institutions Matter? The Adjustment Experience in Latin America and the Caribbean, *Labour*, 9: S243–S268.

Tzannatos Z. (1995). Labour Policies and Regulatory Regimes, in C.R. Frischtak (ed.): *Regulatory Policies and Reform: A Comparative Perspective*, Washington, D.C., World Bank, chapter 9, pp. 170–190.

CHAPTER IV

Trade and Integration as a Strategy for Growth

Anneke Jessen and Christopher Vignoles

A. Introduction

Barbados is a small, open island economy with one of the highest trade-to-GDP ratios in the Western Hemisphere. Trade, because it plays such a dominant role in the Barbadian economy, also substantially determines the country's development prospects. Exports are particularly important in this respect: export income is needed to create and sustain jobs, cover the cost of imports, pay off foreign debt, and maintain a healthy balance in the country's external accounts. All of these are necessary to achieve sustainable levels of economic growth. Successful international insertion, through trade facilitation and related measures, should therefore be a central aim of the IDB's support strategy for Barbados, particularly at a time when the country is facing the rapid erosion of trade preferences long enjoyed by its exporters in major world markets.

This chapter discusses recent trends in Barbados' foreign trade, as well as related policy developments and economic integration efforts undertaken by the country at both the regional and global levels. The aim is two-fold: to identify existing bottlenecks to the country's successful international insertion, and to advance policy recommendations for removing such bottlenecks.

Section B briefly highlights the importance of trade in the Barbadian economy. Sections C and D look at developments in merchandise and services trade over the past decade, using different indicators to measure the country's export performance. Section E discusses Barbados' trade and economic integration policies, focusing on the various trade agreements it has recently signed or is in the process of negotiating.

Section F examines the national trade policymaking process and the principal institutions involved in this process. Section G summarizes the main difficulties faced by

The authors would like to thank Desmond Thomas and Henry Gill for their valuable comments on an earlier version of this paper, which was published by the IDB Institute for the Integration of Latin America and the Caribbean (IDB-INTAL) in December 2004 (INTAL/ITD, Occasional Paper No. 28).

Barbados in its efforts to achieve successful international insertion, and points to some possible solutions. This section also briefly reviews the support given to Barbados by the Inter-American Development Bank (IDB) in the area of trade and integration and the activities of other multilateral and donor agencies. Two appendixes complete this chapter. Appendix I presents some complementary trade data, while Appendix II provides an overview of Barbados' trade agreements with partner countries and regions.

B. The Importance of Trade in the Economy

One way of illustrating the crucial role of trade in the Barbadian economy is by looking at the value of the country's external transactions relative to its total output—a measure referred to as trade openness. Barbados displays a high degree of openness: its trade to GDP ratio is over 100 percent.[1] Openness has clear benefits for a small economy in that it can diversify risk. But when coupled with a narrow export base, as in Barbados, openness makes the economy vulnerable to external shocks such as fluctuations in international commodity prices, a downturn in global demand for tourism, or policy changes abroad. It also means that any significant expansion or contraction in the country's foreign trade will have an immediate effect on its GDP.

Another way of illustrating the importance of trade in the national economy is by looking at how trade flows affect the country's balance of payments. Between 1992 and 1996, Barbados recorded significant trade surpluses, with net earnings from services trade far outweighing persistent deficits in merchandise trade. As a result, the current account was positive throughout the period. Between 1997 and 2004, this trend was reversed as a result of a continued deterioration in the merchandise trade balance coupled with weaker services exports in some years owing to a slowdown in tourism. In 2004, the current account deficit reached an estimated 10.5 percent of GDP.

Barbados has financed its current account deficits with large capital and financial account surpluses resulting from heavy government borrowing and some income from privatization. These sources of finance will likely continue to be available to Barbados in the short term; further divestment in the hotel and infrastructure sectors is certainly possible. It is worth noting, however, that total external public debt has risen by one third since 2000, reaching over 27 percent of GDP in 2004. Ultimately, stronger export performance will be crucial to maintain a healthy balance in the country's external accounts.[2]

---

[1] Trade-to-GDP ratio equals exports plus imports of goods and services divided by GDP. By comparison, the average trade-to-GDP ratio is 97 percent for CARICOM, 39 percent for the Andean Community and 26 percent for Mercosur.

[2] For more detailed Balance of Payments (BOP) information, see IMF, *Barbados: Article IV Consultation – Staff Report,* August 2005.

C. Merchandise Trade: Trends and Performance Indicators

Similar to other Caribbean islands, Barbados exports mostly services. Goods account for only 20 percent of the country's total exports. They make up around two-thirds of total imports, and just over 45 percent of the country's total trade. This section deals with merchandise trade only. Services trade will be covered in Section D.

Growth and Direction of Trade

In the past decade, Barbados' merchandise exports have been characterized by modest overall growth and high volatility. Between 1994 and 2004, total exports grew by an average 4.3 percent per year, in a context of strong growth in world trade during that period (7.8 percent). Export growth fluctuated significantly from year to year, ranging from a high of +31 percent in 1995 to –17 percent in 2002.

It is important to note that around one-third of Barbados' total merchandise exports are "re-exports", that is, goods previously imported into Barbados that are then exported in the same state, without any value added. Most of these are related to Barbados' role as transshipment and regional distribution centre, with fuels representing more than half of the total and medicaments, vehicles and other products for regional distribution accounting for another 20–30 percent. Luxury items sold in duty-free shops make up the remainder of the total. Excluding re-exports, growth in merchandise exports averaged just 2.6 percent a year in the last decade, and –2.2 percent a year between 2000 and 2004.

Import growth averaged 5.9 percent a year between 1994 and 2004, but fluctuated almost as strongly as export growth, from +25 percent in 1995 to –8 percent in 2004. This volatility is mainly related to imports of manufactured goods, led by cars from Japan. Figure IV-1 illustrates these trends while, at the same time, highlighting Barbados' significant merchandise trade deficit with the world.

Figure IV-1. Merchandise Trade, 1994–2004

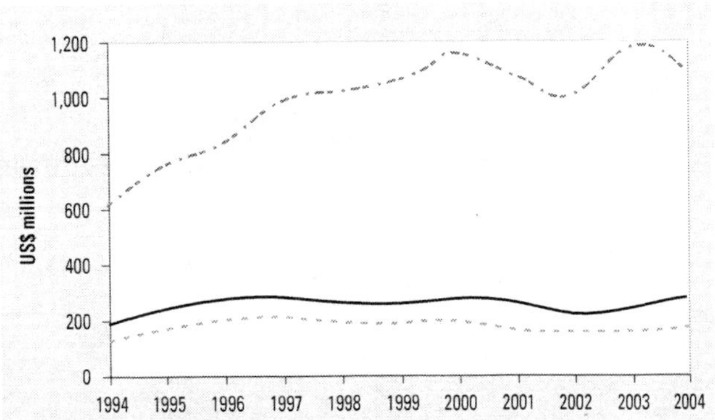

Source: See Appendix Tables A-IV-1 through A-IV-3.

Barbados relies increasingly on Caribbean markets as a destination for its merchandise exports (Figure IV-2). After the United States, Barbados' main export markets in the Western Hemisphere are all Caribbean - Trinidad and Tobago,

Jamaica and St. Lucia, in that order.[3] Over the last five years, 43 percent of Barbados' merchandise exports went to CARICOM, up from 37 percent in the mid-1990s. Barbados now exports more to its Caribbean neighbors than to the United States and the EU combined. These markets each absorb around 15 percent of the country's total exports. The growing share of CARICOM markets in Barbados' total exports is mostly the result of a weak export performance to other destinations (Europe, Latin America and Canada), rather than strong export growth to CARICOM – although, at an average 5.4 percent a year since 1994, such growth was *relatively* fast compared to Barbados' overall export performance.

Figure IV-2. Merchandise Exports by Destination, 1994–2004

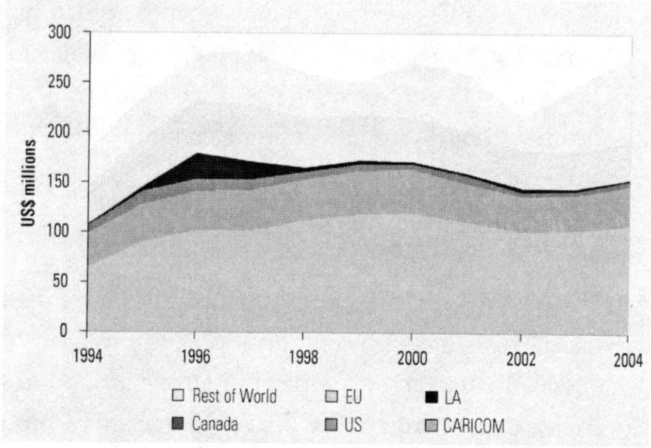

Source: See Appendix Table A-IV-1.

While the US share has remained fairly constant, the EU has become a less important destination for Barbadian exports in recent years. Canada and Latin America together absorb less than 4 percent of total exports, while exports to the rest of the world consist mostly of re-exports in the form of fuels and other supplies to ships and aircraft transiting the island.[4] The fuel price factor largely explains the rapid growth in these exports in the last two years.

Imports are mainly sourced from the United States, which supplies over 40 percent of the total. Another 28 percent come from CARICOM (mainly Trinidad and Tobago) and other Western Hemisphere countries, while the EU supplies about 17 percent. Imports from the rest of the world make up the remaining share and originate mainly in Japan.[5]

It is interesting to note that, within CARICOM, the small island economies of the Organization of Eastern Caribbean States (OECS) – Antigua and Barbuda, Dominica, Grenada,

[3] Total for the period 2002–04.

[4] The destination "Bunker", which measures goods (mostly fuel) delivered to ocean-going ships or aircraft engaged in international traffic, accounts for roughly two thirds of total exports to the rest of the world. Excluding re-exports, the share of Barbadian exports going to CARICOM is 52 percent, the combined share going to the United States and the European Union is 39 percent, and exports to the rest of the world are only 6 percent of the total.

[5] Similar to exports, which include "re-exports", imports include "re-imports". These, however, are not separated by statistics databases such as COMTRADE and can therefore not be analyzed separately.

Montserrat, St. Kitts and Nevis, St. Lucia and St. Vincent and the Grenadines – constitute an important export destination for Barbados. In the period 2000–04, these islands together absorbed US$ 234 million worth of Barbadian merchandise exports, equal to 43 percent of the country's total exports to CARICOM and far exceeding sales to Trinidad and Tobago[6] (which took 27 percent) or to Jamaica (15 percent). OECS members also accounted for over half of all re-exports from Barbados to CARICOM. Since Barbados imports very little from the OECS, it runs a significant trade surplus with these islands, in contrast to large deficits in its trade with the world and with major partners such as the United States, the EU, and Trinidad and Tobago. For more specific data on the growth and direction of Barbados' merchandise trade, see Appendix I, Tables A-IV-1 to A-IV-3.

Market Access

Barbados' modest export performance in the area of goods trade is worrying in light of the significant trade preferences it enjoys in its major export markets. Access to the EU and North American markets is very favourable. Apart from those goods entering duty-free under most favored nation (MFN) rules, many products exported to these markets face zero or reduced tariffs under the Cotonou Agreement (EU), CARIBCAN (Canada), the US Caribbean Basin Initiative (CBI) and the Generalized System of Preferences (GSP).[7] In addition, exports to CARICOM face zero tariffs and are protected from foreign competition by the Community's common external tariff (CET). We have calculated that, currently, more than 50 percent of Barbados' merchandise exports to the world (in value terms) enjoy some form of preferential treatment, in addition to the almost 40 percent that receive MFN duty-free treatment.[8]

In all these markets, however, preferences are being eroded by global tariff reductions resulting from the Uruguay Round of multilateral trade talks, and from bilateral trade initiatives involving third parties—initiatives such as US and Canadian free trade agreements with Latin American countries, CARICOM's own recent agreement with the Dominican Republic and the EU's *Everything But Arms Initiative* for the least developed countries (LDCs). Under the latter initiative, for example, the EU will grant duty- and quota-free access to sugar imports from all LDCs starting in July 2009. The expected increase in sugar

---

[6] Over the last decade, Barbados' merchandise trade deficit with the world, as well as with each of its main trade partners individually (the United States, the European Union and CARICOM), doubled in absolute terms.

[7] Apart from preferential access to the Canadian and EU markets, Barbados receives GSP preferences from Australia, Bulgaria, the Czech Republic, Hungary, Japan, New Zealand, Norway, Poland, Russia, the Slovak Republic and Switzerland. Barbados graduated from the US GSP program in January 2006 owing to its high development level. However, the country's trade preferences in the US market will not be affected given that the CBI treatment will remain.

[8] See INTAL/ITD Occasional Paper No. 28, op. cit.

exports from LDCs to the EU as a result of this initiative is likely to push down internal EU sugar prices, and might therefore encourage the EU to negotiate lower prices with ACP producers. In November 2005, EU agriculture ministers reached agreement on a wide-ranging reform of the EU sugar regime, including a 36 percent cut in the guaranteed price for white sugar over four years—a measure viewed with considerable concern by CARICOM governments. Lower prices are expected to erode the economic rent received by Barbados under its current export quota. In anticipation of these problems, Barbados has already taken steps to adjust the sector to the new market realities but, along with its CARICOM partners, is urging the EU to honor its commitments under the Cotonou Agreement to support economic development and adjustment in the region.

This trend in preference erosion is likely to continue in the coming years because of expected further trade liberalization under the WTO and between countries in the Western Hemisphere, as well as the conclusion of a free trade agreement between CARICOM and the EU, which would reduce Barbados' market access advantages in the Caribbean market. In such a context, questions of export performance and competitiveness become even more relevant.

Barbados' modest export performance in the past decade has been attributed to several factors, including a steady appreciation, between 1995 and 2002, of its real effective exchange-rate (REER) and, since 1999, a combination of declining labour productivity and increasing real wages that led to an increase in real unit labour costs (RULCs) of about 11 percent between 1999 and 2004.[9]

Product Composition

Product composition, and more specifically, the strong concentration of exports in just a few products, is another determining factor of the country's export performance. Figure IV-3 shows the sectoral composition of Barbados' merchandise exports to the world (excluding re-exports). In the period 2000–04, manufactured goods account for 50 percent of exports, while another 40 percent were food items, and the remaining 10 percent were divided among fuels, ores and metals, and non-specified goods. Exports of food and manufactured products grew markedly in the late 1990s, but have contracted since 1999; fuel products, consisting mainly of crude petroleum exports to Trinidad and Tobago, have grown by an average 6.3 percent per year over the last decade.

Analysis of export flows by destination shows that food is an increasingly important sector in exports to the United States and Canada, and that fuel exports to CARICOM have performed well. Food products still account for the bulk of Barbados' exports to the EU

[9] IMF, Barbados: Article IV Consultation – Staff Report, August 2005.

(80 percent) and Canada (70 percent), while manufactures are the dominant category in exports to the United States (67 percent) and CARICOM (56 percent).

A closer analysis of product composition in the country's merchandise exports reveals a high concentration in just a few products. Table IV-1, which excludes re-exports, shows that of a

Figure IV-3. Sector Composition of Exports, 1994–2004

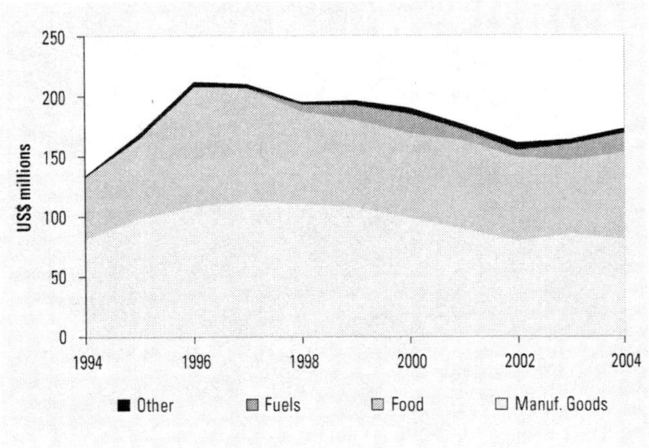

Source: See Appendix Table A-IV-4.
Note: Excluding re-exports.

Table IV-1. Top 20 Exports to the World and CARICOM, 2000–2004

World			CARICOM		
Rank	Product Description	Share (%)	Rank	Product Description	Share (%)
1	Sugars, beet and cane, raw, solid	12.8	1	Portland cement, ciment fondu, slag	9.3
2	Spirits and distilled alcoholic bevs.	10.5	2	Food preparations, n.e.s.	8.7
3	Resistors, fixed or variable	7.3	3	Insecticides packed for sale etc.	8.3
4	Portland cement, ciment fondu, slag	5.9	4	Petroleum oils, crude	7.2
5	Insecticides packed for sale etc.	5.2	5	Other fuel oils	5.9
6	Food preparations, n.e.s.	4.9	6	Casks, drums, boxes of sheet or plate	5.7
7	Petroleum oils, crude	3.7	7	Medicaments cont. other substances	5.0
8	Other fuel oils	3.1	8	Margarine	4.4
9	Medicaments cont. other substances	3.0	9	Paper and paperboard labels	3.4
10	Casks, drums, boxes of sheet or plate	3.0	10	Other paints & enamels	3.3
11	Margarine	2.3	11	Sanitary towels & tampons of paper	3.3
12	Paper and paperboard labels	2.2	12	Pastry, biscuits, cakes	2.3
13	Other paints & enamels	1.8	13	Structures & parts of aluminum	2.2
14	Sanitary towels & tampons of paper	1.7	14	Flour of wheat or of meslin	2.1
15	Pastry, biscuits, cakes	1.5	15	Sausages & the like, of meat	1.8
16	Structures & parts of aluminum	1.2	16	Lemonade,flavoured spa waters	1.5
17	Wrenches and spanners	1.1	17	Soybean oil	1.5
18	Flour of wheat or of meslin	1.1	18	Spirits and distilled alcoholic bevs.	1.3
19	Lemonade, flavoured spa waters	1.0	19	Builders' carpentry and joinery	1.2
20	Sausages & the like, of meat	0.9	20	Articles for conveyance or packing	1.1
Top 20		74.2	Top 20		79.2
Other 926 Products		25.8	Other 503 Products		20.8

Source: IDB Integration and Regional Programs Department using UN-COMTRADE.
Note: SITC Rev. 2, leaf level of aggregation.

total of 946 products exported by Barbados in the period 2000–04,[10] the top 20—led by sugar and spirits—accounted for almost 75 percent of total exports (in value terms). The share of the top 20 in total exports has remained quite constant over the years, as has the list of products included in the top 20. Product concentration is high in all markets, but especially so in the EU market, where the top two products (sugar and spirits) make up 77 percent of total export value, and the share of the top 20 reaches almost 95 percent. Exports to the United States and Canada are also highly concentrated, with the top two products in each market representing 56 percent and 65 percent, respectively, and the share of the top 20 reaching 86 percent and 87 percent, respectively, of total export value.

In exports to CARICOM, the product composition includes some food and manufactured items that are not among the main products exported to the world. The number of products exported to CARICOM is also significantly higher than that exported to Barbados' other major markets, and has risen in the last decade. But even in that market, product concentration remains high, with the top 20 products accounting for almost 80 percent of total exports in value terms.

Barbados' narrow export base compounds the country's vulnerability to external shocks. Export diversification should therefore be a priority for Barbados, but it may be difficult to achieve this in merchandise trade. As indicated in Section D of this chapter, the future for Barbados appears to lie in the services sector, to which the country has already shifted most of its export activity. But even in the goods sector, there should be some room for diversification; there is a clear need to restructure agriculture and manufacturing activities in order to foster better export performance in these sectors. The best strategy in this regard would be to shift export supply towards products that face growing demand in world markets. This would increase Barbados' capacity to expand exports over time. Conversely, for a country whose exports are either uncompetitive or face mostly stagnant or declining demand in world markets, there is little opportunity for growth.

In the following section, we will look at some indicators that analyze both supply and demand conditions for Barbados' merchandise exports and, by doing so, shed light on the level of competitiveness of its exports.[11] As explained further on, none of these indicators is perfect, and they should therefore be used cautiously. Most importantly for Barbados, these indicators do not isolate policy-induced from real competitive advantages, and can therefore erroneously conclude that a country is competitive in exporting a specific product when the country's only competitive advantage stems from preferential market access.

[10] Includes all products exported in at least one year of period 2000–04, aggregated at the SITC Rev. 2 leaf level.

[11] The analysis includes re-exports. These products should normally be excluded from a competitiveness analysis because they are not produced in the country. At the time of writing, however, there were problems isolating the detailed product data for re-exports from the global export data in the COMTRADE database. Including re-exports does not alter the main conclusions of the analysis.

These rather crude measures should therefore be taken only as very broad indicators of competitiveness.

Competitiveness and Specialization

Winners and Losers

Figure IV-4 divides Barbados' top 30 exports into four categories, with the size of each "bubble" depicting the corresponding product's export value:

- *Winners in growing markets* (upper right quadrant). These are the "champions": global demand for these products is expanding (for some goods, faster than the average growth in world trade) and Barbados has increased its share in world exports. Promotional efforts should focus on further expanding supply, as well as efforts to capture new export markets.
- *Winners in declining markets,* or "achievers in adversity" (lower right quadrant). Barbados has managed to increase its share of world trade, but demand for these products is declining. Niche marketing strategies may be the best way of expanding export opportunities in otherwise declining markets.
- *Losers in growing markets,* or "underachievers" (upper left quadrant). These products face growing demand in world markets, but Barbados has not been

Figure IV-4. Competitiveness of Top 30 Exports, 1998–2003

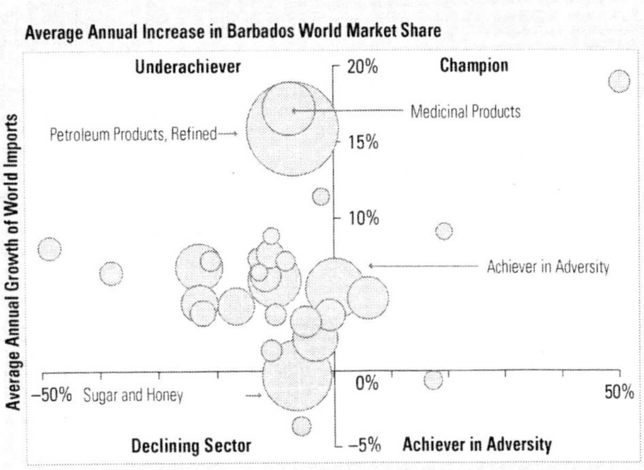

Source: IDB Integration and Regional Programs Department using UN-COMTRADE.
Note: Top 30 exports by category (ranked by export value, in descending order): *Champions (4)*—Alcoholic beverages; lime and cement; petroleum oils (crude); and optical goods. *Achiever in adversity (1)*—Aircraft and associated equipment. *Underachievers (23)*—Petroleum products (refined); medicinal and pharmaceutical products; electric apparatus such as switches and relays; edible products and preparations; disinfectants and insecticides; paper and paperboard; printed matter; metal containers; margarine and shortening; pigments, paints and varnishes; cereal preparations; tools for use in the hand or in machines; thermionic transistors and photocathode valves; soap, cleansing and polishing preparations; watches and clocks; electrical machinery and apparatus; structures and parts of structures of iron; other articles of plastics; meat and edible offal (prepared and preserved); passenger motorcars for transport; component articles made of textiles; jewelry; and non-alcoholic beverages. *Declining sectors (2)*—Sugar and honey; meal and flour of wheat. Average annual growth of petroleum oils (crude) exceeded 50 percent.

able to maintain its share of those markets because its exports have either declined or grown less dynamically than world trade. Supply factors, rather than weak demand, are the bottleneck, and promotional efforts should aim at eliminating these.

- *Losers in declining markets* (lower left quadrant). These products face both supply and demand constraints. World demand has stagnated or declined, and Barbados has been unable to maintain its share of a shrinking market. Efforts to promote products in this sector may be the least cost-effective in terms of expanding export revenues.

A division of a country's exports along these lines can be useful in that it helps identify the varying degrees of global competitiveness that the country's exports have achieved, the nature of constraints faced by different export products (demand or supply-side), and possible export promotion strategies using the results of the above.

As Figure IV-4 shows, most of Barbados's top 30 exports are "underachievers". There are only a few champions and, not surprisingly, one of the country's main traditional exports—sugar—is not among them. Repeating the analysis for all 212 product groups exported during the 1998–2003 period results in the following classification:[12]

- Champions: 76 product groups (representing 16 percent of the value of the country's total exports). It is interesting to note that 40 percent of these exports (in value terms) go to the CARICOM market, with another 40 percent going to the US and EU.
- Achievers in Adversity: 10 groups (just 1 percent of exports). Half of these go to destinations other than CARICOM, the United States, Canada or the EU.
- Underachievers: 112 product groups (71 percent of exports). Two-thirds of these go to CARICOM and the United States.
- Declining Sectors: 14 groups (representing 11 percent of exports). Almost all of these exports go to the EU.

In addition to "declining products", the high share of "underachievers" in Barbados' merchandise exports raises concern because it points to a lack of competitiveness. To obtain more specific data, the analysis can be repeated at the sector level (for example, by looking only at agricultural goods), or for different export markets. In all such research, the level of product aggregation is important. Here, we used an intermediate level of aggregation,

[12] This number excludes 16 product groups that were not exported either at the beginning (1998) or the end (2003) of the period, because it was not possible to establish "trends" for those groups.

the SITC three-digit product-group level. At this or higher levels, some important winners or losers may be missed. The disadvantage of using more detailed data, however, is that at that level, trade flows may be more sensitive to policy interventions such as restrictive (or preferential) trade policies in the importing country or industrial policies in the exporting country. Such interventions distort trade and may lead to false conclusions about competitiveness. It is also important to point out that the analysis does not capture *potential* champions: products that are not yet being exported by Barbados, but which could become important foreign exchange earners in the future.

Export Specialization

Another way of analyzing Barbados's export performance is by looking at revealed comparative advantage (RCA), an indicator of international trade specialization. It measures a country's level of specialization in a particular product by dividing that product's share in a country's total exports by its share in world exports.[13] The link with competitiveness is based on the assumption that if a given product's share in a country's exports is greater than its share in world exports (that is, RCA > 1), then the country is specialized in, and therefore a relatively efficient producer of, that product. Here, too, the level of aggregation is important. For purposes of consistency, we use the same level as above, namely the three-digit level of the SITC.

Table IV-2 shows that of the 225 product groups exported to the world in the period 2000–03, Barbados appears to be relatively efficient in 42 groups (RCA > 1). In 14 of these, it did not have comparative advantage at the beginning of the 1990s, but developed it during the decade, while another 13 product groups increased their RCA over the period.[14] There was no change in RCA for five products, while RCA declined for ten. Together, the 42 product groups (which include most of the country's top 30 exports) account for 85 percent of the country's total exports in value terms. For the 183 remaining groups, Barbados shows no particular specialization (RCA < 1), although for six of these, it did so at the beginning of the decade. It is quite possible, of course, that there are individual products among these broader product groups that have an RCA > 1. We could identify these by repeating the analysis at a more disaggregated product level.

---

[13] Revealed Comparative Advantage (RCA) is calculated: *RCA (Xijk)* = (*Xijk* / *Xij* total) / (*Xwjk* / *Xwj* total); where *Xijk* is the exports of country i to country/region *j* of product *k*, *Xij* total is the total exports of country *i* to country/region *j*, *Xwjk* is the exports of the world to country/region *j* of product *k*, and *Xwj* total is the total exports to country/region *j*. Revealed comparative advantage measures how important each product (group) is in the exports from one market to another versus the total importance of that product (group) in world exports to the destination market. In this case, RCA was measured at the SITC Rev 2, 3-digit product group level of aggregation.

[14] In our analysis, we define an "increase" in RCA as >10 percent growth in the RCA indicator, a "decrease" as >10 percent decrease in the indicator, and "no change" as no more than +/– 10 percent movement.

Table IV-2. Comparative Advantage in Exports to the World, 1990–93 and 2000–03

Product	Share (%) 2000–03	RCA 1990–93	RCA 2000–03
Margarine and shortening	1.8	45.7	65.9
Animals, live (including zoo animals)	0.4	23.6	63.2
Sugar and honey	8.8	56.3	48.5
Lime and cement	4.2	4.8	23.5
Meal and flour of wheat	0.7	0.7	23.5
Disinfectants, insecticides, fungicides	3.9	16.0	22.3
Metal containers for storage	2.2	17.7	19.4
Other cereal meals and flours	0.1	9.3	15.8
Alcoholic beverages	7.6	8.2	15.0
Edible products and preparations	4.5	6.3	14.9
Meat and edible offal prep./pres.	0.8	3.5	8.4
Petroleum products, refined	18.7	10.6	8.0
Non-alcoholic beverages	0.7	13.5	6.6
Cereal preparations	1.6	4.8	5.3
Paper and paperboard (cut to size)	2.2	6.0	4.6
Printed matter	2.3	2.4	4.6
Pigments, paints, varnishes	1.8	5.6	4.4
Jute and other textile fibres	0.0	0.0	4.2
Structures and parts of iron	0.9	4.4	4.0
Watches and clocks	1.1	0.2	3.6
Electrical apparatus such as switches	5.1	5.5	3.5
Glassware	0.6	1.3	3.3
Tools, used in the hand or in machines	1.1	3.8	3.3
Tea and mate	0.1	0.0	3.2
Medicinal products	6.3	2.0	2.6
Fixed vegetable oils, crude	0.4	0.0	2.6
Other optical goods	0.8	0.0	2.2
Wire products and fencing grills	0.2	2.5	2.2
Component articles made of textiles	0.6	1.9	2.0
Soap, cleansing and polishing	0.4	13.4	1.9
Food processing machines	0.2	0.2	1.8
Fruit, preserved and prepared	0.4	0.6	1.7
Other wood manufactures	0.5	1.2	1.7
Jewelry	0.6	0.1	1.6
Live animals chiefly for food	0.2	0.8	1.6
Cotton	0.1	0.8	1.4
Fish, fresh	0.4	0.2	1.2
Printing and bookbinding machines	0.2	0.5	1.1
Tobacco (manufactured)	0.3	1.0	1.1
Stone, sand and gravel	0.1	1.9	1.1
Articles made from plastics	1.0	1.0	1.0
Civil engineering and contractors plants	0.6	0.3	1.0
Share of exports with RCA > 1	84.6		

Source: IDB Integration and Regional Programs Department using UN-COMTRADE.

Note: Products are ranked by RCA 2000–03, in descending order.

Trends in RCA can help identify emerging advantages in exports and thus point to areas where promotional efforts might produce positive results. They can also highlight variations in export performance across different markets. Table IV-3, for example, shows that in exports to CARICOM, Barbados is a relatively efficient producer in 37 products—fewer than at the world level. In this market, Barbados became specialized in eight new products during the 1990s, and increased its existing RCA in 13 others, but saw an erosion of RCA levels for 15 product groups and lost RCA for an additional 13 products. This trend merits attention in light of the planned opening of CARICOM markets to greater external competition, and could indicate that, unlike Trinidad and Tobago, Barbados has not been very successful in exploiting its preferential access to the CARICOM market to develop export competitiveness in new products.

In the US market, Barbados gained new RCA in 13 products and increased its existing RCA in another 9, while reducing its RCA in eight products and losing it in nine products. In the EU market, despite significant preferences, Barbados appears to be specialized in only 21 product groups, but it has gained in 19 products and lost in only one. In Latin America, which represents only a tiny fraction of Barbados' total exports, Barbados has gained RCA in 22 product groups but lost it in two. Table IV-4 summarizes the RCA analysis for all five markets discussed above.

The same analysis of trade specialization can be done at the sub-regional level, by dividing a product's share in a country's intra-regional exports by its share in total intra-regional exports. Barbados' exports to CARICOM seem more specialized relative to intra-regional trade than to total world trade with CARICOM, with 94 product groups (of a total of 191 exported in the period 2000–03), showing an RCA > 1. Of these, 30 did not have RCA at the beginning of the decade. In comparison, Trinidad and Tobago exhibits intra-regional specialization in 70 products, of which 28 did not have RCA a decade ago.

As mentioned earlier, the two indicators used to determine the competitiveness of Barbados' merchandise exports—"winners" and "losers" and product specialization—may be subject to significant margins of error. The preferences that Barbados enjoys in its major export markets probably distort the analysis, at all levels of product aggregation.[15] We can nevertheless draw some important conclusions from the above analysis of trade flows, product composition and export competitiveness.

- Barbados has not been a successful merchandise exporter in the past decade. Excluding re-exports, sales to all its major export markets (except CARICOM) have remained stagnant or declined, and there has been little product or market diversification.

[15] Alternatives, such as looking at specialization in production rather than in exports, are available, but they are more demanding of data and have their own drawbacks.

Table IV-3. Comparative Advantage in Exports to CARICOM, 1990–93 and 2000–03

Product	Share (%) 2000–03	RCA	
		1990–93	2000–03
Margarine and shortening	4.1	20.8	27.0
Disinfectants, insecticides, fungicides	7.4	17.4	25.8
Metal containers for storage	4.9	22.7	18.4
Live animals chiefly for food	0.5	11.1	17.0
Tea and mate	0.3	0.0	12.9
Lime and cement	8.0	4.7	12.7
Medicinal products	12.1	6.3	10.9
Pigments, paints, varnishes	3.7	12.5	9.5
Edible products and preparations	9.1	4.9	9.2
Meat and edible offal prep./pres.	1.9	2.5	7.6
Meal and flour of wheat	1.5	0.2	6.7
Printed matter	4.2	4.1	5.9
Paper and paperboard (cut to size)	4.7	8.6	5.1
Other cereal meals and flours	0.3	4.3	4.9
Glassware	1.3	1.9	3.6
Animals, live (including zoo animals)	0.0	2.6	3.6
Structures and parts of iron	2.1	8.3	3.4
Cereal preparations	2.8	4.6	3.4
Fixed vegetable oils, crude	0.9	0.0	2.9
Armored fighting vehicles	0.0	0.0	2.8
Non-alcoholic beverages	1.2	12.7	2.6
Photo and cinematographic supplies	0.1	1.4	2.6
Wire products and fencing grills	0.4	3.4	2.3
Alcoholic beverages	1.9	3.3	2.3
Other wood manufactures	1.0	2.1	2.1
Fruit, preserved and prepared	0.8	1.4	2.1
Outer garments for men	0.4	2.4	1.9
Soap, cleansing and polishing	1.0	15.4	1.7
Misc. chemical products	0.8	0.9	1.7
Articles made from plastics	1.8	2.5	1.6
Pearls, precious and semi-precious	0.0	0.0	1.5
Stone, sand and gravel	0.1	5.8	1.4
Component articles made of textiles	0.3	1.5	1.2
Synthetic organic dyestuffs	0.0	0.7	1.1
Medical instruments and apparatus	0.1	1.4	1.1
Other crude minerals	0.1	0.3	1.1
Perfumery, cosmetics	0.5	3.3	1.0
Share of exports with RCA > 1	80.4		

Source: IDB Integration and Regional Programs Department using UN-COMTRADE.

Note: Products are ranked by RCA 2000–03, in descending order.

Table IV-4. RCA Trends by Destination, 1990–93 to 2000–03

	Global RCA					Intra-regional RCA
RCA Trend	World	CARICOM	U.S.	EU	Latin America	CARICOM
Increase	27	21	22	19	22	62
Food/Tobacco	12	9	7	6	6	16
Crude Materials	3	5	3	1	2	10
Manuf. Goods	12	7	12	12	14	36
No Change	5	1	0	1	1	6
Food/Tobacco	2	0	0	1	1	1
Crude Materials	0	0	0	0	0	1
Manuf. Goods	3	1	0	0	0	4
Decrease	10	15	8	1	3	26
Food/Tobacco	2	3	2	0	1	3
Crude Materials	4	4	0	0	0	2
Manuf. Goods	4	8	6	1	2	21
No RCA*	183	154	132	119	65	97

Source: IDB Integration and Regional Programs Department using UN-COMTRADE.
Note: Increase = RCA increased by more than 10%; No Change = RCA changed by no more than ± 10%; Decrease = RCA contracted by more than 10%.
* Some of these products had an RCA > 1 in the early period (1990–93) but lost it later on (2000–03).

- Most of Barbados' merchandise exports appear to be uncompetitive (underachievers or in declining sectors). In the absence of existing trade preferences in the country's main export markets, the above indicators would probably reveal an even less promising picture for its merchandise exports.
- With the exception of the OECS market, Barbados does not appear to have exploited its CARICOM preferences to establish an important presence in the regional market.

These are worrying trends, not least in light of the changing market access conditions that Barbadian exporters will face in the coming years, including the erosion and possible elimination of current preferences that undoubtedly have facilitated export growth into some of the country's most important markets.

Against this background, the government should assist the private sector with the implementation of a transition strategy involving, first, a gradual move away from the production of goods that depend mostly (or exclusively) on preferences for their "competitive" advantage in international markets; and, second, targeted export diversification and promotion efforts, concentrating on products that face growing demand in world markets.[16]

---

[16] One promising product is *sea island cotton*. Between 2000–03, exports of cotton (SITC Rev 2, Code 2631) grew by 33 percent a year on average, while international demand also increased (3.4 percent a year over the same period). Although currently accounting for a small share of Barbadian exports, the island holds natural advantages necessary for production, making it a sector of potential growth.

Export promotion efforts should not only focus on identifying promising products and niche markets and fostering product innovation among local producers and exporters, but also target new markets. Efforts to achieve greater overall competitiveness in the economy should be strengthened, particularly in areas that are crucial to export performance (telecommunications, transport and services infrastructure, etc.). This would also facilitate growth in Barbados' services industries, which have become the fastest growing and most promising area of export growth in recent years.

D. Trade in Services

The effective provision of services is of crucial importance to economic growth in Barbados. Services sectors contribute over 70 percent of the country's GDP, and account for almost 80 percent of exports and 75 percent of employment.[17] The importance of services extends beyond the sector itself: because services industries provide important inputs into the domestic production of goods, they also determine the level of competitiveness of the goods sector. This section examines recent trends in the country's services exports. It is important to note, however, that the scarcity of reliable data on such trade—the result of a deficient system of data collection and dissemination in the country—does limit the scope of our analysis.

General Trends

Services exports represent a significant share of total exports (78 percent) and GDP (44 percent)—both for 2003.[18] These shares have remained relatively consistent over time, demonstrating that Barbados' services exports have been and will continue to be a crucial contributor to the economy. Between 1990–2003, Barbados' services exports grew at an annual average of 4.5 percent, similar to the growth rate for CARICOM as a whole, yet below the world's average growth of 6.7 percent a year for the same period.[19] The value of services exports grew consistently in every year during the 1990s, contracted somewhat between 2001–02, and recovered strongly with growth of 12 percent in 2003.

Travel continues to represent the most important sector in the country's services portfolio. Commercial services, however, have recently increased their significance. From 2000–03, travel receipts accounted for 65 percent of total services exports, down from 75 percent a

[17] Data on the share of services in GDP, exports and employment are from World Bank, IMF and ILO, respectively.

[18] In comparison, Jamaica's and Trinidad and Tobago's services exports as a share of total exports equal 60 and 12 percent, respectively; services exports as a share of GDP equal 24 and 7 percent, respectively (2003).

[19] Growth rates calculated using WTO Statistics Database.

decade earlier. Commercial services increased their share in total services exports by 10 percentage points to reach 30 percent over the same period. The remaining areas, transportation and government services, have maintained marginal shares of 2 and 3 percent, respectively. Figure IV-5 demonstrates the general sectoral trends in services exports.

Figure IV-5. Services Exports by Area, 1990–2003

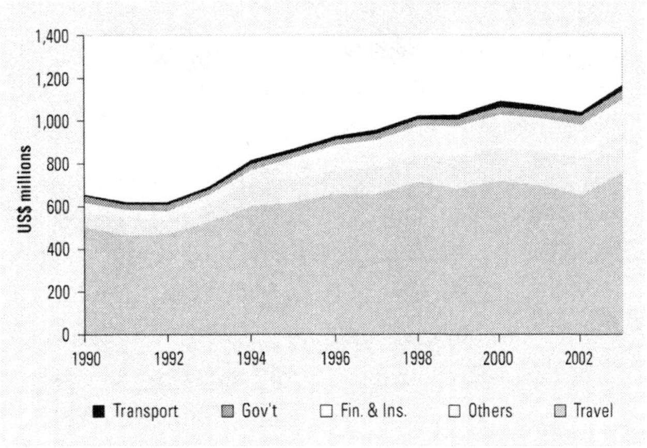

Source: See Appendix Table A-IV-5.

As mentioned above, Barbados' services sector is not only an important foreign revenue earner, but also the leading source of employment on the island. From 1997–2002, the latest years with data available, three out of every four employed persons worked in services-related industries.[20] These industries together created 11,700 jobs over the same period, while the manufacturing and agriculture sectors witnessed a net reduction of approximately 2,600 jobs.[21] The tourism industry accounted for 11 percent of employment and added, directly, almost 2,000 net jobs to the economy, in addition to the employment created through its strong linkages to other services sectors such as transportation and wholesale and retail trade. Other job-creating sectors were financial, insurance and business (+2,800 jobs), and government services (+2,500 jobs).[22] This shows the importance of services industries, many directly related to trade, as a promoter of economic growth, employment and poverty reduction.

Unlike goods, which are traded across borders, services exports can be exchanged through four different modes of supply. The General Agreement on Trade in Services (GATS) defines these as: Mode 1 (cross-border trade) is the supply of a service from the territory of one country into that of another, such as an international telephone call; Mode 2 (consumption abroad) is the movement of one country's consumer into the territory of the country providing the service, such as tourism; Mode 3 (commercial presence) is the service provided by foreign suppliers (for example, a foreign-owned bank) who establishes in the territory of the country concerned; and Mode 4 (presence of natural persons) is the

[20] Here, services industries include wholesale and retail trade, tourism, transport and communications, finance and insurance, business services, general services, and government services.

[21] Between 1997 and 2002, the economy as a whole created 12,500 net jobs, reaching 128,600 employed persons.

[22] Calculations using ILO Caribbean Labour Statistics database.

service supplied by foreign nationals who enter the territory of the country concerned on a temporary basis (less than one year).

Because services trade is so important for Barbados, the stakes in the services negotiations currently taking place at the regional and multilateral level are high. Services liberalization has potentially positive effects on economic growth. A more efficient provision of services in, among others, the financial, telecommunications and transportation sectors drives down transaction costs and improves the performance of sectors (including goods) across the economy. One example is further opening to service suppliers via Mode 3 (commercial presence/foreign direct investment), stimulating the transfer of technology and skills to improve national productivity (Mattoo, 2001).

These effects are more pronounced in a small economy like Barbados, where the services sector employs a large share of the labour force. Services liberalization should therefore be a key element of such countries' trade policies, but the pace of liberalization must take account of the specific vulnerabilities of small developing countries. In the following sub-sections, we discuss the country's different services sectors and their medium-term prospects.

Travel Services

Figure IV-5 shows the overwhelming importance of travel in the country's services export portfolio. Earnings in this sector come mostly from personal travel (i.e., tourism, health and education) rather than business travel, as the latter group represents only 9 percent of visitor arrivals and less than 1 percent of total travel receipts.[23] From 2000 to 2003, the last year for which data is available, Barbados experienced little growth in travel services exports, with average annual increases of just 1.6 percent. This slower-than-normal growth (3.6 percent annual average in the 1990s) can be attributed to lower tourism receipts, which were affected by external events such as economic slowdown in major consumer markets like the United States and Europe and the events of 11 September 2001.

The United Kingdom is the most important consumer market for Barbados' travel industry, accounting for 40 percent of all stopover arrivals (average for 2000–2003). Arrivals from the UK nevertheless declined by an average 3.7 percent per year over this period, among other things owing to increased competition from lower-cost destinations in the Hispanic Caribbean. The US market is the second most important, with a 23 percent share of all stopover visitors. From 1992 to 2000, arrivals grew by just 0.2 percent per year; they nevertheless rebounded over the next three years (averaging 5 percent growth a year), owing in large part to the "Best of Barbados" incentive program.[24] Barbados has benefited from growth in intra-re-

[23] For the period 1996–2003.

[24] Launched in 2002, the "Best of Barbados" incentive program is sponsored by the Barbados Tourism Authority and includes such offers as US$200 credits in airfare and first nights free at certain area hotels.

gional arrivals, as CARICOM stopovers have increased by an average of almost 6 percent per year since 1992. The majority of these arrivals come from OECS countries and Trinidad and Tobago, and are linked to the increasing popularity of cultural and music festivals such as Cropover (Figure IV-6).[25]

Figure IV-6. Stopover Arrivals by Origin, 1992–2003

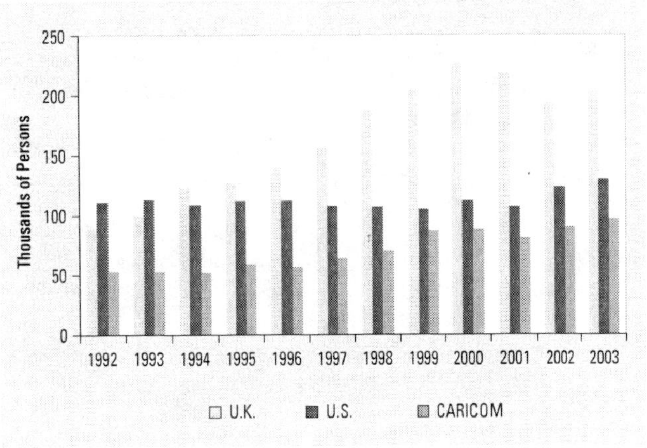

Source: Appendix Table A-IV-6.

Tourism

Barbados' tourism industry receives mainly two types of visitors: stopover tourists who stay at least one night and up to a year, and cruise ship passengers who usually stay less than a day. Yachting excursionists constitute a third type, although no data exist in Barbados for distinguishing this category of tourist arrival. Stopover arrivals rose by an average 4.4 percent a year between 1992 and 2000, reaching a total 544,696 visitors (double the number of permanent residents on the island). The years 2000–03 saw a 1 percent average annual contraction, partly because of falling global demand for tourism and increased competition from other Caribbean destinations.

The other type of visitor is the excursionist who arrives via cruise ship. In the period 2000–03, cruise ship passenger arrivals accounted for half of total visitors; in other words, a number equal to that of stopover tourists. However, cruise ship passengers stay less than 24 hours and consume much less onshore than stopover visitors (WTO, 2002). In the 1990s, cruise ship passengers accounted for just 7 percent of Barbados' personal travel earnings (compared to a 92 percent share for stopovers). However, it is important to note that these receipts grew at an average rate of 5 percent per year, compared to 3 percent growth in stopover tourism receipts over the same period. Barbados could develop a strategy to increase income derived from cruise ship calls by improving the quality and quantity of services targeting those passengers, thus creating the incentives to spend more money on the island. Tourism's performance and impact on the Barbadian economy can also be measured using a relatively new methodology, the tourism satellite account or TSA (Box IV-1).

Barbados is currently working on measures to increase tourist and cruise ship passenger arrivals. Tourists arriving by air will see increased capacity in the short term, with

[25] Calculations using the Barbados Ministry of Tourism data.

Box IV-1. Barbados's Tourism Satellite Account (TSA)

The tourism satellite account (TSA) is a statistical methodology to measure the impact of the tourism sector on a country's national accounts. It is beneficial because a variety of "sectors" and "industries" (i.e., transportation, hotel, food and beverage, etc.) contribute to create one tourism product. Since tourism does not supply one homogenous product, the TSA is calculated from the demand-side of economic activity, and allows for comparisons between countries and sectors.

The external component of the TSA is "visitor exports" or spending by *international visitors* on goods and services within a resident economy. In Barbados, visitor exports account for 57 percent of all exports of goods and services. The island ranks seventh in the world in terms of its dependency on the tourism sector for export receipts. Tourism exports displayed moderate growth (4 percent a year) compared to the Caribbean (almost 7 percent) in the 1990s; Barbados's performance has improved markedly since 2000, with growth of 6 percent a year versus 4 percent for the region as a whole.

The TSA methodology also uses the demand-side aggregates to construct supply-side accounts such as tourism GDP, the measurement of direct and indirect value-added of tourism to the resident economy. Barbados' tourism GDP, estimated at US$1.3 billion in 2004, accounts for half of total output, up roughly 10 percentage points from five years earlier. Similarly to visitor exports, the country is relatively more dependent on tourism for domestic output than its Caribbean neighbors. (The regional share is 16 percent.) The TSA is a valuable tool for policymakers and researchers to understand the performance and economic impact of tourism on the small island economies in the region.

Source: For more on Barbados' TSA see (WTTC, 2005).

an expansion in seat capacity from added flights by Continental and Delta Airlines and bigger planes operated by British Airways, Virgin Atlantic and Air Canada. Furthermore, a Bds$50 million (US$25 million) cruise ship pier project (to house more and larger cruise ships such as Cunard's "Queen Elizabeth 2") and a major airport improvement project will address growing transport infrastructure capacity concerns. Developments are also in place to increase hotel capacity. The Bds$212 million (US$106 million) 350-room Barbados Hilton, inaugurated in the summer of 2005, is likely to attract more American tourists and business visitors given its brand-name appeal. New attractions are planned to increase the attractiveness of Barbados as a tourist destination. The government is supporting a Bds$460 million (US$230 million) redevelopment of the main cricket ground (Kensington Oval) for the 2007 Cricket World Cup. A museum will moreover be built to house the recently acquired British Airways Concorde that provided service between the island and the UK for many years.

In Barbados, private operators are the main providers of tourism services. The government's role is to provide the regulatory environment to attract investment in the tourism industry, and to assist in financing projects that are not attractive to foreign or domestic capital. The Ministry of Tourism (MOT) formulates and implements tourism policy in collaboration with the Barbados Tourism Authority (BTA), Barbados Tourism Investment Inc (BTI) and Needhams Point Development Inc (NPD). The BTA is in charge of marketing the island as a top vacation destination and the BTI is responsible for attracting the investment, while the NPD deals with the development of the hotel sector. Even though Barbados has not committed its tourism industry to liberalization under the WTO regime, market access conditions are fairly liberal for those foreign firms interested in establishing a commercial presence on the island (WTO, 2002).

The development of Barbados' tourism sector is important for future economic growth and stability. At the same time, the country must address some important bottlenecks to eliminate constraints. First, Barbados' southern location in the Caribbean and its high prices make it an expensive travel destination for consumers. Second, high operating costs – in factors like labour, land and equipment – have a direct impact on tourism given that most providers are small and medium-size enterprises. Third, potential environmental problems such as shortages of fresh water and ocean pollution could be major roadblocks for further development of the industry, and especially so in leisure activities such as golf and scuba diving. Finally, Barbados is under increased competition from cheaper regional destinations (i.e., Mexico, Puerto Rico, the Dominican Republic and Cuba) that offer a similar tourism product.

Barbados has been actively addressing these constraints. One strategy is to pursue the high-end tourist niche market more actively, an approach that would increase Barbados' regional competitiveness and shield against future drops in demand.[26] Another strategy is the government's implementation of the Tourism Development Act of 2002. This focuses on competitiveness by promoting foreign investment through fiscal and tax incentives; sustained government support through infrastructure and transportation projects; and the recognition of innovation and productivity based on the provision of high-quality service. The MOT has set specific targets to measure the strategy's performance through 2010 (UN-ECLAC, 2003).

Health

Another sector within travel services that merits attention is the provision of health and elder-care-related tourism. Barbados has the potential for growth in this sector because it enjoys the characteristics needed for successful development. These include an attractive climate, skillful health practitioners, reliable telecommunications and transportation infrastructure, and an established tourism services sector. The supply of health tourism in Barbados is mostly through consumption abroad (Mode 2). Facilities on the island regu-

---

[26] Research shows that the income elasticity of tourism exports—in the world and more so in the Caribbean—is high (UN-ECLAC, 2003). In other words, when world income falls the demand for tourism falls sharply, and when income rises the demand rises sharply. However, the provision of high-end tourism services is more income inelastic, helping to dampen fluctuations in demand.

larly treat foreign visitors who fall ill while on vacation, and Barbados is already an established medical destination for cruise ship lines traveling in the Caribbean. There is limited commercial presence in health tourism (Mode 3), and some cross-border trade (Mode 1) mainly in laboratory shipments to the United States. The income from health tourism is negligible, and there is room for expansion. Potential for growth within the sector could be in preventative care methods such as holistic healing, and cosmetic surgery given the target high-end tourist market (Gonzales, 2001).

The demand for elder care is growing worldwide given the aging population. In Barbados, visitor arrivals of seniors (over 50 years of age) have increased from a 28 to 32 percent share of total arrivals, while the number of visitors between ages 20 and 49 contracted from 59 to 55 percent.[27] These numbers could point towards a possible gradual shift towards an older population traveling to Barbados, and pose an excellent opportunity to market elder-care facilities. However, like tourism, the health and elder-care sector also faces constraints, particularly high costs of operation, a reliance on foreign investment, water scarcity, institutional capacity concerns in the Ministry of Health, and problems related to the portability of insurance limiting patient access. In addition, there is a sense among residents that the development of health and elder-care travel will be at the expense of the national health-care system (Gonzales, 2001). Despite these challenges, the introduction of the right incentive structure coupled with government and donor support, could facilitate a diversification of travel services and stimulate additional export receipts.

Education

International trade in education services is also a growing market, given the increased demand worldwide for higher education and a new push from international policymakers promoting this form of trade (Larsen, 2001). Barbados has participated in supplying these services since 1963, when the University of the West Indies Cave Hill campus was founded. Even though education-related travel receipts are relatively small (less than 1 percent of travel services over the last decade), they have grown rapidly at 10 percent a year (over the same period). The future of Barbados' education services looks bright. Plans for a University College Barbados campus, for example, will add an internationally recognized institution to the island's higher education system and could attract a significant number of students from the Caribbean region and beyond. The development of educational services is also capacity enhancing as it attracts and develops domestic human capital. This is an interesting area of potential growth for Barbados' services exports and one that merits further research.

---

[27] For the period 1997–2003, using Barbados Ministry of Tourism data.

Transportation Services

Exports of transport services in Barbados are very limited as they accounted for only 2 percent of total services earnings over the last decade.[28] However, this sector has seen the most extensive growth during the same period, expanding at an average 10 percent per year. Barbados consistently runs a negative balance on trade in transport services given that it does not house a national maritime or airline fleet.

There are currently 16 foreign-owned shipping companies offering maritime transport services to and from Barbados. The port at Bridgetown Harbour serves as a transshipment point for merchandise destined to smaller Caribbean islands. However, Barbados does not have any public- or private-sector shipping lines in operation. The potential of maritime transport as a sector of growth for Barbados merits further research, given the island's geographical advantage and established port infrastructure. In air transport, Barbados has one international airport, fully owned by the Government of Barbados, with facilities to accommodate aircraft of any size. As mentioned before, the competitiveness of the country's publicly owned transport infrastructure should be evaluated against the possible benefits of privatization, especially given the sector's importance throughout the economy. There is no national airline in operation, but the Government does hold 10 percent ownership in Leeward Islands Air Transport (LIAT).

Commercial Services

Communication and Information

The communication and information services sector is attracting growing attention throughout the Caribbean region as a potential source of export revenue.[29] In the past, this sub-sector of commercial services was not a very important one. Between 2000 and 2003, it accounted for only 9 percent of commercial services receipts and less than 3 percent of total services exports. Communications exports have grown by an average of 5 percent a year over the last decade. These earnings were primarily derived from incoming international calls (Mode 1, cross-border supply), which, according to settled accounting standards, require the originating carrier to compensate one-half of the total cost of completing the call to the terminating carrier.

---

[28] Transportation services are international transactions via air, sea and other modes involving carriage of goods (freight), passenger services (fares), and cargo handling, navigation and maintenance fees.

[29] Communication and information services cover postal, courier and telecommunications services. The latter include services delivered via transmission of sound or images by telephone, telex, telegram, cable, broadcasting, satellite, e-mail, facsimile, teleconferencing, and voicemail; and information services such as online storage and retrieval, data processing including transactions, transcription services, credit verification, etc.

Cable & Wireless (C&W) was, until 2004, the sole provider of telecommunications services in Barbados. The government has not held any ownership in telecommunications firms since 1991, when it sold its industry shares to C&W and granted the company an exclusive license—monopoly status—to operate nationally and internationally until 2011. The Telecommunications Act of 2001 designated the Fair Trading Commission (FTC) and the Ministry of Economic Development (MED) as regulators, responsible for oversight and industry development, respectively.

Barbados has stated its commitment to telecommunications liberalization and agreed with C&W on a gradual opening of the sub-sector. Phase I enabled full competition in cellular mobile services, provision of telephone equipment, and use of equipment in call centres. Three additional cellular phone providers (Digicel, Cingular and Sunbeach) are now operating on the island. Phases II and III opened local and international telecommunications services, respectively. A new license for domestic landline services was awarded to TeleBarbados Inc in late 2005; there are currently four major license holders, in addition to C&W, in international telecommunications services (Digicel, Cingular, Sunbeach and TeleBarbados Inc).[30] The liberalization of telecommunications is a crucial step in developing services trade and reducing the cost of doing business in Barbados.

The information services sub-sector is clearly on Barbados' economic development agenda. The island has a strategy to build an information sector around call and data-processing centres, transcription services, credit processing and e-business transactions to cater to the regional information and communications industry. The prospect for implementing such a strategy is favourable. For this development to occur, the country needs to focus on four core requirements:

(i) an infrastructure framework with good access, high capacity and low cost;
(ii) human capacity with the required technical skills;
(iii) a transparent and strong policymaking process; and
(iv) the appropriate legal framework to protect interests, yet facilitate access to capital.

Barbados appears to fare well in all categories with the exception of relatively high costs (Cleland, 2003).

Financial and Insurance

The financial services sector in Barbados is a well-regulated industry offering both domestic and international (offshore) banking services. Between 2000 and 2003, financial

[30] See Barbados Telecommunications Unit at www.telecoms.gov.bb.

services earnings accounted for a 23 percent share of commercial revenues or over 6 percent of total services exports. Barbados is a net exporter of financial services, with the sector consistently performing as the third most important foreign exchange earner in the country, after tourism and insurance. Since 2000, this sector has experienced stagnant growth (–0.7 percent), relative to growth of 5 percent for communications and 6 percent for other business services.

Barbados' financial sector history is rooted in the 1965 International Business Companies Act, which, in conjunction with subsequent legislation, created the incentives for foreign nationals and firms to invest on the island. The industry is divided into two areas, those providing services to residents and those managing foreign funds for foreign persons (offshore). In 2001, there were 56 licensed offshore banks with assets equal to 11 times the country's GDP. Barbados' niche in financial services was the Foreign Sales Corporations (FSCs) market, with a reported 2,975 companies in operation.[31] In that same year, the WTO ruled that, given US foreign income tax laws, Barbados' tax privileges towards US corporations mirrored a hidden export subsidy, limiting the prospects for the FSC market. Securities trading takes place through the Barbados Stock Exchange, with 22 companies listed and a market capitalization of Bds$10.4 billion (US$5.2 billion) in 2004. Cross-border trading in securities is limited, with only three Barbadian companies listed in other regional stock exchanges. Deeper regional integration through implementation of the CSME is likely to promote more cross listing, and perhaps the creation of a regional stock exchange (WTO, 2002 and Henry, 2003).

The future holds some challenges for the development of financial services in Barbados, particularly in offshore banking. In 2000, an OECD report identified 35 jurisdictions (including Barbados) as tax havens with harmful tax practices. Barbados disputed the claim and campaigned to keep its taxation system in place as a tool for the development of its financial services sector. The OECD has subsequently eliminated Barbados from its tax haven list, citing that the country enjoys a wide international network of tax agreements and has passed legislation to increase transparency in its tax and regulatory regimes. Nevertheless, doubts about the extension of bilateral tax treaties and the introduction of a more level playing field in the incentive structures that countries can provide will affect Barbados' competitiveness vis-à-vis more developed financial services sectors. In addition, domestic banking institutions' access to extra-regional markets will be difficult, given the high fixed costs of foreign entry and the relatively limited liquidity of these (small) institutions compared to the larger and more efficient firms in Canada, the US and the EU (Henry, 2003).

[31] Barbados was the largest FSC market in the Caribbean, with St. Kitts and Nevis as the second biggest market with 75 FSCs in operation (Suss, 2002). Also, see (IMF, 2003a).

The preservation of offshore financial services in Barbados is very important given the sector's contribution to the economy. A deterioration of the sector would have a marked effect not only on foreign exchange earnings, but also on tax revenues. It is estimated that offshore activities contribute almost 40 percent of the government's corporate tax revenue. The outlook for offshore activities is uncertain. In the medium-term, the development of Barbados' financial services seems to be linked to the implementation of the CSME. Planned liberalization of exchange controls, with the OECS first, and then with CARICOM as a whole, should provide efficiency gains and opportunities for diversification. Continued efforts to modernize and strengthen the financial sector would help solidify the country's regional position and prepare for increased competition (IMF, 2003b).

As for insurance services, revenues in 2000–03 were slightly higher than for financial services, accounting for 27 percent of Barbados' commercial services exports or 8 percent of its total services exports. As with financial services, the insurance industry is segmented into international and domestic providers. In 2000, the latest year for which data are available, there were 19 domestic and 200 active international insurance companies in Barbados. Insurance services grew at an average 4.3 percent a year between 2000 and 2003, largely owing to a boom in life insurance and pension fund revenues. Barbados is currently fully committed to liberalization only in reinsurance services, and not in life or non-life insurance, under the WTO (WTO, 2002). Within the Caribbean, insurance services are considered vulnerable and uncompetitive, mainly owing to a shortage of quality long-term assets that leads to inflated premiums. This sector, like the financial services one, has potential for growth in Barbados if it can provide the environment for firms to compete at the regional level with foreign providers.

Prospects for Services Exports

As mentioned earlier, it is difficult to obtain detailed and reliable data on services trade for the Caribbean countries, including Barbados. Comparisons across the region are moreover hampered by the fact that collection and reporting methods differ from country to country. A comprehensive system of data collection, management and reporting in services trade should be implemented to ensure that the region's policymakers have the most reliable and up-to-date information on which to base their decisions—not least in the region's external trade negotiations. Even with these constraints, some conclusions regarding Barbados' services trade can be drawn from the above analysis.

- Barbados is a successful exporter of services. Services exports have consistently accounted for almost 80 percent of total exports and more than 40 percent of GDP, clearly demonstrating their importance to the economy.

- The travel industry, particularly in the high-end tourism segment, appears to be internationally competitive. Recent legislation outlining a strategic plan for the industry's development is likely to facilitate further growth. Areas such as education and health-related travel have the potential to become important sources of income.
- Financial and insurance services have been prominent sectors in Barbados' export portfolio; however, they will face increased competition from other, more efficient locations. It is perhaps within a regional context that these two sectors will be able to compete and bring further growth.
- Continued liberalization of the telecommunications sector is crucial to developing the services sector and bringing down the costs of doing business on the island. Conclusion of the liberalization agenda will facilitate improvement in the sector's efficiency and transparency.

Current multilateral trade negotiations in services have potentially significant implications for market access in this rapidly growing sector of the world economy. Barbados' engagement in these negotiations, and its general trade policy objectives and actions, are the subject of the next section.

E. Trade Policy Objectives: Global Integration, Special Treatment

Barbados' trade policy is shaped by both a firm belief in the merits of trade liberalization and global integration, and a strong conviction that the vulnerabilities of small island developing states (SIDS) must be recognized and sufficiently addressed in the pursuit of those goals. Following a prolonged recession in the early 1990s, Barbados took a number of steps to open up and deregulate its economy. It implemented unilateral trade reforms, gave growing support to multilateral and regional trade initiatives and became a leading force behind the revitalization of integration in CARICOM. At the same time, the government maintained high levels of protection for some import-competing industries, as well as various forms of financial support to domestic production. Coupled with a stable political environment characterized by regular, formal consultations among the government, trade unions and the private sector, these policies spurred almost a decade of economic growth and have helped sustain high living standards on the island, well above those of most developing countries.

In international trade fora, Barbados has actively argued in favor of special and differential (S&D) treatment for SIDS to compensate for their particular vulnerabilities to price and supply fluctuations, higher fixed costs of production and marketing, and susceptibility to natural disasters. Barbados has argued that S&D treatment should, among other things, involve longer transition periods for opening up domestic markets and the right to maintain domestic support for local production in order to promote non-trade objectives such as food security, rural development and poverty alleviation. Developed countries, meanwhile, should eliminate export subsidies and trade-distorting domestic support measures in their own markets. In addition, they should agree to binding provisions of technical and financial assistance to SIDS in order to facilitate their successful insertion into the global economy. Barbados has insisted, moreover, that unilateral trade preferences granted by developed countries play a vital role for small developing countries and should therefore be maintained. (As mentioned previously, however, existing preferences are being eroded by growing trade liberalization worldwide and, even if maintained, are likely to yield fewer benefits in coming years.)

Barbados' trade policy is formulated within the context of its membership both of CARICOM and the WTO, as well as existing and planned trade arrangements with countries in Europe and the Americas. (See Appendix II for an overview of trade agreements and preferential arrangements governing the country's external trade relations.)

CARICOM Membership

Barbados is a founding member of CARICOM, which was established in 1973 to foster economic integration, cooperation and foreign policy coordination among its now 15 members. CARICOM has a population of 15 million and a combined GDP of US$40 billion.[32] The group, excluding The Bahamas, is currently in the process of establishing a Caribbean Single Market and Economy (CSME), which includes the right of establishment, free movement of goods, services, capital and skilled persons within the sub-region, growing harmonization of economic and regulatory policies, and a common external tariff and trade policy. Thus, in the area of trade, CARICOM membership has important implications for Barbados.[33]

Preferential Access to, and Participation in, the CSME

CARICOM's free trade area in goods, in place since the early years of the integration process, allows virtually free, preferential access to the sub-regional market for Barbadian merchandise exports that meet CARICOM rules of origin. Current efforts in the region focus on the elimination of a few remaining non-tariff barriers (NTBs). Intra-regional trade nevertheless remains somewhat constrained, accounting for only 17 percent of the group's total exports, and only 11 percent of its imports. Inefficient regional transport facilities constitute a major

---

[32] Calculations using IMF-WEO and WB-WDI databases.

[33] For a more detailed overview of progress achieved so far in the implementation of the CSME, see (Brewster, 2003) and (INTAL, 2005).

bottleneck to the free flow of goods, as do the small size of the regional market and similar product specialization in a number of Caribbean countries. Only a limited number of companies in the region have thus far managed to overcome these constraints by establishing a lasting presence in the sub-regional market.

As mentioned earlier, Barbados appears to have drawn some benefits from intra-regional trade liberalization and the tariff preferences resulting from the application of the CET to extra-regional imports. From 1994 to 2004, its merchandise exports to CARICOM grew by some 5.4 percent a year on average, much faster than its exports to other markets. But unlike Trinidad and Tobago, which almost doubled its share of the CARICOM market in the last ten years and is the origin of over 70 percent of all intra-group exports, Barbados has struggled to maintain its small share of the regional market, and has lost market share in several countries. (See Table IV-5.)

Among CARICOM countries, Barbados still accounts for the second-largest share of all intra-regional exports (9 percent), after Trinidad and Tobago. It is uncertain, however, whether the country will be able to maintain its share of the CARICOM market once that market opens up to greater competition from Europe and other trade partners. Much will depend on Barbados' ability to pursue a successful transition to freer trade, but, as indicated earlier, the outlook for its merchandise exports is not encouraging. The regional services

Table IV-5. Barbados' Share in CARICOM Countries' Imports

	Imports from Barbados (US$ million)		Imports from World (US$ million)		Barbados Market Share (%)	
	1990–92	2002–04	1990–92	2002–04	1990–92	2002–04
Antigua & Barbuda	10	22	1,001	1,803	1.0	1.2
Bahamas	3	7	7,030	17,184	0.0	0.0
Belize	3	6	730	1,471	0.4	0.4
Dominica	10	16	350	624	2.8	2.6
Grenada	12	24	329	695	3.7	3.5
Guyana	8	23	991	1,677	0.8	1.4
Haiti	1	1	1,604	3,842	0.1	0.0
Jamaica	27	50	5,519	11,715	0.5	0.4
St. Kitts & Nevis	9	22	776	690	1.1	3.2
St. Lucia	24	39	728	1,293	3.3	3.0
St. Vincent & Grenadines	16	23	400	824	3.9	2.8
Suriname	1	13	1,552	1,957	0.0	0.7
Trinidad & Tobago	59	95	4,307	12,797	1.4	0.7
CARICOM	183	342	25,316	56,573	0.7	0.6

Source: IDB Integration and Regional Programs Department using IMF-DOTS.

Note: Barbados and Montserrat are not included in CARICOM data. Values represent totals for the period.

market may provide more immediate opportunities for Barbados.[34] So would other aspects of the regional integration process.[35]

Six member states—Barbados, Belize, Guyana, Jamaica, Suriname and Trinidad and Tobago—met the December 2005 deadline for implementing the main provisions of the CSME relating to services trade, right of establishment and movement of capital and labour. Other member states are expected to follow suit by mid-2006. To reduce transaction costs in the CSME, member countries have moreover sought to accelerate the process of harmonizing and upgrading regulatory frameworks within CARICOM. The aim is to identify key areas affecting investment decisions and other sectors of economic activity where regional harmonization is most urgent. While a lack of technical and financial resources has thus far precluded concrete progress in this area, member states recognize it as vital for fulfilling one of the main objectives of the CSME, which is to strengthen the international competitiveness of Caribbean economies.[36]

By fully participating in the CSME, Barbados is likely to benefit from opportunities in the travel and commercial services markets, given that it is relatively more efficient and developed in these sectors than other regional competitors. In addition, CSME integration can be used as a catalyst for greater global insertion—in terms of more effective penetration of external markets for health, education and high-end tourism services. As one of the stronger economies in the sub-region, Barbados could gain much from the CSME, and has made timely implementation of its various provisions a key part of its trade-policy agenda. To date, the implementation process has been rather slow across the region, perhaps understandably so, given the large number of countries in the group and the varying levels of development among them. In light of the changing external context, however, there is growing recognition among government leaders that more needs to be

---

[34] Lack of reliable data on intra-regional services trade may in the past have led policymakers and analysts to underestimate the importance of the CSME for CARICOM countries. Anecdotal evidence suggests that services trade within the CSME is picking up, and that opportunities for such trade are growing. Barbados is relatively well placed to expand its participation in such trade. It appears to have a regional competitive advantage in professional services areas such as accountancy, legal services (especially business-related) and financial management, as well as construction and engineering services. Barbadian professionals have won many services contracts in OECS countries, a fact that further illustrates the importance of the OECS sub-region to the Barbadian economy.

[35] Among other things, Barbados' stable political environment and relatively advanced social and physical infrastructure make it an attractive location for regional institutions and the provision of regional services in CARICOM. Many regional institutions are based in Barbados, among them the Caribbean Development Bank (CDB), the Caribbean Regional Negotiating Machinery (RNM), the Caribbean Export Development Agency, one of the three main campuses of the University of the West Indies, the Caribbean Regional Organization for Standards and Quality (CROSQ) and the CARICOM Secretariat's CSME Unit. Several international donor organizations servicing the wider Caribbean region also have their central offices in Barbados. As mentioned earlier, moreover, Barbados has become an important regional distribution and transshipment centre.

[36] Delays in the formal integration process have not stopped a budding process of private-sector-led economic integration through growing intra-regional investment, mainly targeting the services sector. Large firms based in

done to speed up the process, and there have been some encouraging signs to this effect in the past year.

Trade Policy Coordination and the CET

By signing on to the Treaty of Chaguaramas in 1973, Barbados committed itself to a progressive coordination of its trade policies with those of its CARICOM partners.[37] In line with the group's common market objective, member countries agreed to establish a common external tariff.[38] In 1993, after much delay, they finally began a four-phased implementation of the CET, to be completed between 1994 and 1998. Given the new outward-oriented direction of the integration process, this process involved a substantial reduction in external protection levels (including those of Barbados), from an average 20 percent to 10 percent for CARICOM as a whole.[39] The pace of implementation has varied greatly among CARICOM countries, with revenue concerns holding back the process in a number of countries. Only two countries, one of which was Barbados, met the 1998 deadline for full implementation of the CET; as of December 2005, all except Antigua and Barbuda, and St. Kitts and Nevis had implemented it.

There are inherent problems to the CET that will not go away even when it is fully implemented across CARICOM. First, while CARICOM tariffs are considerably lower than a decade ago, they are still relatively high, particularly in the food and manufacturing sectors where many products remain highly protected from external competition. This raises concerns about trade diversion and is not conducive to the development of internationally competitive local industries. Second, even when the CET is uniformly applied throughout CARICOM, it will remain rather "uncommon". That is because, in its current form, there is broad scope for tariff suspensions and reductions, as well as for national derogations

---

Trinidad and Tobago, Jamaica and Barbados are the main origin of such flows. Although specific data measuring these investments are not available, anecdotal evidence suggests that such flows are driven by the establishment of intra-corporate links, i.e. "brownfield", rather than "greenfield" investment. A prominent example is Goddards, a Barbadian firm involved in many areas but perhaps best known for its airline catering business. It has operations throughout the Caribbean and in South America. Sagicor – a financial services provider – has operations throughout the Caribbean and in the United States. These and other firms have "gone regional" for a variety of reasons, including diversification, market expansion, and competitive positioning. They are among the most successful firms in Barbados, perhaps further evidence of the importance of the intra-regional market. For more on this subject, see Trevor Farrell, *Caribbean Economic Integration – What Is Happening Now; What Needs to Be Done.* Monograph, 2003.

[37] See Chapter IV of the Treaty's Common Market Annex, Article 34: External Trade Policy, which states that "Member States shall seek a progressive co-ordination of their trade relations with third countries or groups of third countries... Member States undertake to transmit to the Secretariat particulars of any trade or aid agreements entered into after the entry into force of this Annex".

[38] Ibid., Article 31.

[39] Unweighted average tariff rate.

from the CET. This not only complicates the region's joint negotiating efforts *vis-à-vis* third partners, but also, given the implementation of rules of origin to avoid trade deflection, creates additional transaction costs and reduces transparency of market access for exporters targeting the CARICOM market. Third, the level of tariff dispersion in the CET remains high, resulting in higher efficiency costs and further complicating the group's market access negotiations with other countries and regions. Table IV-6 illustrates these three problems. It is worth noting that, among CARICOM countries, Barbados has one of the highest applied tariffs, three percentage points above the CET. Its weighted tariff, at 20.3 percent, is even higher. In fact, it is the highest among all countries in the Western Hemisphere. Despite efforts at liberalization over the past decade, Barbados remains a highly protected economy in many ways.

Table IV-6. CARICOM: CET and National Applied Tariffs, 2003

		Tariff (Simple Average, %)				
HS Section	Product Group	CET	Barbados	Trinidad & Tobago	Guyana	St. Kitts & Nevis
01	Live Animals/Products	24.9	53.3	24.3	27.1	11.5
02	Vegetable Products	18.2	28.0	16.2	18.4	13.2
03	Animal/Vegetable Fats	26.7	32.1	24.0	25.8	21.9
04	Processed Foods/Tobacco	19.7	34.2	16.2	25.0	16.1
05	Mineral Products	4.8	6.9	3.0	6.2	2.4
06	Chemical/Industrial Products	5.4	6.6	2.3	6.1	5.6
07	Plastics/Rubber	7.4	9.1	6.3	8.7	6.7
08	Animal Hides/Skin	8.2	9.6	5.8	9.2	7.6
09	Wood/Wood Articles	9.6	10.6	6.9	9.5	9.7
10	Paper/Cellulose Material	7.3	8.9	5.2	8.0	8.1
11	Textiles	10.4	10.8	7.9	10.8	11.1
12	Footwear/Miscellaneous Articles	16.6	16.2	15.2	16.0	18.5
13	Stone/Glassware	8.8	9.6	8.4	8.8	9.8
14	Precious/Semi-Precious Metals	20.1	29.7	14.7	28.6	14.4
15	Base Metals	5.6	6.8	4.6	6.7	6.2
16	Machinery/Electrical Equipment	6.5	7.8	4.9	7.5	7.7
17	Motor Vehicles/Vessels	9.6	10.0	7.2	9.4	9.7
18	Precision Instruments	11.5	14.4	9.9	14.2	10.8
19	Arms/Munitions	38.1	47.7	22.9	44.7	46.8
20	Misc. Manufactured Articles	16.2	16.2	15.7	15.8	19.3
21	Art/Antiques	20.5	20.0	20.0	20.0	25.0
	Average Tariff (%)	10.1	13.1	7.9	11.0	9.4
	Standard Deviation	14.7	26.4	12.3	12.9	12.1

Source: IDB Integration and Regional Programs Department using UN-TRAINS and FTAA-HDB.

Note: In 2002, the average tariff and standard deviation were 5.9 and 7.9 percent, respectively, for the Central American Common Market (CACM) and 7.0 and 0.0, respectively, for Chile.

In addition to a somewhat uncommon CET, there are other loopholes in CARICOM's common trade regime that weaken the group's external projection as a single market. As indicated earlier, CARICOM's founding treaty sought no more than a "progressive coordination" of members' external trade policies (which, in the absence of a common services regime, focused exclusively on trade in goods), and allowed members freely to negotiate bilateral trade agreements with third countries. The revised treaty of 2001 goes somewhat further towards establishing a common trade policy, but falls short of fully committing member states to this goal. By creating a common services regime, the treaty extends CARICOM's capacity to negotiate and implement joint services agreements with third parties. It moreover reduces the flexibility that individual member states have to negotiate bilateral trade agreements, by obliging members who negotiate such accords to seek the approval of the relevant CARICOM Ministerial Council.[40] It does not, however, expressly prohibit the negotiation of such agreements and is thus at odds with the principle of a customs union (and, by extension, a single market), which requires a truly common trade policy in order to be effective.

The constraints imposed by CARICOM's *not so* common trade policy on national policymaking should be weighed against the benefits that preferential access to the CARICOM market, the creation of the CSME and functional cooperation are providing to Barbados. There is another advantage, namely that foreign policy coordination has given the countries a stronger voice in international trade negotiations. As experience in the Free Trade Area of the Americas (FTAA) negotiations has shown, the voice of 14 countries, however small, is stronger than that of one small country on its own. The creation, in 1997, of the Caribbean Regional Negotiating Machinery (RNM) to formulate and implement joint Caribbean negotiating strategies has facilitated a more efficient pooling of the region's scarce human, technical and financial resources and thus led to more effective participation in external trade negotiations. For Barbados, there is an added benefit: as one of the stronger economies in the group, it is probably better able than many other member countries to shape regional positions in the negotiations.

[40] Chapter V, Article 80 of the revised treaty states that: "The Member States shall coordinate their trade policies with third States or Groups of states. The Community shall pursue the negotiation of external trade and economic agreements on a joint basis in accordance with principles and mechanisms established by the Conference. Bilateral agreements to be negotiated by Member States in pursuance of their national strategic interests shall (a) be without prejudice to their obligations under the Treaty: and (b) prior to their conclusion, be subject to certification by the CARICOM Secretariat that the agreements do not prejudice or place at a disadvantage the position of other CARICOM States *vis-à-vis* the Treaty. Where trade agreements involving tariff concessions are being negotiated, the prior approval of COTED shall be required." Belize obtained certain derogations from these provisions with respect to negotiation of trade agreements with "neighboring economic groupings". [Editors' note: COTED is Council on Trade and Economic Development.]

Western Hemisphere Markets

Barbados, through CARICOM, has signed trade agreements with five Latin American countries (Venezuela, Colombia, Dominican Republic, Cuba and Costa Rica; see Appendix II) in the past decade, allowing it improved, preferential access to some important markets in the region. Because the first two agreements are limited in scope, and the last three were only recently concluded, it is too early to determine the overall effect of these agreements on bilateral trade flows. Barbados trades very little with Latin American countries (the result of a long tradition of doing business primarily with the English-speaking world). Between 2000 and 2004, its merchandise sales to Latin America averaged only US$3 million a year. Barbados exports 15 times as much to the OECS (population just over half a million) as to all Latin American countries combined (population 500 million). Consolidated data on services trade with Latin America is not available, but it is well known that Latin Americans account for only a tiny share of tourism arrivals in Barbados. Considering the size and growth potential of the Latin American market, Barbados should explore possibilities for expanding its trade relations with these countries, particularly in the area of services. Improved penetration of Latin American markets will require a concerted effort by both the government and the private sector in Barbados, in terms of improved market analysis, promotional activities specifically targeted at new Western Hemisphere markets, and efforts to obtain better access to these markets. This is particularly important in light of the current impasse in the FTAA negotiations.

Negotiations for a hemisphere-wide free trade agreement were officially launched in 1998. The goal then was a balanced and comprehensive WTO-consistent agreement by January 2005, covering trade in goods and services, investment, government procurement, dispute settlement, intellectual property, subsidies, competition policy, and antidumping and countervailing duties. The agreement was to take into account the needs, economic conditions and opportunities of the smaller economies of the region, and was to coexist with bilateral and sub-regional agreements (such as CARICOM) to the extent that the rights and obligations under these agreements were not covered by, or went beyond, those of the FTAA. The latter would have had important implications for CARICOM in that, unless substantial progress towards the CSME was made prior to the entry into force of the FTAA, the CARICOM economic integration process could risk being overtaken (and made somewhat redundant) by the hemisphere-wide trade initiative.

The FTAA negotiations stalled in 2003 and, since then, there has been virtually no progress in the talks despite repeated commitments to continue the process. Partly as a result, there has been a proliferation of new bilateral agreements among individual or groups of FTAA countries, including a free trade agreement between the United States and Chile and the recently concluded agreement between the United States and five Central American countries plus the Dominican Republic (CAFTA-DR). The United States is also negotiating bilateral agreements with Colombia, Ecuador and Peru, while Canada hopes to expand its free trade agreement with Costa Rica to include the other members of the Central American Common Market.

These and other developments are putting pressure on CARICOM countries to seek alternative arrangements to the FTAA with their Western Hemisphere partners, in order to prevent a relative deterioration of their access to these markets. For Barbados, which conducts most of its trade in the Western Hemisphere, seeking alternative arrangements to the FTAA, or the revival of those talks, appears to be of particular importance. CARICOM has already sought to accelerate discussions with Canada and is exploring a possible trade agreement with Mercosur, but there is no decision as yet to enter into bilateral negotiations with the United States. Nonetheless, a new trade agreement with the United States is imperative if CARICOM wants to keep its preferences under the US-Caribbean Trade Preference Act, which are set to expire in 2008 unless the FTAA or a comparable free trade agreement between the United States and CBTPA beneficiaries enters into force earlier.

Whatever the configuration of future trade agreements in the Western Hemisphere, they are likely to lead to further erosion of current preferences enjoyed by Barbados in the US, Canadian and Caribbean markets, and in those Latin American countries with which Barbados already has a free trade area. The prospect of tougher competition makes it all the more urgent for Barbadian exporters to exploit their current window of opportunity in these markets. At the same time, however, access to the US and Canadian markets would be more secure under a reciprocal trade agreement with these countries, since it would no longer depend on unilaterally applied "preferences", but rather on contractually agreed rules. In addition, exports that do not currently enjoy preferences or enter duty-free under MFN rules in these markets would gain improved access, and could consequently increase their share in Barbadian exports. A similar trend would apply to any new agreement that CARICOM signs with Latin American countries, although here, too, competition from other countries in the region will be tough if the agreement is hemisphere-wide.

In any such agreement, Barbados will have a significant interest in obtaining better market access for its services exports. At the same time, it will have to liberalize its import market for both goods and services, with important consequences for import-competing industries and fiscal revenues—but also potentially large benefits for consumers and the economy in general, given that Barbados sources most of its imports from Western Hemisphere markets. The gains from trade liberalization (which go beyond trade creation by facilitating ongoing structural reforms and their subsequent "locking in", the establishment of a more secure and transparent business environment, and higher inflows of FDI, among other things) could be substantial for a small country like Barbados. However, the adjustment process will be difficult even if the country succeeds in negotiating longer transition periods for its own market opening.

Relations with Europe

Along with its CARICOM partners, Barbados is currently engaged in negotiations with the EU that will fundamentally alter the current provisions governing EU trade with the region. These provisions are spelled out in the June 2000 EU-ACP Cotonou Partnership Agreement. This agreement foresees the entry into force of Economic Partnership Agreements (EPAs) between the EU and ACP countries by 1 January 2008 at the latest. After an initial phase of all ACP-EU talks (2002–03), bi-regional EU-CARIFORUM negotiations, involving CARICOM plus the Dominican Republic on the Caribbean side, were launched in April 2004. The aim is to produce a draft EPA by December 2006 and a final agreement by December 2007. Meanwhile, the unilateral trade preferences granted by the EU to imports from ACP countries under Lomé IV have been extended through the end of 2007.

Since CARICOM countries—including Barbados—already enjoy duty-free access to the EU market for most of their merchandise exports, the benefits of the agreement for CARICOM will largely depend on the degree to which remaining non-tariff restrictions to such trade are eliminated; to what extent the EU opens up its services market to CARICOM; the timeframe and scope of reciprocal trade liberalization, which should allow CARICOM countries enough time to adjust to both increased competition and declining tariff revenues; and how generous and effective the EU's financial assistance in support of CARICOM's adjustment to freer trade will be. The stakes in the EPA negotiations are high, not only because the resulting agreement will govern trade relations and development cooperation between the two regions for years to come, but also because it will likely influence any agreement that CARICOM—and hence Barbados—subsequently signs with other developed countries.

CARICOM's trade relations with the EU will not only be shaped by a future EPA. As in the case of CAFTA and other bilateral trade initiatives in the Western Hemisphere, new trade arrangements between the EU and third countries or regions could weaken the position of CARICOM countries in the EU market, and thus erode the benefits of an EPA. The Cotonou Agreement commits Europe to consult with the ACP group prior to implementing new liberalization measures. It does not, however, guarantee CARICOM continued "preferential" status in the EU market, either in the transition phase or following the implementation of an EPA. Another factor influencing CARICOM-EU trade relations is the Community's recent eastward enlargement. Upon joining the EU in 2004, the ten new members assumed all EU commitments included in the Cotonou Agreement; they now offer CARICOM the same preferences it already enjoyed in the EU of 15.[41] Along with the acceleration of economic growth expected in the new member countries as a result of their accession, this translates

[41] As mentioned earlier, the Czech and Slovak Republics, Poland and Hungary already grant reduced or zero tariff rates to selected imports from Barbados.

into new export opportunities for CARICOM, perhaps most of all in the area of services (i.e., tourism). It is nevertheless important to point out that, as members of the EU, these countries now participate in, and influence, the ongoing EPA negotiations. For political as well as economic reasons, therefore, it is important for Caribbean countries (including Barbados) to increase their engagement with the new EU members in order to facilitate dialogue, information-exchange and business links between the regions.

WTO Membership

Barbados has been a GATT contracting party since February 1967 and became a founding member of the WTO in January 1995. It accords at least MFN treatment to all its trading partners. As a result of the Uruguay Round of multilateral trade negotiations, it has bound all of its tariffs except on fish and fish products, albeit at ceiling rates. Agricultural tariffs are bound at a minimum of 100 percent, with some products bound at more than double that rate. Tariffs on manufactured goods are bound at rates of at least 70 percent, with considerably higher rates for some specific products.[42] There is a substantial gap between bound rates and applied tariffs (which are set in accordance with the CET and the national exceptions included therein; see Table IV-6 above). NTBs, such as quantitative restrictions, import surcharges and import licences, have been progressively dismantled in line with commitments made in the Uruguay Round.

Under the General Agreement on Trade in Services (GATS), Barbados has scheduled a number of commitments in trade in services, with two horizontal exemptions applying to all sectors. First, it has imposed a restriction on all services delivered via commercial presence (Mode 3) with the Property Transfer Tax Act, which levies taxes on purchases and sales of land, stocks, or shares by foreign investors.[43] Second, it has restricted the services delivered through the presence of natural persons (Mode 4) with the Immigration Act regulating entry and residence of all foreign persons working on the island.

Barbados has also made some sector-specific commitments to services liberalization. These include unlimited market access and national treatment for all foreign providers of legal documentation services, specialized medical services, software implementation, courier services, reinsurance, and entertainment services. In addition, some commitments have been made on basic telecommunications services through the Telecommunications Act of 2001.[44] It is important to note that Barbados is one of the few developing countries

---

[42] The vast majority of tariff rates are ad valorem. Specific rates apply to 57 product lines, most of which are alcoholic beverages, and correspond to high levels of protection. See (WTO, 2002).

[43] This legislation was amended in 1999 to eliminate any differentiation in treatment between foreign and local investors.

[44] The Telecommunications Act of 2001 has not yet been notified to the WTO. See Centre for Trade Policy and Law, *Summary Report: Implementation of Selected WTO Agreements in the Caribbean Community*, 2002.

in the WTO that has not included tourism in its schedule of commitments (partial or full). Even though the sector is fairly liberalized, an official commitment could help attract additional investment.

Currently, Barbados faces two challenges in the WTO. The first relates to the full implementation of the Uruguay Round Agreements. Compared to other Caribbean countries, Barbados is relatively advanced in implementing its Uruguay Round obligations, a difficult process involving a number of legislative and institutional changes (some of which are being handled at regional, rather than national, level in CARICOM). There are, however, some pending issues, for example with respect to notifications; actions needed to satisfy the Agreement on Technical Barriers to Trade (TBT), including upgrading of standards information centres and accreditation of laboratories; upgrading of antidumping laws and legislation on subsidies and countervailing measures; and compliance with the Agreement on Trade-related Investment Measures (TRIMs), including revision of incompatible fiscal and industrial incentives and other provisions.[45]

Participation in the Doha Development Round represents another challenge for Barbados. The Doha negotiations, launched in November 2001, include a large number of areas, most prominent among them agriculture and services, where countries are seeking substantial improvements in market access and, in agriculture, the elimination of distorting domestic support measures. Countries also want to achieve further reductions in tariffs and non-tariff barriers on industrial products, and reach agreement on new issues such as trade facilitation. Implementation issues resulting from the Uruguay Round agreements are also on the agenda—developing countries, in particular, have experienced problems in implementation and have asked for revisions of commitments undertaken in that earlier round of multilateral negotiations.

After a breakdown in negotiations at the 2003 ministerial meeting in Mexico, a package of framework agreements to guide future negotiations was concluded in August 2004, giving renewed impetus to the talks. Since then, however, the negotiations have moved slowly, with agriculture proving to be one of the main stumbling blocs in the talks. At the December 2005 ministerial meeting in Hong Kong, WTO members resolved some issues related to agriculture and non-agriculture market access, and agreed to finish the negotiations by December 2006—an ambitious deadline given that much remains to be solved for a comprehensive new agreement. Throughout the negotiations, Barbados has joined with its CARICOM partners to promote special and differential treatment for developing countries, the principle of "less than full reciprocity" in the formulation of the modalities for tariff

[45] The most recent WTO Trade Policy Review for Barbados was undertaken in 2002, and is therefore somewhat outdated. Barbados' implementation status has also been reviewed in a series of documents commissioned by the CARICOM Secretariat under an IDB-financed TC project entitled "Support for the Implementation of WTO Commitments in the Caribbean Community" (ATN/SF-7075-RG). These reports are based on an analysis conducted during the period January–December 2002.

reduction, and the need to ensure that the negotiations on trade in services facilitate the increasing participation of developing countries.[46]

Given the current impasse in the FTAA negotiations, EPA and WTO negotiations have assumed a prominent place on CARICOM's trade policy agenda. Both negotiations are important for Barbados—not least because they are likely to influence both the pace and outcome of future trade negotiations in the Western Hemisphere. Given the importance of this latter region in its total trade, Barbados should view with some concern the deadlock in the FTAA process, and the absence of significant progress to date in alternative arrangements between CARICOM and its FTAA partners. While other Latin American countries are moving swiftly towards the conclusion of bilateral free trade agreements with each other and with North America, CARICOM countries have been far less active on this front. Barbados should therefore support an intensification of CARICOM's current talks with Canada and Mercosur, as well as efforts to seek a new agreement with the United States.

The Cost of Protection

As mentioned earlier, Barbados has taken a number of steps in recent years to liberalize and simplify its import regime, among others by reducing tariffs, eliminating quantitative restrictions and replacing multiple indirect taxes and levies with a value-added tax (VAT). Border protection nevertheless remains high for imports that compete with domestic production. Without stringent protection from external competition, most of the few existing agricultural and manufacturing activities on the island would likely contract significantly. In the agri-food sector, border protection (for example through non-automatic import licensing) is applied to decrease imports and enhance food security.

Protection is also high in some industries where Barbados has no domestic production. In those cases, the aim is to raise government revenue and/or to protect domestic industries in other CARICOM member states (through the application of the CET, which encourages Barbadians to source their imports regionally).[47] Some import tariffs have actually risen since 1999, first as a result of the conversion of quantitative restrictions on agricultural imports into tariffs ("tariffication", which does not necessarily increase effective border protection), and subsequently, in November 2001, in response to the economic difficulties experienced in the aftermath of September 11th, 2001 (which led the government to raise tariffs on domestically produced manufactured goods from 15–20 percent to 60 percent).

---

[46] CARICOM positions in the WTO negotiations are summarized in the "Caribbean Declaration on the Fifth WTO Ministerial Conference", presented in Cancún, Mexico, in September 2003.

[47] As is well known, the formation of a common market and now the CSME has not prevented trade disputes among Caribbean countries. The current flying fish dispute between Barbados and Trinidad and Tobago is a clear example of this and points to remaining weaknesses in the legal set-up of the CSME.

Special safeguard measures were moreover implemented in July 2002 to protect some sensitive products against import competition.

In addition to tariff protection, many domestic producers of goods and services benefit from tax incentives that provide total or partial exemption of import duties on inputs needed for production. The government moreover gives financial assistance to domestic producers, particularly in the agricultural sector in order to help the embattled sugar industry and, at the same time, promote diversification into new crops (cotton, vegetables, fruit, cut flowers). Support is provided through concessional financing, public funds set up for particular purposes, or technical cooperation and training. International or offshore companies also benefit from substantial tax rebates. There are no available estimates of the budgetary costs of all this support, nor of the cost of duty-exemptions. A comprehensive cost-benefit analysis of such support might be useful in order to determine its real value to the economy and the population as a whole. Meanwhile, barriers to food imports may have affected the international competitiveness of the island's tourism industry by restricting access to the best and most competitively priced inputs (and, in the process, raising the cost of restaurant meals to levels far beyond those of some competing tourism destinations in the Caribbean).

The government is cognizant of the high cost of protection and has already implemented a number of measures aimed at restructuring the economy and making it less reliant on trade preferences, old forms of protection and concessional finance. Such reliance nevertheless remains high and raises concern regarding the private sector's readiness for the CSME, the EPA and, particularly, greater integration among Western Hemisphere economies.

F. Trade Policymaking: Institutional Issues

The Foreign Trade Division of the Ministry of Foreign Affairs and Foreign Trade is responsible for formulating, negotiating and implementing trade policy, investigating all antidumping and subsidies complaints and administering safeguard measures. The Ministry plays an important coordinating role in trade policymaking through close inter-ministerial collaboration and consultation with civil society. As illustrated in Box IV-2, several ministries and government agencies collaborate with the Foreign Trade Division in the development and implementation of trade policy. The trade policymaking process in Barbados moreover enjoys a long tradition of consultation among the government, the private sector and trade unions.

At the regional level, the RNM and the CARICOM Secretariat participate in developing and implementing trade policy. The RNM is responsible for coordinating and representing the negotiating positions of CARICOM members, and works closely with the Ministry of Foreign Affairs and Foreign Trade and other relevant national entities in doing so. All positions presented by the RNM in the various negotiations have to be approved by the Community's

Box IV-2. Participants in National Trade Policymaking

- Ministry of Foreign Affairs and Foreign Trade. The ministry's Foreign Trade Division coordinates trade policy. The ministry's foreign missions play a crucial role in establishing and maintaining trade links with third countries. Barbados has embassies or high commissions in the United Kingdom, Canada, the United States, Belgium, Switzerland, and Venezuela, and permanent missions to the OAS in Washington, the UN in New York, and the EU in Brussels.
- Ministry of Finance and Economic Affairs is responsible for coordinating and implementing the government's economic policy. Its Customs and Excise Department administers the CARICOM CET, rules of origin and other customs procedures.
- Ministry of Industry and International Business (MIIB): its investment arm, the Barbados Investment and Development Corporation (BIDCO), is responsible for export promotion policies and the facilitation of business entry into Barbados. Its Corporate Affairs and Intellectual Property Office (CAIPO) is responsible for company registration and the registration and maintenance of public records relating to trademarks, patents, industrial designs and other intellectual property categories.
- Ministry of Tourism and International Transport formulates policies to develop sustainable tourism. Through its development agency, Barbados Tourism Investment Inc., it promotes investment in the island's tourism and hospitality industries.
- Ministry of Agriculture and Rural Development is in charge of sanitary and phytosanitary standards, plant and animal quarantine, natural resources, soil conservation, irrigation, fisheries, and veterinary services.
- Ministry of Commerce, Consumer Affairs and Business Development has different entities related to trade, among them the Barbados National Standards Institute (BNSI) and the Fair Trading Commission.
- Private Sector. The Barbados Private Sector Trade Team, established in 2003, supports businesses and industries in assessing competitiveness, formulating trade negotiating strategies, and increasing awareness in trade issues. Other important private sector bodies include the Barbados Chamber of Commerce and Industry, the Barbados Manufacturers' Association, the Barbados Coalition of Service Industries, the Barbados Hotel and Tourism Association, and the Barbados International Business Association.
- Trade Unions. The Congress of Trade Unions and Staff Associations of Barbados. Since 1991, it has been an effective voice for union workers and staffers within the framework of Barbados' trade policymaking process.

Council on Trade and Economic Development (COTED), comprising Ministers of Trade and Foreign Affairs of member countries, including Barbados. While benefiting from this regional pooling of resources, Barbados often sends its own national representatives to the negotiations to work alongside RNM officers. The CARICOM Secretariat focuses mainly on intra-regional negotiations and on the implementation of trade agreements already signed by Caribbean countries (CSME and WTO). The Barbados Prime Minister's Office is the lead entity responsible for the administration of CSME policies, working closely with Secretariat personnel to achieve this objective.

For a small country like Barbados, maintaining a large public sector is unrealistic. All ministries and agencies engaged in trade policymaking have to work under significant human-resource and budgetary constraints. Maximizing the efficiency of these limited resources is therefore crucial, particularly in the current context of multiple simultaneous and technically complicated trade negotiations and significant new obligations assumed in the WTO and the CSME. A comprehensive analysis of the country's institutional infrastructure in the area of trade may be useful in this respect, since it would focus attention on possible weaknesses or bottlenecks to efficient trade policymaking or administration. Institutional strengthening can be achieved, among other things, through more effective intra- and inter-agency coordination, human resource training, elimination of duplication of activities among government agencies, improved access to technical expertise and use of modern communications systems.

G. Trade and Integration: Challenges and Strategies

Export Growth and Diversification

In the area of trade, Barbados' first and foremost challenge is to achieve higher and sustained export growth. The potential for growth exists mainly in services exports. Tourism is likely to remain the country's leading export in the foreseeable future. The continued development of the travel industry is of crucial importance to Barbados, but it will only be possible if the country remains competitive *vis-à-vis* other tourist destinations both in the Caribbean and worldwide. To do this, Barbados needs to address some development bottlenecks by improving price competitiveness, keeping operating costs down, developing a sustainable water policy, and improving infrastructure. It should continue to develop the high-end tourism segment, a proven competitive export in the past. Diversification within the travel industry is also an important strategy; here, Barbados has two areas of potential growth. One is education-related travel, linked to increased global demand in this sector; the other is the development of health-related services given the strong link between high-end tourism and preventative and cosmetic healthcare. The government can play an important role in facilitating this growth, and it has begun to do so.

Diversification is important not only within the travel industry, but also with respect to exports as a whole. Barbados' dependence on the tourism sector is overwhelming—and therefore risky: in the last 20 years or so, tourist arrivals have largely determined changes in the country's real GDP. Barbados should therefore explore ways of decreasing the economy's dependence on this sector by expanding export potential in other services sectors. One area that merits attention is Barbados' role as transshipment and regional distribution centre. There could be potential to develop competitive advantages in this area, but available data are scarce and more thorough analysis would be needed to make specific recommendations in this respect. Financial and insurance services are another area of potential growth. Although Barbados does not appear to be competitive *vis-à-vis* developed countries in these services, it does enjoy a regional presence and could further develop that presence within the CSME.

As regards merchandise trade, continued efforts need to be made to move away from export activities that are not internationally competitive, and export promotion efforts should limit themselves to targeting products that face growing demand in world markets and that could be exported competitively even in a context of declining trade preferences. Apart from some niche products, possibilities in this area are likely to be limited.

Although the main actors in the process of diversification will be private companies, the government can support the process through assistance to the various government agencies charged with facilitating private-sector development (particularly in areas such as development of niche markets and specialized products, consumer and market surveys, training in product development and innovation, etc.). The government can also assist with development of the tourism industry and other services sectors, including further liberalization of the telecommunication, transportation and financial-services markets. An opening of services sectors could encourage technology transfer, spur innovation, increase transparency and predictability, and lower the cost of doing business across the island, given that services are often key inputs both to the production of goods and the provision of other services.

A related challenge is to diversify, and gain improved access to, export *markets*, both in the Western Hemisphere and beyond. Again, it is important to remember that it is companies, not governments that trade. Companies, therefore, will have to do most of the work to reduce Barbados' dependence on its traditional export markets in North America, Europe and the English-speaking Caribbean. But the government can help by negotiating and implementing trade agreements that offer Barbadian exporters increased access to both existing and new markets, and by supporting market intelligence programs and private-sector-led export promotion campaigns through BIDCO and the BTA.

A Heavy Negotiating Agenda

For Barbados, active participation in all the negotiations currently underway between CARICOM and its various trade partners is of vital importance, and very difficult. Like other small Caribbean countries, Barbados faces significant resource constraints. The trade ministry is tiny compared to those of the country's main external trade partners. With just a dozen or so trade specialists (compared to between 100 and 300 in the relevant agencies of the United States, Canada and the EU), the Foreign Trade Division of the Foreign Affairs Ministry is struggling to complete the necessary tasks for securing an effective voice in the negotiations: market/sector analysis to determine the country's competitiveness *vis-à-vis* its trade partners, studies on the implications of trade liberalization on domestic export and import-competing industries, review of partner countries' offers in the negotiations, preparation of national offers, and so on. The creation of the RNM has eased some of the pressures on CARICOM governments in terms of technical preparation for the negotiations, but the RNM can only be effective if member states contribute actively to the process.

Effective participation in complex trade negotiations requires a considerable level of human, technical and financial resources. It would not, however, be realistic for a small country like Barbados to significantly expand the size of its trade policymaking apparatus. But through *efficient resource allocation*, specific interventions aimed at *institutional strengthening* and some *external support*, the government could maximize its available resources without increasing its size. In addition, Barbados and its CARICOM partners should further strengthen their efforts to pool scarce resources at the regional level, not just through continued support to such mechanisms as the RNM, but also through greater cooperation at the level of embassies and foreign trade missions.

It will be important for Barbados to regularly re-assess and, if necessary, modify its various *integration and market opening strategies*, including the way in which it uses alliances such as CARICOM to promote its national development agenda. For a small country with scarce resources, there are many benefits to be derived from political and economic cooperation with neighbouring countries, but there are some costs, too.[48] The pooling of resources at the regional level is one way of overcoming the constraints of being small. Establishing clear priorities for policy intervention is another: since the Western Hemisphere accounts for around 60 percent of Barbados' merchandise trade, as well as a large portion of its tourism arrivals, then that is perhaps where most of the country's negotiating resources should go.

Implementation of Agreements

Once trade agreements are negotiated and signed, Barbados must ensure their effective and timely implementation in order to reap the benefits (and minimize the costs) for its economy. This involves complicated revisions to the country's legal and administrative apparatus. How difficult that process can be is illustrated by the fact that Barbados is still in the process of implementing the GATT Uruguay Round agreements, 10 years after they were signed. Along with these, Barbados will have to implement its commitments resulting from CARICOM's agreements with the Dominican Republic, Cuba and Costa Rica. With the WTO Doha and EPA negotiations scheduled for completion in December 2006 and 2007, respectively, and with new agreements likely to emerge between CARICOM and

---

[48] As indicated in Section E above, membership in CARICOM has conferred a number of benefits on Barbados, principal among which are privileged access to neighbouring markets and the benefits derived from the pooling of scarce resources across the region (greater leverage in international fora, cost savings, etc.). But preferences may in the long term prove to be a mixed blessing unless Barbadian companies use them to upgrade their export supply not only in quantity but also in qualitative terms. Meanwhile, however, there is much room to expand cooperation among CARICOM members in a number of strategic areas related to trade and economic integration. And, like other countries in the group, Barbados could benefit from this as it confronts the many challenges of globalization. In addition, timely implementation of the CSME is likely to provide tangible benefits for Barbados. All of this points to the importance for Barbados of developing and maintaining a clear strategy for its CARICOM membership.

other FTAA countries, Barbados is likely to face tremendous difficulties in securing effective implementation without committing more resources to this endeavour. Again, this could be achieved through further public-sector reform that would allow a more efficient allocation of existing resources, and use of external assistance where possible, rather than an expansion of government.

Indeed, such assistance will be necessary for Barbados to meet the various challenges of implementation. Specific needs identified by the government include those related to sanitary and phytosanitary (SPS) issues (accreditation of the Ministry of Agriculture Laboratories for international trade, development of a fish inspection regime, needs assessment for animal and plant health inspection services); technical barriers to trade (upgrading the Mass Metrology Laboratory Facilities and renovating the Soil and Materials Testing Facility of the Barbados National Standards Institution (BNSI); and intellectual property (improvement of Corporate Affairs and Intellectual Property Business Facilitation Services). The government also wants to establish trade reference centres in strategic, easily accessible locations. As with the negotiating effort, some implementation issues (particularly those related to WTO) might be handled more efficiently—and at lower cost—at the regional, rather than the national, level; Barbados should explore such possibilities with its CARICOM members as soon as possible.

Achieving Competitiveness in a More Liberalized Trading Environment

Product and market diversification, and the benefits deriving from free trade, will be neither achievable nor sustainable without a *business-friendly environment,* particularly one that encourages and rewards innovation, initiative and risk-taking, while at the same time offering transparent laws and regulations and a stable macroeconomic environment.

Both the government and the private sector must prepare themselves for the significant changes that will result from trade liberalization, not only within the country but in the global economy as well. Production and investment strategies in the Western Hemisphere are likely to change significantly in the coming years. A similar process is already underway globally, and Barbados will have to compete more fiercely for both markets and capital. The country's heavy reliance on a limited number of export products, some of which are clearly not internationally competitive, raises some concerns in this respect—hence the importance of diversification. Once trade barriers come down, Barbados' import-competing sectors will have to adjust to greater competition at home, and many traditional exporters will be unable to compete once their preferences disappear. Barbados' presence in the CARICOM market, for example, is certain to come under attack once the group lowers its tariffs on imports from North America and Europe.

The government will have to play an active role in this transitional process by facilitating productivity and export growth through prudent macroeconomic management, better infrastructure (particularly in services and transport, but also in R&D) and, as mentioned above, more concerted efforts (with the private sector) at export diversification. The country's *National Strategy for Trade Related Capacity Building* (2003) identifies a number of projects aimed at facilitating the country's adaptation to more liberalized trade (competitiveness enhancement programs for private-sector entities, Small Business Association five-year project to expand markets, and an agricultural marketing enhancement program, among others).

Sharing the Costs and the Benefits

The creation of efficient social safety nets and other such services in order to soften the impact of adjustment will be critical to the government's efforts to support the transition to free trade. Equally important will be the way in which the benefits of free trade are distributed among the Barbadian population. Export diversification, access to new markets, regional cooperation and a strong trade policymaking process should all facilitate economic growth. But higher growth is a means to an end, not an end in itself. Any strategy to increase and diversify exports should have as its ultimate goal the equitable and sustainable economic development of the country's population, which requires, but is not solely based on, growth itself.

In its effort to maximize the gains from trade for the majority of the population, should the government target and support specific export industries—those that produce the highest value added, create the greatest number of new jobs, pay the highest salaries? Or should it follow a more market-based approach, aimed at improving the general business climate without picking winners, and designing appropriate social and fiscal policies to encourage a better distribution of the gains from trade? Addressing these questions would go beyond the limits of this paper, but at the very least we want to raise them here.

Donor Support and Coordination

Donor strategies for Barbados should support the country's efforts to achieve higher growth and development levels within an increasingly more liberalized and competitive global economic environment.

Given the multiple trade-related challenges outlined above, it is a matter of concern that, among the IDB's Caribbean members, Barbados currently has one of the least active portfolios with regard to trade-related operations. Barbados has yet to take advantage of the Bank's various national lending and non-lending instruments that directly support trade and integration-related issues. One mechanism—already used by Suriname and Trinidad and Tobago—is a Trade Facility offering small loans of up to US$5 million for comprehensive institutional strengthening of trade-related ministries and other agencies. A simplified approval and fast-track disbursement process provides immediate solutions to urgent needs in training and technical support for trade negotiations, institutional support for the implementation of trade agreements, mechanisms to foster trade policymaking coordination among agencies, consultation between public, private and civil society actors, and export promotion activities. Another mechanism is the Lending Program for Trade, Integration and Competitiveness. This offers a new approach to the mainstreaming of the different instruments and loan processing procedures needed to address the challenges of trade liberalization into one package, simplifying and expediting the programming process. Support is also available to the private sector from the Multilateral Investment Fund (MIF), particularly in areas that foster innovation, competitiveness and increased capacity to access traditional and new markets.

While few of the IDB's national interventions directly target trade, Barbados does benefit from a number of regional projects financed by the Bank in this area. One example is the ongoing support provided to the RNM in its preparation of regional negotiating positions and training of national trade officials. The Bank has also provided support to the CARICOM Secretariat in areas related to the implementation of WTO commitments, harmonization of investment and government procurement rules in the region, revisions to the CET, and the creation of the Caribbean Court of Justice to oversee the implementation of intra-regional liberalization commitments. Two additional regional programs include support to the Caribbean Regional Technical Assistance Centre (CARTAC) for tax and customs reform, and customs valuation and business facilitation in the Caribbean.

In order to maximize the potential benefit of such support, careful coordination between national and regional-level interventions will be needed. National interventions—for example, through a Trade Facility Loan or a MIF operation—should be consistent not only with the Bank's country strategy for Barbados but also with its regional strategy for CARICOM. The latter supports a regional approach to economic opening through:

(i) improvement of regulatory frameworks to match international best practices, supporting appropriate regional harmonization;
(ii) regional coordination of external trade negotiations and implementation of new trade agreements;
(iii) development of human resources through more efficient education, training, and R&D activities oriented towards greater competitiveness in international markets; and
(iv) improvement in the region's capacity to collect, analyze and disseminate relevant and comparable social and economic data, through both regional and national interventions.[49]

---

[49] IDB-Integration and Regional Programs Department, *Regional Programming Paper for CARICOM,* 1999.

IDB support to Barbados in the area of trade and integration should also be closely coordinated with that of other multilateral institutions and bilateral donors. Apart from the Bank, the European Commission (EC) is one of the most active donors in Barbados through its National and Regional Indicative Programs. Regional programs focus on the area of trade/export promotion (managed by the Caribbean Export Development Agency-CEDA), tourism development, and private-sector development (through the BIDCO). The European Investment Bank (EIB) also plays an important role in private-sector development with its facilitation of credit lines to the Barbados Development Bank (BDC) and the Industrial Credit Fund (ICF) to finance small and medium enterprises in industry and tourism.[50] Other donors focus more on regional development programs such as training in trade negotiations, institutional strengthening in the implementation of trade agreements, and support to the transition towards freer trade. They include the Caribbean Development Bank (CDB), the United States Agency for International Development (USAID), the UK Department for International Development (DFID), the Canadian International Development Agency (CIDA), the WTO Secretariat, the Organization of American States (OAS) and some UN agencies. As part of its National Strategy for Strengthening Trade-related Capacity, Barbados should consider setting up a mechanism by which its trade ministry and other relevant agencies—as well as donors—have regular access to updated information on the various trade and integration-related assistance programs currently underway in the country and, at the regional level, in CARICOM.

Appendix I

(Appendix Tables A-IV-1 through A-IV-6 appear on the following pages.)

[50] EC, *Barbados Country Strategy and National Indicative Programme for the Period 2002–2007,* March 2003.

Table A-IV-1. Barbados: Merchandise Exports to World and Selected Partners, 1994–2004

												Share (%)			Avg. Ann. Growth (%)		
(US$ millions)	**1994**	**1995**	**1996**	**1997**	**1998**	**1999**	**2000**	**2001**	**2002**	**2003**	**2004**	**94–04**	**94–99**	**00–04**	**94–04**	**94–99**	**99–04**
World	182	238	278	283	259	251	273	259	215	250	278	100	100	100	4.3	6.6	2.1
United States	35	38	39	41	42	44	43	39	36	36	39	16	16	15	1.2	4.9	–2.4
Canada	8	13	12	10	7	7	6	7	5	4	5	3	4	2	–4.2	–3.2	–5.2
CARICOM	65	90	102	102	112	119	120	111	102	102	109	41	40	43	5.4	13.0	–1.8
Latin America	1	5	26	18	4	4	3	4	4	3	2	3	4	1	7.1	36.7	–16.1
FTAA	108	146	179	172	165	174	172	160	146	146	155	62	63	61	3.6	9.9	–2.3
EU (25)	39	49	53	57	50	44	45	41	38	37	39	18	20	16	0.1	2.7	–2.5
Rest of World	35	43	46	54	43	33	56	58	32	67	85	20	17	23	9.2	–1.3	20.8
CARICOM												**Share (%)**			**Avg. Ann. Growth (%)**		
(US$ millions)	**1994**	**1995**	**1996**	**1997**	**1998**	**1999**	**2000**	**2001**	**2002**	**2003**	**2004**	**94–04**	**94–99**	**00–04**	**94–04**	**94–99**	**99–04**
Guyana	4	7	8	8	6	6	7	6	9	6	7	7	7	6	6.5	10.7	2.5
Jamaica	11	17	25	20	20	19	19	20	15	15	14	17	19	15	2.1	10.8	–6.0
OECS	30	41	41	46	49	52	49	45	44	46	50	44	44	43	5.3	11.8	–0.8
Grenada	4	5	5	6	7	7	7	7	7	7	7	6	6	7	6.0	12.5	–0.2
St. Lucia	9	12	12	13	13	15	14	14	11	12	14	12	13	12	4.6	9.8	–0.4
St. Vincent	5	7	8	9	9	10	9	9	9	9	10	8	8	8	5.8	12.7	–0.6
Trinidad & Tobago	17	22	20	19	27	33	36	29	24	28	29	25	23	27	5.5	13.9	–2.3
Other CARICOM	3	3	7	8	9	9	9	11	10	7	9	7	7	8	12.7	27.9	–0.7
Total	65	90	102	102	112	119	120	111	102	103	109	100	100	100	5.4	13.0	–1.8
Latin America												**Share (%)**			**Avg. Ann. Growth (%)**		
(US$ millions)	**1994**	**1995**	**1996**	**1997**	**1998**	**1999**	**2000**	**2001**	**2002**	**2003**	**2004**	**94–04**	**94–99**	**00–04**	**94–04**	**94–99**	**99–04**
Central America	0.5	1.1	1.0	1.7	0.7	0.2	0.2	0.7	1.4	1.2	0.5	12	9	25	0.9	–18.3	24.4
Chile	0.0	0.0	0.0	0.1	0.0	0.0	0.0	0.0	0.0	0.0	0.0	0	0	1	9.7	29.0	–6.6
Dom. Rep.	0.1	0.1	0.1	0.1	0.5	0.6	1.8	1.1	1.5	0.9	0.7	11	3	38	21.5	43.3	3.0
Mexico	0.1	0.1	0.1	0.0	0.0	1.0	0.3	0.4	0.0	0.5	0.1	4	2	9	1.5	66.7	–38.2
MERCOSUR	0.1	0.1	0.2	0.2	0.2	0.0	0.0	0.1	0.2	0.2	0.1	2	1	4	7.3	–11.8	30.4
Andean Comm.	0.1	3.1	24.2	16.3	2.7	2.1	1.0	1.2	0.9	0.3	0.2	71	84	23	6.2	88.4	–40.2
Total	0.8	4.6	25.7	18.4	4.1	4.0	3.3	3.6	4.0	3.2	1.6	100	100	100	7.1	36.7	–16.1

Source: IDB Integration and Regional Programs Department using UN-COMTRADE and Barbados Statistical Service data (Jan. 2006).
Note: Figures include domestic exports and re-exports.

Table A-IV-2. Barbados: Merchandise Re-exports to World and Selected Partners, 1994–2004

												Share (%)			Avg. Ann. Growth (%)		
(US$ millions)	1994	1995	1996	1997	1998	1999	2000	2001	2002	2003	2004	94–04	94–99	00–04	94–04	94–99	99–04
World	47	69	66	72	63	54	83	83	54	85	104	100	100	100	8.2	2.8	13.9
United States	5	8	6	6	7	5	6	7	7	5	10	9	10	8	7.8	1.8	14.1
Canada	1	4	3	1	0	1	1	1	1	0	1	2	2	1	−2.7	0.7	−6.0
CARICOM	11	17	16	13	15	20	22	22	17	16	17	24	25	23	4.6	13.5	−3.7
Latin America	0	1	1	5	1	1	1	1	1	2	0	2	2	1	−10.7	17.9	−32.3
FTAA	17	29	26	24	23	27	30	30	26	24	28	36	39	34	5.2	10.3	0.3
EU (25)	1	4	1	2	3	2	5	5	5	5	2	5	4	5	0.1	10.0	−8.8
Rest of World	29	36	39	46	37	25	48	48	23	56	75	59	57	61	9.9	−3.3	24.9
CARICOM												Share (%)			Avg. Ann. Growth (%)		
(US$ millions)	**1994**	**1995**	**1996**	**1997**	**1998**	**1999**	**2000**	**2001**	**2002**	**2003**	**2004**	**94–04**	**94–99**	**00–04**	**94–04**	**94–99**	**99–04**
Guyana	0.3	0.7	0.3	0.2	0.2	0.4	0.4	0.3	1.7	0.3	0.9	3	2	4	10.5	5.6	15.5
Jamaica	1.2	2.2	4.2	1.5	2.1	2.0	2.8	4.2	1.7	1.8	1.6	14	14	13	2.8	10.4	−4.4
OECS	6.4	8.2	6.7	7.1	8.8	11.4	11.3	10.7	9.5	9.8	10.1	54	53	55	4.7	12.2	−2.4
Grenada	0.9	0.8	0.8	0.9	1.4	1.3	1.5	1.5	1.5	1.4	1.7	7	7	8	6.4	7.7	5.1
St. Lucia	1.9	1.6	1.9	2.3	2.8	3.6	4.4	4.1	2.9	2.8	3.9	17	15	20	7.4	13.6	1.5
St. Vincent	1.0	1.6	1.8	1.3	1.7	2.2	1.8	2.0	1.6	1.9	2.0	10	10	10	6.8	15.7	−1.5
Trinidad & Tobago	2.4	5.6	3.0	3.4	2.7	5.0	5.9	4.5	2.6	3.1	2.4	22	24	20	0.1	16.0	−13.7
Other CARICOM	0.4	0.5	1.3	0.9	1.3	1.4	1.3	1.9	1.7	1.3	1.8	7	6	9	15.9	28.5	4.5
Total	**10.7**	**17.2**	**15.5**	**13.1**	**15.2**	**20.3**	**21.7**	**21.6**	**17.2**	**16.3**	**16.8**	**100**	**100**	**100**	**4.6**	**13.5**	**−3.7**
Latin America												Share (%)			Avg. Ann. Growth (%)		
(US$ millions)	**1994**	**1995**	**1996**	**1997**	**1998**	**1999**	**2000**	**2001**	**2002**	**2003**	**2004**	**94–04**	**94–99**	**00–04**	**94–04**	**94–99**	**99–04**
Central America	0.2	0.7	0.9	1.6	0.6	0.1	0.1	0.3	0.9	0.8	0.1	45	49	40	−8.0	−12.7	−3.0
Chile	0.0	0.0	0.0	0.0	0.0	0.0	0.0	0.0	0.0	0.0	0.0	1	2	1	—	−32.6	—
Dom. Rep.	0.0	0.0	0.1	0.0	0.1	0.1	1.2	0.2	0.2	0.0	0.0	14	3	31	−16.8	20.3	−42.4
Mexico	0.0	0.0	0.0	0.0	0.0	0.0	0.0	0.3	0.0	0.5	0.0	7	1	15	—	—	−33.1
MERCOSUR	0.0	0.0	0.1	0.1	0.0	0.0	0.0	0.1	0.1	0.1	0.0	4	3	5	−16.8	−20.5	−13.0
Andean Comm.	0.1	0.0	0.0	2.8	0.1	0.6	0.0	0.0	0.1	0.2	0.0	29	43	7	−20.4	51.1	−58.1
Total	**0.4**	**0.7**	**1.1**	**4.5**	**0.9**	**0.9**	**1.4**	**0.9**	**1.3**	**1.7**	**0.1**	**100**	**100**	**100**	**−10.7**	**17.9**	**−32.3**

Source: IDB Integration and Regional Programs Department using UN-COMTRADE and Barbados Statistical Service data (Jan. 2006).
Note: Bunkers (fuel sales to ships and aircraft) make up a majority of re-exports to the Rest of World category.

Table A-IV-3. Barbados: Merchandise Imports from World and Selected Partners, 1994–2004

												Share (%)			Avg. Ann. Growth (%)		
(US$ millions)	1994	1995	1996	1997	1998	1999	2000	2001	2002	2003	2004	94–04	94–99	00–04	94–04	94–99	99–04
World	614	766	829	995	1,022	1,067	1,156	1,068	997	1,195	1,094	100	100	100	5.9	11.7	0.5
United States	247	312	361	452	427	454	480	449	440	453	477	42	43	42	6.8	12.9	1.0
Canada	38	39	42	39	42	46	48	40	37	42	52	4	5	4	3.3	3.8	2.8
CARICOM	117	123	124	124	163	163	230	218	158	285	125	17	15	18	0.6	6.9	–5.2
Latin America	40	52	64	76	52	54	60	49	55	59	68	6	6	5	5.4	6.3	4.6
FTAA	442	525	591	691	684	717	818	757	690	839	722	69	69	69	5.0	10.2	0.2
EU (25)	100	132	138	149	173	176	179	179	174	201	177	16	16	17	5.9	12.0	0.2
Rest of World	73	108	101	156	165	175	159	132	133	155	194	14	15	14	10.3	19.1	2.1

CARICOM												Share (%)			Avg. Ann. Growth (%)		
(US$ millions)	1994	1995	1996	1997	1998	1999	2000	2001	2002	2003	2004	94–04	94–99	00–04	94–04	94–99	99–04
Guyana	8	9	8	9	8	9	9	10	11	12	16	6	6	6	7.1	1.9	12.4
Jamaica	18	17	14	12	11	11	10	10	9	10	11	7	10	5	–5.1	–8.8	–1.2
OECS	11	13	11	11	12	13	15	14	13	13	13	8	9	7	1.3	2.6	0.0
St. Lucia	2	2	3	2	3	5	6	7	6	5	5	3	2	3	11.0	22.9	0.3
St. Vincent	6	6	5	4	4	3	4	4	4	4	4	3	3	2	–3.2	–11.0	5.3
Suriname	0	0	1	0	1	5	5	8	7	12	1	2	1	3	9.0	84.3	–35.6
Trinidad & Tobago	79	83	89	91	131	124	190	174	116	236	83	76	73	79	0.6	9.5	–7.6
Other CARICOM	1	1	1	1	1	1	2	1	2	2	2	1	1	1	6.2	10.0	2.6
Total	117	123	124	124	163	163	230	218	158	285	125	100	100	100	0.6	6.9	–5.2

Latin America												Share (%)			Avg. Ann. Growth (%)		
(US$ millions)	1994	1995	1996	1997	1998	1999	2000	2001	2002	2003	2004	94–04	94–99	00–04	94–04	94–99	99–04
Central America	7	7	6	9	13	16	14	11	12	15	14	20	17	23	6.8	17.6	–2.9
Chile	0	0	1	1	1	1	3	1	2	2	2	2	1	4	16.4	16.6	16.2
Dom. Rep.	2	2	2	4	4	3	2	3	3	3	3	5	5	5	6.5	15.9	–2.1
Mexico	1	1	5	10	11	12	11	11	10	11	18	16	12	21	30.9	59.0	7.8
MERCOSUR	9	9	8	19	12	12	20	13	18	19	23	26	20	32	10.4	6.8	14.2
Andean Comm.	21	32	42	34	12	10	10	10	9	8	9	31	45	16	–8.6	–13.6	–3.3
Total	40	52	64	76	52	54	60	49	55	59	68	100	100	100	5.4	6.3	4.6

Source: IDB Integration and Regional Programs Department using UN-COMTRADE.

Table A-IV-4. Barbados: Composition of Trade, 1994–2004

Exports to World (US$ millions)	1994	1995	1996	1997	1998	1999	2000	2001	2002	2003	2004	Share (%) 94–04	Share (%) 94–99	Share (%) 00–04	Avg. Ann. Growth (%) 94–04	Avg. Ann. Growth (%) 94–99	Avg. Ann. Growth (%) 99–04
Food	51	66	100	94	76	73	71	74	69	62	73	41	41	40	3.6	7.5	–0.1
Ag Raw Mat's	0	2	1	1	0	0	0	0	1	1	0	0	0	0	–0.9	–5.8	4.3
Ores & Metals	0	1	1	1	1	1	0	0	0	0	2	0	0	0	13.2	7.9	18.8
Fuels	0	1	0	0	6	11	16	9	6	12	15	4	2	7	84.6	220.4	6.3
Manuf Goods	82	99	108	113	111	108	98	89	80	85	81	53	56	50	–0.1	5.6	–5.5
Goods n.e.s.	0	1	1	1	1	3	4	4	5	3	2	1	1	2	19.8	53.8	–6.6
Total	135	168	212	210	195	197	190	176	161	165	174	100	100	100	2.6	7.9	–2.4

Exports to CARICOM (US$ millions)	1994	1995	1996	1997	1998	1999	2000	2001	2002	2003	2004	Share (%) 94–04	Share (%) 94–99	Share (%) 00–04	Avg. Ann. Growth (%) 94–04	Avg. Ann. Growth (%) 94–99	Avg. Ann. Growth (%) 99–04
Food	15	22	28	28	31	30	29	29	29	22	24	30	31	29	5.0	14.9	–4.1
Ag Raw Mat's	0	0	0	0	0	0	0	0	0	0	0	0	0	0	21.8	24.7	19.0
Ores & Metals	0	0	0	1	0	0	0	0	0	0	1	0	0	0	11.2	–3.2	27.7
Fuels	0	0	0	0	6	11	16	9	6	12	15	8	3	13	86.9	228.5	6.3
Manuf Goods	39	50	59	60	60	57	52	51	48	51	51	61	65	56	2.8	8.0	–2.3
Goods n.e.s.	0	0	0	0	0	1	1	1	1	1	0	0	0	1	52.7	137.7	–1.9
Total	54	73	87	89	97	99	99	89	85	86	92	100	100	100	5.5	12.9	–1.4

(continued on next page)

Table A-IV-4. Barbados: Composition of Trade, 1994–2004 *(continued)*

Imports from World												Share (%)			Avg. Ann. Growth (%)		
(US$ millions)	1994	1995	1996	1997	1998	1999	2000	2001	2002	2003	2004	94–04	94–99	00–04	94–04	94–99	99–04
Food	126	140	146	176	171	174	178	183	188	204	220	18	18	18	5.7	6.6	4.8
Ag Raw Mat's	17	18	22	27	28	29	27	24	26	23	25	2	3	2	3.7	11.0	–3.2
Ores & Metals	6	9	9	10	11	16	12	11	9	10	14	1	1	1	9.1	22.6	–2.9
Fuels	53	65	82	83	82	66	133	124	63	184	14	9	8	9	–12.5	4.2	–26.5
Manuf Goods	409	532	566	698	728	781	802	723	707	771	817	70	70	69	7.2	13.8	0.9
Goods n.e.s.	3	2	3	2	3	2	3	3	3	4	4	0	0	0	5.5	–6.6	19.1
Total	614	766	829	995	1,022	1,067	1,156	1,068	997	1,195	1,094	100	100	100	5.9	11.7	0.5
Imports from CARICOM												**Share (%)**			**Avg. Ann. Growth (%)**		
(US$ millions)	**1994**	**1995**	**1996**	**1997**	**1998**	**1999**	**2000**	**2001**	**2002**	**2003**	**2004**	**94–04**	**94–99**	**00–04**	**94–04**	**94–99**	**99–04**
Food	33	36	32	36	35	40	41	45	44	49	54	24	26	23	5.0	3.8	6.3
Ag Raw Mat's	2	2	2	3	3	3	3	4	5	6	6	2	2	2	12.7	11.2	14.2
Ores & Metals	0	0	0	0	1	2	1	1	1	1	1	0	0	0	20.4	52.3	–4.9
Fuels	35	30	38	31	69	61	129	119	59	179	9	41	32	49	–12.7	11.9	–32.0
Manuf Goods	47	55	51	53	55	57	56	50	50	51	54	32	39	26	1.5	4.1	–0.9
Goods n.e.s.	0	0	0	0	0	0	0	0	0	0	0	0	0	0	–9.4	–18.8	1.0
Total	117	123	124	124	163	163	230	218	158	285	125	100	100	100	0.6	6.9	–5.2

Source: IDB Integration and Regional Programs Department using UN-COMTRADE and Barbados Statistical Service data (Jan. 2006).
Note: Excludes re-exports.

Table A-IV-5. Barbados: Services Exports by Area, 1990–2003

															Avg. Ann. Growth (%)			
(US$ millions)	**1990**	**1991**	**1992**	**1993**	**1994**	**1995**	**1996**	**1997**	**1998**	**1999**	**2000**	**2001**	**2002**	**2003**	**90–03**	**90–95**	**95–00**	**00–03**
Transportation	7	9	9	10	14	16	18	21	21	23	25	22	21	23	10.2	20.1	8.6	–2.1
Travel	508	467	470	534	603	622	659	663	712	687	723	697	658	758	3.1	4.1	3.0	1.6
Commercial	112	118	111	119	168	205	224	249	262	287	308	313	324	343	9.0	12.8	8.4	3.7
Communication	22	24	25	20	23	25	26	26	27	27	28	29	31	32	3.0	2.7	2.1	5.0
Insurance	55	35	42	41	54	50	60	65	68	75	80	85	87	90	3.9	–2.0	9.8	4.3
Financial	—	—	—	—	—	50	55	59	64	68	75	71	70	74	—	—	8.4	–0.7
Other Business	35	59	44	58	91	80	83	98	102	117	125	128	136	147	11.6	17.8	9.4	5.5
Government	27	24	28	27	29	23	26	27	29	32	35	36	38	42	3.5	–3.2	8.9	6.2
Total	654	618	619	689	814	867	927	959	1,024	1,029	1,090	1,069	1,041	1,166	4.5	5.8	4.7	2.3
															Shares (%)			
Share (%)	**1990**	**1991**	**1992**	**1993**	**1994**	**1995**	**1996**	**1997**	**1998**	**1999**	**2000**	**2001**	**2002**	**2003**	**90–03**	**90–95**	**95–00**	**00–03**
Transportation	1.0	1.4	1.5	1.4	1.8	1.9	1.9	2.1	2.1	2.2	2.3	2.1	2.0	2.0	1.9	1.5	2.1	2.1
Travel	77.7	75.6	76.0	77.5	74.1	71.8	71.1	69.2	69.5	66.7	66.3	65.3	63.2	65.0	69.7	75.2	69.0	65.0
Commercial	17.2	19.2	17.9	17.2	20.6	23.7	24.2	25.9	25.6	27.9	28.2	29.3	31.2	29.4	25.0	19.5	26.0	29.5
Communication	3.4	3.9	4.0	2.9	2.8	2.9	2.8	2.7	2.6	2.7	2.5	2.8	3.0	2.8	2.9	3.3	2.7	2.8
Insurance	8.4	5.7	6.8	5.9	6.7	5.8	6.5	6.8	6.7	7.3	7.3	7.9	8.4	7.7	7.1	6.5	6.7	7.8
Financial	—	—	—	—	—	5.8	6.0	6.2	6.3	6.6	6.9	6.6	6.7	6.3	4.7	1.2	6.3	6.6
Other Business	5.4	9.6	7.1	8.4	11.1	9.2	9.0	10.3	10.0	11.3	11.5	11.9	13.1	12.6	10.4	8.6	10.3	12.3
Government	4.1	3.8	4.6	3.9	3.5	2.6	2.8	2.8	2.8	3.1	3.2	3.4	3.6	3.6	3.4	3.7	2.9	3.5
Total	100.0	100.0	100.0	100.0	100.0	100.0	100.0	100.0	100.0	100.0	100.0	100.0	100.0	100.0	100.0	100.0	100.0	100.0
Memorandum:																		
Services Exports	**1990**	**1991**	**1992**	**1993**	**1994**	**1995**	**1996**	**1997**	**1998**	**1999**	**2000**	**2001**	**2002**	**2003**				
As % of GDP	38.2	36.6	39.0	42.0	47.1	46.6	46.7	43.8	43.3	41.7	42.3	42.2	41.1	44.4				
As % of total exports	74.9	74.9	72.0	75.3	78.0	73.9	72.9	73.0	76.1	77.1	75.4	75.7	79.4	77.7				

Source: IDB Integration and Regional Programs Department using IMF-BOPS (November 2005).

Table A-IV-6. Barbados: Tourism Statistics, 1992–2003

Visitor Arrivals by Origin

Persons													Shares (%)				Avg. Ann. Growth (%)			
(thousands)	1992	1993	1994	1995	1996	1997	1998	1999	2000	2001	2002	2003	92–03	92–95	95–00	00–03	92–03	92–95	95–00	00–03
Stopover	385	396	426	442	447	472	512	515	545	507	498	531	49.1	48.2	49.6	49.3	3.0	4.7	4.3	–0.8
U.K.	89	100	123	127	140	156	187	203	227	217	193	203	17.0	12.8	17.5	19.9	7.8	12.6	12.4	–3.7
U.S.	111	113	109	112	112	108	106	105	112	107	123	129	11.7	13.0	11.1	11.2	1.4	0.4	0.0	4.9
CARICOM	53	52	51	59	57	64	70	86	87	80	90	97	7.3	6.3	7.1	8.4	5.7	3.5	8.3	3.5
Canada	50	49	52	53	55	59	60	57	60	52	47	50	5.6	6.0	5.8	4.9	–0.1	2.2	2.4	–6.1
Others	83	82	89	91	84	86	89	63	58	51	45	53	7.6	10.1	8.0	4.9	–4.0	3.2	–8.6	–3.2
Cruise	400	429	460	485	510	518	507	433	533	528	523	559	50.9	51.8	50.4	50.7	3.1	6.6	1.9	1.6
Total	785	825	885	927	957	990	1,019	947	1,078	1,035	1,021	1,090	100.0	100.0	100.0	100.0	3.0	5.7	3.1	0.4

Visitor Arrivals by Purpose of Visit

Persons													Shares (%)			Avg. Ann. Growth (%)		
(thousands)	1992	1993	1994	1995	1996	1997	1998	1999	2000	2001	2002	2003	96–03	96–00	00–03	96–03	96–00	00–03
Stopover	385	396	426	442	447	472	512	515	545	507	498	531	100.0	100.0	100.0	2.5	5.1	–0.8
Tourism	—	—	—	—	416	422	444	435	462	428	417	436	85.9	87.4	83.8	0.7	2.6	–1.9
Education	—	—	—	—	2	3	3	4	4	4	4	4	0.6	0.6	0.7	10.3	22.2	–3.8
Business	—	—	—	—	22	34	39	51	56	53	54	61	9.2	8.1	10.8	15.5	25.8	3.1
In transit	—	—	—	—	6	13	26	8	7	10	8	11	2.2	2.4	1.8	8.8	4.7	14.5
Others	—	—	—	—	1	1	1	18	16	12	14	19	2.0	1.4	2.9	67.6	135.0	6.8

Source: IDB Integration and Regional Programs Department using Barbados Ministry of Tourism data.

Appendix II

Table A-IV-7. Barbados: Trade Agreements

Partner Signature Date (Date Entered into Force)	Type of Arrangement	Implementation Status
WTO April 1994 (January 1995)	Multilateral trade agreement covering goods, services, and trade-related issues.	1994 Uruguay Round Agreements being implemented; Doha Round initiated in 2002.
CARICOM July 1973 (August 1973)	Broad integration arrangement including single market and economy (CSME), covering free movement of goods, services, capital and skilled persons, CET, right of establishment, macroeconomic policy coordination, harmonization of economic policies, and common sector policies (agriculture, industry, services, and transport).	Free trade in goods and CET established; single market partially implemented. Single economy pending.
Venezuela October 1992 (January 1993)	Preferential partial-scope agreement with CARICOM, offering improved market access to the Venezuelan market.	In force.
Colombia July 1994 (January 1995)	Preferential partial-scope agreement with CARICOM, offering improved access to the Colombian market. Revised May 1998 to include reciprocity for MDCs.	In force.
Dominican Republic August 1998 (December 2001)	Reciprocal FTA with CARICOM MDCs and non-reciprocal with LDCs. Trade: free for commodities; MFN for sensitive goods; services: reciprocal, but no timetable set. Includes investment and government procurement provisions.	In force.
Cuba July 2000 (December 2002)	Reciprocal trade liberalization (partial-scope) agreement with CARICOM, covering goods. Trade liberalization according to positive list approach. Provisions for trade promotion and special treatment of goods from export-processing zones (EPZs).	In force.
Costa Rica March 2004	Reciprocal FTA with CARICOM MDCs and non-reciprocal agreement with LDCs. Goods trade: free with some exceptions. Also provisions for dispute settlement, application of anti-dumping measures, and enhancement of SPS regulations.	Will enter into force as soon as member states complete administrative procedures for implementation.
EU/ACP Cotonou June 2000 (April 2003)	Partnership agreement maintaining non-reciprocal trade preferences for CARICOM until December 2007, and introducing negotiations toward an EPA. Immediately abolishes STABEX (compensatory finance scheme to stabilize export earnings), SYSMIN (mineral export assistance scheme), and Rum Protocol.	In force.
EPA between EU and CARIFORUM Signature pending	Reciprocal trade between EU and Caribbean region, with provision of aid. Will come into force in January 2008. Trade provisions will be imposed over a period of 10–12 years.	Negotiations are expected to conclude in December 2007.
FTAA Signature pending	Reciprocal FTA among 34 Western Hemisphere countries. Includes goods and services, government procurement, intellectual property, investment, AD/CVD, dispute settlement, and competition policy.	Negotiations began in April 1998 but are currently stalled.

CHAPTER V

Maximizing Tourism's Potential

Auliana Poon and Desmond Thomas

A. Introduction: Questions in Need of Answers

No analysis of Barbados' economy can afford to ignore the country's tourism industry. The industry has played a fundamental role in the economic transformation that has occurred over the last 40 years and that continues to be the very backbone of Barbados' economic performance. With the emergence of tourism, the Barbados economy has undergone a diversification of sorts from one dominated by agriculture, mainly sugar, to a predominantly service-oriented one. It now contributes directly 15–20 percent of total value added, and its actual impact on economic well-being in Barbados is considerably more pervasive. It has provided the foundation for an economic performance that has resulted in moderately but steadily rising living standards and job generation, improving social conditions and macroeconomic stability.

As Barbados strives to raise economic performance to meet development needs and the challenges of growing competitiveness in a liberalizing international environment, the tourism industry will continue to play a central role. For a small country like Barbados, meeting these challenges will require answers to a number of critical questions. In the first place, there is the question of the steps necessary to revitalize the industry through the increased exploitation of traditional strengths and the exploration of untapped potential, in order to satisfy current market tastes. These steps call for attention to the question of what strategic areas to emphasize and invest in, having regard to new attractions, niches and marketing plans.

A second question is how tourism can be a springboard to greater diversification, through increased linkages within the domestic economy and through the utilization of the supply of well-trained human resources. Diversification is an imperative for Barbados for two main reasons:

(i) its role in reducing economic vulnerability resulting from the concentrated production structure; and

(ii) the physical limits on the expansion of tourism (or any other single industry, for that matter) resulting from the small size of the country. In this connection, diversification needs to be pursued within the industry itself, in terms of the range of attractions and types of tourism offered, as well as through linkages with related industries.

Thirdly, attention has to be paid to the institutional setting for tourism to promote efficiency and an adequate support climate for investment. Attention must also be paid to the creative development of the industry. Finally, there is the question of what adjustments need to be made in the industry to be able to take full advantage of the proposed arrangements under the new CARICOM Single Market and Economy (CSME) as well as the Free Trade Area of the Americas (FTAA), whenever the FTAA materializes.

The context for these considerations is one that Barbados shares, typically with other small countries. As a small country, its vulnerability is high, partly as a result of its relatively undiversified production structure. The aftermath of the 9/11 attacks in the US has exposed the underlying vulnerability and fragility of the industry and of the economy as a whole, and has confirmed the need to strengthen competitiveness in order to withstand such shocks. The country's vulnerability has also been brought into focus by the recent spate of highly active hurricane seasons that have spared Barbados any serious damage but have wreaked severe destruction in neighbouring islands. The context for analysis of the Barbados tourism industry includes an evaluation of its features and special characteristics, which the Barbadians have nurtured for their industry and which have helped it to strive so far. Also crucial is an evaluation of the weaknesses that need to be overcome.

There also has to be a strong awareness of the economic environment within which the Barbadian product exists in terms of the performance, activities and conditions of the industry's international rivals. Consequently, this study pays careful attention to comparative and competitive analysis, taking account of the international environment. This study is informed by a review of relevant studies of the industry in Barbados and other Caribbean countries. In addition, given the pervasive nature of the industry in Barbados, the study takes into account the macroeconomic and social factors that impact significantly on the competitiveness of the industry. The study is also consistent with the emphasis placed by the Barbados authorities on human resource development, and ensures that the obligations and opportunities of social groups are accounted for explicitly.

A final underlying element worth stressing in the context of Barbados is its natural environment. As a small country, Barbados has to be concerned about its carrying capacity in terms of additional pressure on its natural environment resulting from tourism, and care has to be taken not to overextend its infrastructure. Issues like possible beach and land erosion, waste management in all forms, and air pollution all assume major proportions in the restricted island conditions of Barbados. In this context, growth of the industry has to be based primarily on added value through quality rather than through volume.

Methodology

An analysis of the competitiveness status and requirements of the tourism industry in any one country faces one major problem at the very outset. Tourism is not a homogeneous product but rather a complex package of sub-products, each with its own unique attributes and appeal, and there are strong subjective factors determining the appeal of the product. Costs are determined by a variety of independent factors (e.g., the role of location in transportation costs), and different characteristics and sub-products carry unequal weights in different places. Ultimately, the competitive context for the Barbados industry is the global market, especially given the relatively liberalized nature of this market. Inevitably, however, for practical purposes, there is the tendency to focus on the performance of the Barbados industry in the Caribbean context. Except for a few passing references to competitors outside the Caribbean, this analysis will focus primarily on competition with other regional players.

This chapter relies mainly on interviews and survey techniques to gather information about the characteristics, performance and prospects of the Barbados tourism industry. The people surveyed may be divided into three groups: (1) tour operators in important markets serving as sources of visitors for Barbados—the UK, the US and Germany; (2) key stakeholders and experts on the industry from the public and private sectors in Barbados; and (3) tourists visiting Barbados. The UK is the largest market for stopover visitors to Barbados, and the US is the second largest market, so tour operators from these areas could provide valuable evaluations. Continental Europe represents a promising market in terms of the numbers of actual and potential visitors, hence the importance of the German surveys.

The surveys aimed mainly to:

- obtain feedback from clients on the strengths of Barbados as a tourism destination;
- determine the support required in order to better promote and sell Barbados;
- examine the opportunities and constraints encountered;
- find out how Barbados is rated as a tourism destination; and
- determine which countries are perceived to be Barbados' competitors;

A list of sources that were consulted is attached as Appendix 2.

The survey instrument used to gather information was discussed with the Barbadian authorities before being finalized and administered in Barbados, the UK, the US and Germany. According to the list received from the London office of the Barbados Tourism

Authority (BTA), there are more than 50 tour operators and wholesalers (mainly web-based companies) in the UK that offer holidays to Barbados. Of these tour operators, about half can be considered generalists, one-third long-haul specialists, one-quarter Caribbean specialists and just a handful of smaller operators, villa specialists, and others. In terms of the response rate, 30 out of 54 UK tour operators surveyed responded. The survey in Barbados was carried out through personal interviews and by e-mail. There was a 40% response in terms of the number of hotels but a 30% response in terms of the number of rooms represented. Representatives of the Barbados Hotel and Tourism Association (BHTA) were also interviewed for the Association's perspective.

Secondary research and the analysis of existing information also formed an integral component of the market research that was carried out in order to determine key trends and developments in the sector that impinge on Barbados' competitiveness. Statistical analyses were also carried out from available data in order to determine the current and historical performance of the country's tourism sector.

Organization of the Chapter

Section B of this chapter presents recent performance trends and forecasts of the Barbados tourism industry, including the composition of arrivals and the pattern of behaviour and preferences of tourists. Section C uses the survey data to identify Barbados' relative position with respect to its main competitors. Section D identifies strengths and weaknesses in the provision of Barbados' tourism services and Section E provides recommendations for improving the efficiency and effectiveness of the sector.

B. Recent Trends

The tourism sector plays a crucial role in the economic development of Barbados. The 500,000-plus visitor arrivals spend millions of dollars in the Bajan[1] economy. According to the World Travel and Tourism Council (WTTC) 2004 Travel and Tourism Economic Research, Barbados' travel and tourism was expected to generate Bds$3,242.6 million (US$1,621.3)[2] of economic activity in 2004. In terms of direct impact, the industry generated 28,040 jobs or 19.8% of total employment and US$420.3 of Gross Domestic Product (15.8% of total GDP). However, utilizing the Tourism Satellite Account (TSA) framework in measuring the sector—since travel and tourism touches all sectors of the economy, direct and indirectly—one finds that the impact is much greater. According to the TSA research for Barbados, travel and tourism directly and indirectly accounted for 82,426 jobs or 58.3%

---

[1] Bajan: a fond way of saying Barbadian, especially used in Caribbean circles.

[2] US$1.00 = Bds$2.00.

of total employment and US$1.3 billion of the GDP, equivalent to 52.2% of the total GDP. Given the fact that tourism has been traditionally measured by the contribution of the hotels and restaurants sector, the TSA research needs to be continued so that the measurement of tourism in terms of its direct and indirect impact might help stakeholders to understand the wider importance of tourism and to carry out critical planning.

Arrivals

Following modest beginnings in the late 1950s, the modern tourism industry in Barbados received a significant boost with the construction of a major hotel project in the 1960s. At the same time, the Government established the Barbados Board of Tourism, which represents an important milestone in terms of the decision to give policy support to the promotion of tourism. Since then, the industry has grown steadily as indicated by visitor arrivals, eventually overtaking other productive sectors in terms of contribution to total GDP. Stopover visitor arrivals grew on average by 4 percent per annum from 1993 to 2004, despite a cumulative 9 percent contraction in 2001 and 2002, while cruise passenger arrivals grew by 5 percent annually. Significantly, the tourism industry advanced in a climate of general macroeconomic stability most of the time, interrupted by relatively brief episodes of fiscal and balance-of-payments instability. Since the early 1990s, the growth of the industry has helped to establish a pattern of falling unemployment, reflecting its labour-intensive character, as the rate went from an average of 16 percent in the 1980s to 9 in 2005.

Arrivals follow a seasonal pattern as Barbados receives 44% of its annual arrivals in the winter months from December to April. July and August are also good months, accounting for a total of 19% of annual arrivals. High visitor arrivals in July and August partly reflect the significant contribution to Barbados tourism by returning nationals living abroad. However a fairly even pattern of arrivals is emerging with May, June, September and October being the only months with arrivals below 8 percent of the annual total. The seasonal pattern underlines Barbados' image as a tropical escape for visitors from the temperate zones during the winter months and hence its susceptibility to changes in weather conditions during the winter season. Not surprisingly, the months with the most activities, holidays and events receive the highest percentage of visitors—March (Easter/Opera), July (Kadooment/Crop Over) and December (Christmas)—reflecting the role of 'special events' in boosting the industry. (See Figure V-1.)

Closer examination reveals some other significant features of the Barbados industry. The industry has a two-tiered structure with two distinct product lines described colloquially as the West Coast and South Coast products. The West Coast properties and attractions cater to a luxury market while the South Coast caters to a more moderately priced market, providing a range of accommodations and attractions. This two-tiered structure represents a form of diversification within the tourism industry that helps to give the industry some resilience as the two markets are not equally affected by business cycles and economic shocks.

In terms of markets, the United Kingdom yields the largest number of Barbados' tourist arrivals—two-fifths of the total. The United States follows with nearly a quarter of all visitors. Canada generates nearly one tenth, Europe another 5% and the Caribbean and Rest of the World the remaining 22%.

Figure V-1. Seasonally Adjusted Percentage of Arrivals

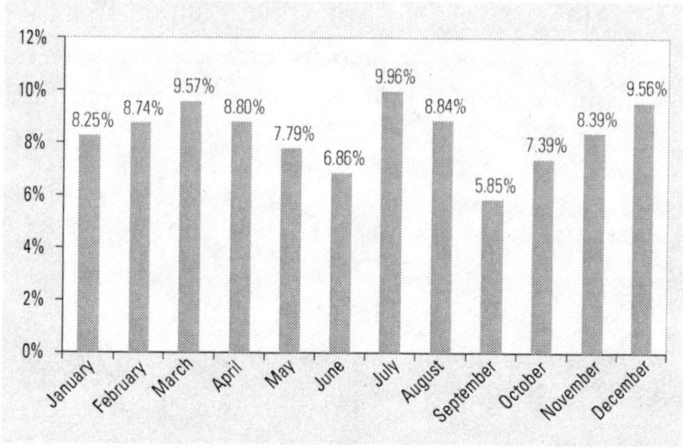

Source: Tourism Intelligence International, 2005.

Among the positive signs that can be seen in Barbados are strong emphases on:

- the conservation of the environment;
- the promotion of heritage tourism;
- measures aimed at involving local communities in the tourism sector;
- consensus and buy-in of stakeholders in tourism policy and planning processes; and
- a wider economic development strategy that recognizes and exploits tourism as a lead sector with a strong focus on developing the wider services sector (telecommunications, medical services, business and professional services, information technology), and major efforts aimed at supporting the small, intimate Barbados-owned hotels.

In addition, key product improvements—such as the South Coast Sewage System, a complete facelift to the St. Lawrence Gap and the development of the Graeme Hall Swamp—continue to add value, quality and variety to the Barbados tourism offering.

In terms of performance forecasts, tour-operator surveys provided positive projections of growth in Barbados tourism. According to the UK Tour Operator Survey, over 50% of the respondents expected Barbados to be a source of just 0–10 percent growth for their companies in the next three years; another 20 percent expected growth of 11–20 percent; 7% indicated that their companies would grow by 21–30 percent; and 11 percent thought that Barbados would be for them a source of growth of more than 30 percent. None of the respondents expected a decline in the number of passengers to Barbados.

In the US market, 40 percent of the respondents expected Barbados to be a source of growth for their companies of just 0–10 percent, however 20 percent expected 11–20 percent growth, 20 percent expected 21–30 percent growth and 10 percent expected 30 percent growth over the next three to five years. In the German market over 60 percent of the respondents expected Barbados to be a source of growth of just 0–10 percent for their companies in the next three years. Limited airlift capacity from Germany to Barbados was identified by 40 percent of respondents as a major constraint to the growth of visitor arrivals from that market.

Evidently, the future prospects for tourism arrivals to Barbados are encouraging. Taking account of survey results, Tourism Intelligence International forecasts that international tourism arrivals will grow approximately 22 percent between 2004 and 2010 (an average of 4.4 percent annually). According to the Tourism Satellite Account research, total travel and tourism demand is also forecast to grow to US$3.1 billion in 2014, with direct jobs expected to grow to 39,973 in 2014. Rising visitor arrivals could place significant pressure on Barbados' carrying capacity, necessitating the examination of strategic choices for raising value added and employment through qualitative changes rather than through increases in visitor arrivals.

Visitor Profile and Trip Characteristics

The average visitor to Barbados is one who resides in the UK and visits Barbados for vacation. He or she will be on his/her first, fourth or greater visit and will definitely come to Barbados again. This visitor travels as part of a couple and stays an average of 12 days. He or she spends an average of US$159 per day, 61% of it on accommodation. Seventeen percent (17%) is spent on meals and drinks, 7 percent on shopping, 5 percent on transportation, 4 percent on entertainment and the remaining 6 percent on souvenirs and other items. (See Figure V-2.) In terms of average daily expenditures, the biggest spenders are visitors from the "other" category of market, followed by the US visitor with US$168.50, other Europe US$161.01 and the UK with US$159.01. Canadian and Caribbean visitors both spend under US$140 each per day on average.

Figure V-2. Percentage Visitor Expenditure by Item

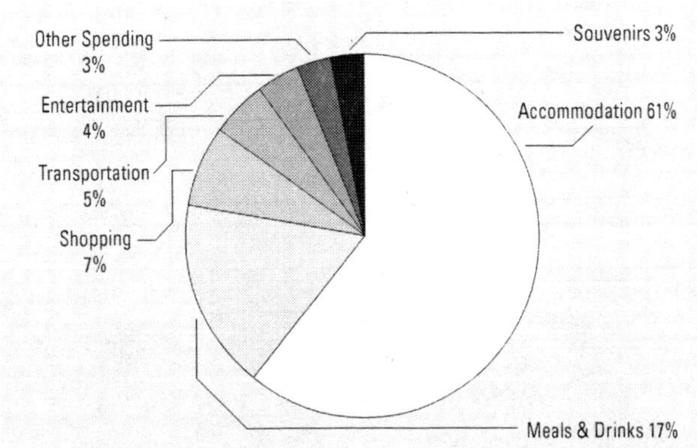

Source: Barbados Stayover Visitor Survey 2003 and 2004 Quarterly Publications.

An important feature of the Barbados tourism product is the customer loyalty it inspires, a loyalty reflected in the high proportion of repeat visits. In fact, more than 40 percent of the visitors are on repeat visits, and nearly a quarter of them are on their fourth visit, at least. Consistent with this repeat characteristic, feedback from the destination survey indicated a high level of customer satisfaction with the Barbados experience. Nearly all visitors, and over 90 percent of respondents to the UK Tour Operators Survey, indicated satisfaction. Nearly 50 percent of the visitors to Barbados travel with their spouses or partners, nearly 30 percent travel with their families, and just over 10 percent each travel either alone or in a group. The Canadian visitor stays the longest, 12.5 days, followed by the UK visitor with 12.1 days. They are followed by the average visitor from other European markets with 10.9 days while the US visitor stays an average of 9.2 days. Overall, on average, a visitor to Barbados spends 10.5 days.

Ultimately, what matters is the total visitor expenditure per stay. In that regard, we can obtain an estimate by combining the average length of stay with the average daily spending of individuals in each group. On that basis, the UK visitor comes out in the lead with over $1,900 spent per stay, followed by visitors from continental Europe with $1,755 and the Canadians with $1,750. This information is relevant and valuable for the purpose of planning and determining correct strategies for promotion of the industry.

In terms of the interests and tastes of visitors indicated by the Barbados Stayover Visitor Survey, more than 70

Figure V-3. Client Satisfaction According to Destination Survey

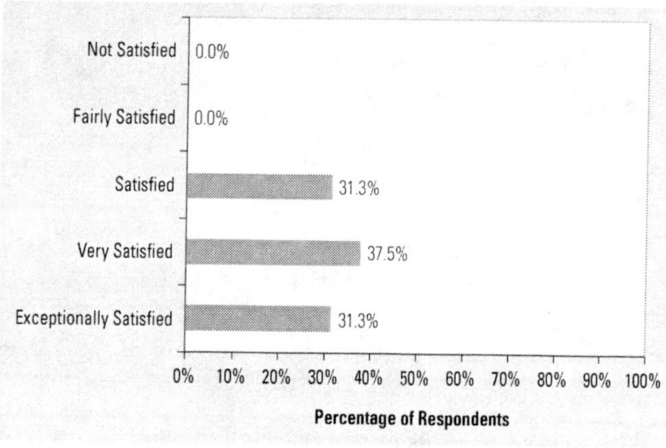

Source: Tourism Intelligence International Destination Survey, 2005.

Figure V-4. Major Interests of Visitors to Barbados

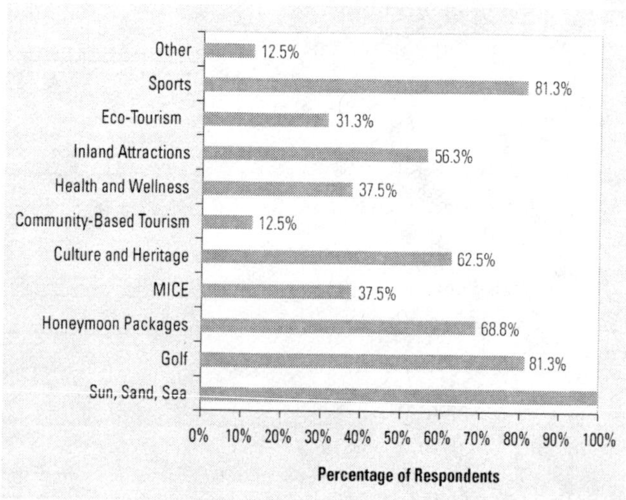

Source: Tourism Intelligence International Destination Survey, 2005.

percent of Barbados' visitors travel for vacation, 6.7 percent travel for business, 5.8 percent for honeymoon/wedding, 4.7 percent under the category of visiting friends and relatives (VFR) and 4.6 percent for vacation and business combined, with the rest split among meetings, incentives, conventions and exhibitions (MICE), golf, festivals, sports and other. According to the destination survey, the vacation element is further broken down by major interests (see Figure V-4). The major interests for visitors were sun, sand and sea followed by golf, sports, honeymoon packages, culture and heritage, and inland attractions.

C. Competitors and Competitiveness

Key Competitors

Compared to goods and other services, the tourism industry operates in a relatively competitive international market insofar as visitors are free to travel widely with relatively few official restrictions. The main endowment factors would be location advantages, transport facilities, safety considerations relating to national conflicts, and significant health considerations. Performance in terms of visitor arrivals and expenditure depends typically also on attractions, natural and contrived, transport infrastructure (access via air, sea, land), institutional support with respect to customs and immigration, tourism investment and marketing costs, and market conditions in the countries where the visitors typically originate. In this kind of global market, national tourism bodies, not surprisingly, tend to devote considerable resources to promotion and marketing aimed at raising market penetration and market share.

In the case of Barbados, key initial considerations, apart from its natural attractions, are its proximity to the large North American market, its English-speaking status and its historical and cultural links to the UK. Consequently, the Barbados industry has developed on the basis of a strong dependence on the US and UK markets. Diversification in terms of marketing efforts to increase penetration in other markets is an important option to sustain the growth of the industry.

Against this background, Barbados has to strengthen its capacity in all facets of the industry in order to maintain market share and the growth of its economy. There is a general recognition that as a 'mature' destination, Barbados has to pay attention to the ongoing revitalization of attractions in line with customer demands. In addition, competition in the tourism industry at large and from the Caribbean in particular is growing as new emphasis (including investment activity) is placed on tourism in other destinations such as Cuba and the Dominican Republic. Improved infrastructure, service orientation and provision and institutional support will be vital to industry performance.

Depending on which group was surveyed, whether Barbados' stakeholders in the destination survey or the tour operators' surveys in the US, UK or German markets, the main competitors to Barbados were identified as St. Lucia, Antigua, Jamaica, Cuba, Mexico (Cancun), the Dominican Republic and Dubai. The Cayman Islands, St. Maarten and Aruba also ranked highly as competitors in the perception of US tour operators. The destination survey identified the Dominican Republic, Jamaica and Cuba as the top three competitors followed by Mexico, St. Lucia and Dubai. The main reason for the competitive advantage of these destinations was lower cost, or, as one respondent put it, "more service for less price".

Figure V-5. Main Competitors to Barbados

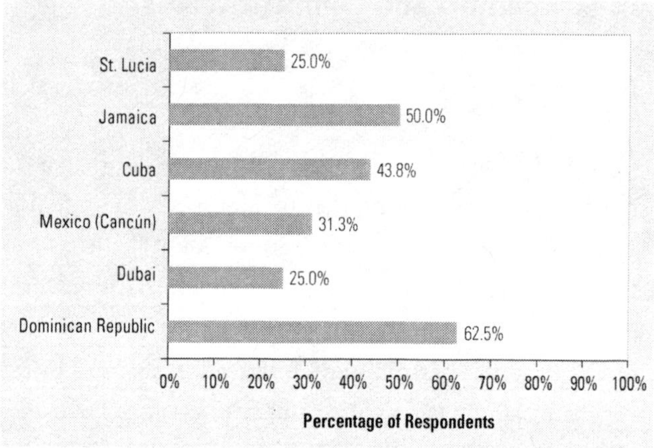

Source: Tourism Intelligence International Barbados Destination Survey, 2005.

Interestingly, the top competitors identified by tour operators were not the same as those mentioned in the destination survey. In Barbados, there is a perception that the Dominican Republic and Cuba are Barbados' major competitors while in the marketplace Antigua and St. Lucia are seen as the top competitors. This demonstrates the multi-faceted nature of the tourism industry and market, and the fact that competitive performance depends on a complex range of factors. It may be noted also that Barbadian respondents identified Dubai as a competitor and tour operators interviewed did not. Most tour operators have specialized departments handling specific regions. Consequently, tour operators tend to see competitors within the Caribbean region (their area of competence) rather than outside. However, it is critical to take account of competitive challenges to Barbados from outside the region, including destinations as far away as Dubai, Mauritius and Thailand.

In terms of growth of stayover arrivals, if we use 1993 as a base year, Barbados is fifth in terms of its performance vis-à-vis its competitors, behind Cuba, which has performed exceptionally well, St. Lucia, the Dominican Republic and Cancun. The relatively flat growth of arrivals in the Barbados case may be attributed partly to a strategy that places low priority on mass tourism and also underlines the physical size constraints of the island. It also serves to underline the importance of qualitative service in any future development strategy for the industry.

In terms of market share for arrivals, the highest belongs to the Dominican Republic (14.7%), Cancun (10.3%), Cuba (8.9%), the Bahamas (7.9%) and Jamaica (6.7%). Barbados received 2.6% of the 19 million arrivals to the Caribbean in 2002. In terms of market shares of visitor expenditure, the highest belong to the Dominican Republic (14.5%), Cuba (9.5%), the Bahamas (9.3%), Mexico (7.6%), and Jamaica (6.4%). Barbados received 3.4% of the US$18.8 million in visitor expenditure to the Caribbean in 2002. Barbados' low market shares are not surprising, given the small size of the island. In fact, if population size is used as a scaling factor, Barbados' market shares come out well ahead of those of the other countries. Another important factor is that Barbados is the leader among Caribbean competitors with regard to average visitor expenditure. Barbados receives US$1,301.06 per visitor compared to Dominican Republic with US$979.31 and Mexico US$726.98. The high visitor expenditure in Barbados has to do with a range of factors including the average lengths of stay and the mix of countries from which visitors originate. It also underlines the characterization of Barbados' tourism in general as an 'up-market' product.

Figure V-6. Relative Performance of Selected Competing Destinations and Barbados, 1993–2003

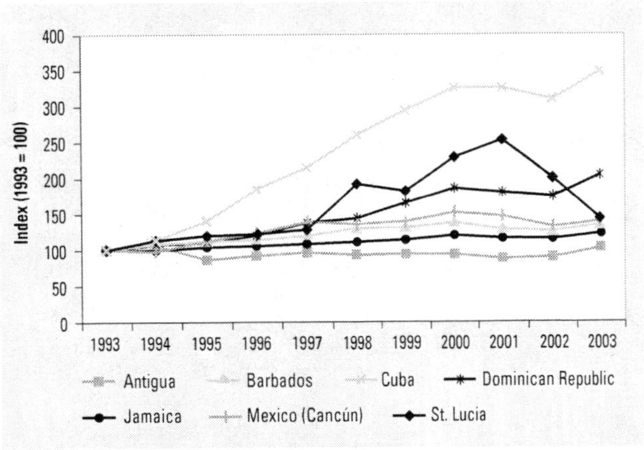

Source: Caribbean Tourism Statistical Report, various years.

Figure V-7. Average Visitor Expenditure Per Tourist by Barbados and Its Competitors, 2002

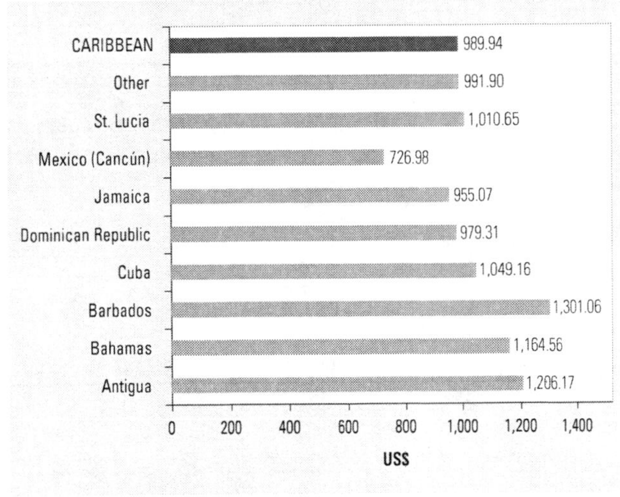

Source: Caribbean Tourism Statistical Report, 2003.

Sources of Competitiveness

The study examined the competitive performance of Barbados' tourism with respect to a range of product characteristics and market niches surveying the opinions of the tour operators and local stakeholders. The product characteristics were selected to include things that related to the quality of attractions, safety, facilities, and processes such as immigration and customs. Market niches related to broad objectives that tourists aim to experience, including health and wellness, eco-tourism, culture and heritage, etc. Barbados was ranked against its seven closest competitors in these areas. With regard to some features, the rating varied significantly among markets. For example, Barbados received a high rating for airline connections from the UK tour operators, but a low rating from the US operators. In this way, the surveys were useful in identifying specific weaknesses to be worked on.

In terms of comparisons with its major competitors, the surveys placed Barbados consistently in the lead. As Table V-1 shows, Barbados ranked first with respect to nine out of 11 product characteristics and first, second or third out of eight destinations in eight out of nine market niches. These results serve to underline the high quality of the Barbadian tourism product over a wide range of characteristics. Significantly, the main area where Barbados has a low score is with regard to 'value for money'. This score also underlines the perception of Barbados as a relatively high-cost destination and the need to focus on measures to improve service quality, attractions and productivity in order to remain competitive. In terms of overall rating with each product characteristic equally weighted, Barbados comes out ahead of the pack followed by St. Lucia and the Bahamas.

Figure V-8. Rating of Barbados Product Characteristics on Destination

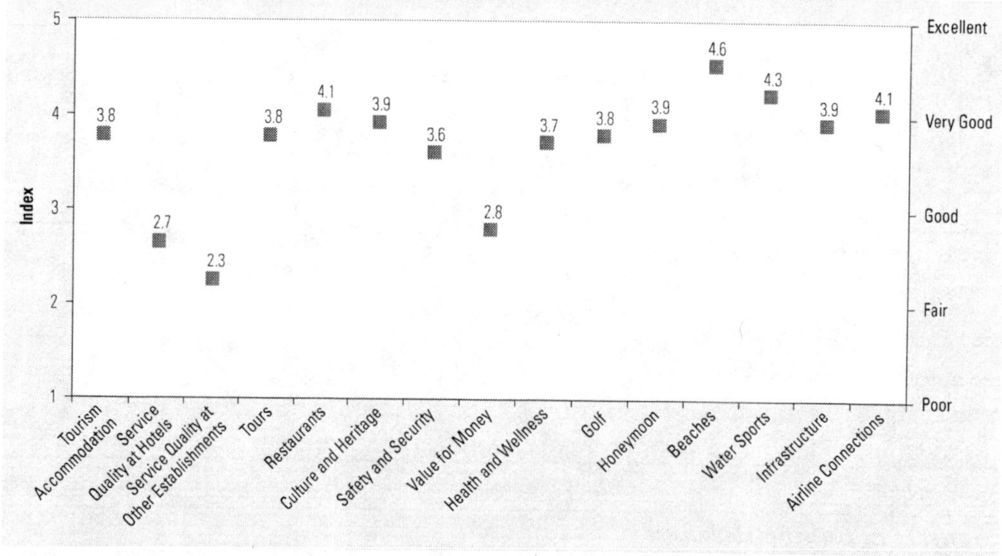

Source: TII Barbados Destination Survey, 2005.

Table V-1. Benchmarking of Barbados by Product Characteristics—All Tour Operators

Product Characteristic	Barbados	Antigua	Bahamas	Cuba	Dom. Rep.	Jamaica	Mexico	St. Lucia
Value for Money	6th	7th	8th	5th	**1st**	3rd	2nd	4th
Service Quality	**1st**	3rd	4th	8th	7th	5th	6th	2nd
Safety & Security	**1st**	2nd	3rd	8th	7th	6th	5th	4th
Beaches	3rd	**1st**	2nd	8th	5th	4th	7th	6th
Accommodation	**1st**	4th	6th	8th	7th	2nd	3rd	5th
Sightseeing & Attractions	3rd	6th	7th	5th	8th	**1st**	2nd	4th
Airline Connections	**1st**	4th	3rd	8th	7th	2nd	5th	6th
Immigration & Customs	**1st**	4th	3rd	8th	7th	5th	6th	2nd
Restaurants	**1st**	6th	2nd	8th	7th	4th	3rd	5th
Watersports	**1st**	6th	3rd	8th	7th	2nd	4th	5th
Environment	**1st**	3rd	4th	8th	7th	5th	6th	2nd
Overall	**1st**	5th	3rd	8th	7th	4th	6th	2nd

Table V-2. Benchmarking of Barbados by Market Niche—All Tour Operators

Market Niche	Barbados	Antigua	Bahamas	Cuba	Dom. Rep.	Jamaica	Mexico	St. Lucia
Eco-tourism	3rd	2nd	5th	3rd	7th	8th	4th	**1st**
Health & Wellness	**1st**	3rd	5th	7th	8th	4th	6th	2nd
Honeymoon	**1st**	2nd	4th	7th	8th	5th	6th	3rd
Culture & Heritage	2nd	5th	7th	**1st**	8th	4th	3rd	6th
Sun, Sand & Sea	3rd	**1st**	2nd	7th	5th	4th	8th	6th
Inland Attractions	4th	6th	8th	2nd	7th	3rd	**1st**	5th
Community Based	2nd	8th	5th	2nd	6th	**1st**	3rd	4th
Golf	**1st**	7th	3rd	8th	6th	2nd	5th	4th
MICE	3rd	6th	2nd	8th	7th	4th	**1st**	5th

In terms of overall rating with each niche equally weighted, Barbados comes out ahead for health and wellness, honeymoon and golf.

Competitor Assessment: Input Costs

One of the most significant input costs within the tourism sector, as well as in many other sectors, is that of labour. Wages within the tourism sector in Barbados are among the highest in the region, lower only than Antigua's. For example, monthly wages in the tourism sector in Barbados are more than 130% greater than in Jamaica, for an equivalent 40-hour work week. (See Table V-3.)

Relatively high wage costs are a feature of some Caribbean countries, notably the ones where average standards of living are high. Indeed, as Table III-21 shows, wage costs for selected categories of workers are consistently lower in Barbados than in the Bahamas and not much higher than those in Antigua. High wage costs reflect the strength of organized labour unions and an approach to achieving an equitable distribution of growth gains. However, Barbados faces an additional challenge of inflexibility in the labour market (tough regulations on the hiring and firing of staff and low flexibility in job descriptions). Labour inflexibility affects productivity levels in the hotel industry by restricting the ability of employers to utilize labour resources efficiently. Labour-market regulations and conditions in the tourism sector need to be addressed in order to improve the competitiveness of the industry.

Table V-3. Minimum Monthly Wage in the Tourism Sector, 2003

Country	Minimum Monthly Wage Tourism Sector	Hours Per Work Week
Antigua	US$405.00	40 hours
Barbados	US$360.00	40 hours
Cancún	US$221.00	48 hours
Dominican Republic	US$165.00	44 hours
Jamaica	US$155.00	40 hours
St. Lucia	US$352.00	40 hours

Source: The Internet.

High wages and other input costs, such as utilities, food and beverages, and import duties, in the Caribbean tourism industry in general, and in Barbados' in particular, have an impact on levels of profitability and rates of return in the tourist accommodation sector. Unfortunately there are limited data available with which to quantify the extent to which these costs impact on the profitability of hotels. The latest available data are from a Panell, Kerr, Foster study done on the Caribbean hotel industry in 1994. It is important, however, that the type of data generated from this study be captured annually so that Barbados can effectively benchmark itself against its competitors. A sample of the data from 1994 is provided in Table V-4.

According to the foregoing data, Barbados' costs as a percentage of revenue are similar to those of other Caribbean islands. While it is necessary to reduce operating costs and restore price competitiveness, Barbados has to continue to be competitive in terms of quality.

Table V-4. Comparative Revenue and Cost Factors

	Caribbean	Barbados	Antigua & Barbuda	Jamaica	Cancún	St. Lucia
Revenues						
Rooms	45.95%	53.40%	43.95%	53.65%	60.1%	29.6%
Food & Beverage	29.45%	37.1%	37.75%	34.8%	32.75%	34.65%
Other Operated Departments	24.60%	9.5%	18.3%	11.55%	7.15%	35.75%
Total Revenues	100.0%	100.0%	100.0%	100.0%	100.0%	100.0%
Departmental Costs & Expenses						
Rooms	13.1%	19.2%	12.4%	14.1%	13.05%	8.15%
Food & Beverage	23.45%	31.8%	34%	22.95%	22.65%	34.65%
Other Operated Departments	13.55%	5.0%	7.85%	3.7%	3.2%	13.7%
Total Dept. Costs & Expenses	50.1%	56.0%	54.25%	40.75%	38.9%	56.50%
Total Operated Departments' Income	49.9%	44.05%	45.7%	59.2%	61.15%	51.7%

Source: Pannell, Kerr, Foster study, 1994.

Pricing and Packaging by Barbados and Its Competitors

Given the high proportion of European visitors to Barbados and other Caribbean destinations and the high cost of air transportation from European countries, high airfare expenditure is a significant cost factor. Barbados is the second most costly Caribbean destination in terms of airfare from the UK via British Airways (February 2005). Antigua is first and St. Lucia is third. The range of costs of tour packages to Barbados reflects the two-tiered structure of the industry—the moderate prices of the South Coast product versus the luxury offerings of the West Coast product. In this connection, the continuing competitiveness of the industry requires that productivity and service be at exceptional levels in the luxury section and be at least comparable with competitors in the other section. In addition, there is evidence of the scope for investment in and expansion of both the West Coast and South Coast products. Future directions for the industry are linked to decisions about the future of the sugarcane industry, which may result in the release of more land for alternative uses.

Customer Satisfaction Compared

After generating an average rating for all tour operators sampled in the survey, one finds that Barbados has emerged as the leader in the majority of product characteristics. The main area of weakness reported by the surveys is 'value for money'. However, from a casual observation of the data, there appears to be an inverse relationship between average cost levels of destinations and value-for-money performance, indicating a misconception of the two concepts as essentially referring to the same thing. The challenge facing Barbados is to ensure that service and productivity are consistent with high value for money at all levels of the industry.

Figure V-9. Average Rating of Barbados among All Tour Operators

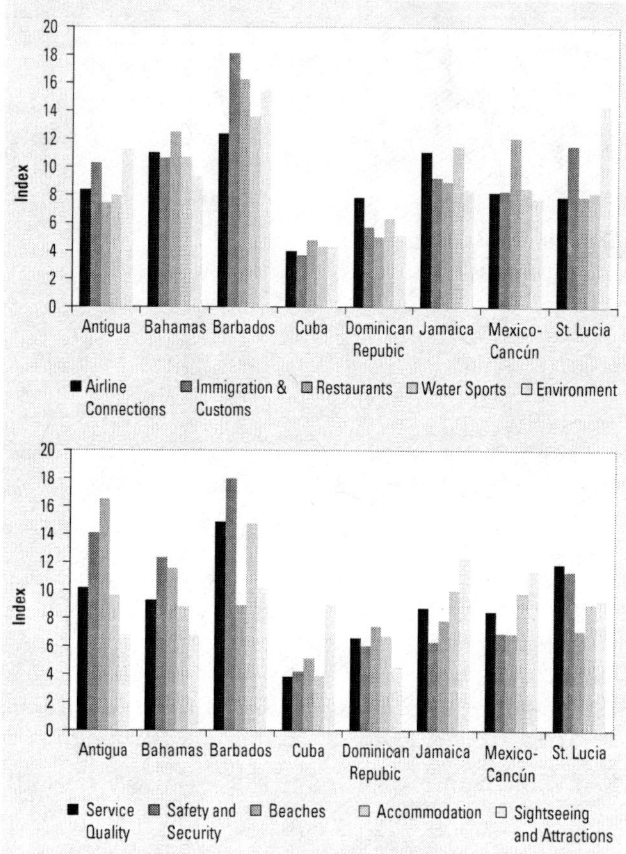

Source: Tourism Intelligence International Tour Operator Surveys, 2005.

D. Strengths and Weaknesses in Tourism Services

Results from the Surveys Regarding Top Market Niches

For the destination survey, key stakeholders in Barbados were asked to rank the top three types of holidays (in order of importance) that Barbados has the most potential to offer. This was done to determine current strengths for ongoing attention and areas of potential growth that could benefit from new investment. The results show that sun, sand and sea was the top type of holiday, followed by honeymoon, culture and heritage and MICE. (See Figure V-11.)

According to the UK Tour Operator Survey, nearly all respondents (96%) indicated that they offered beach holidays (sun, sand and sea) as part of their current program. This was closely followed by honeymoon packages (77%) and, thirdly, health and wellness (54%).

Furthermore, only four respondents indicated that they offered sports tourism, one offered culture and heritage tourism and one offered eco-tourism. All of these responses confirm that the current market shares for these types of holidays are relatively small. This is even more true for market niches not mentioned (i.e., MICE, community-based tourism

Figure V-10. Rating of Barbados on Value for Money —All Tour Operators

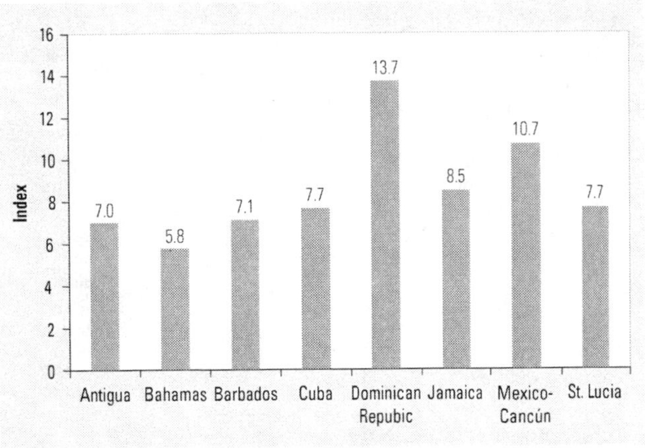

Source: Tourism Intelligence International Tour Operator Surveys, 2005.

and inland attractions). Using all survey data, we see that the top types of holidays with growth potential are sun, sand and sea, health and wellness, and honeymoon.

One area of high potential singled out in the surveys was health and wellness tourism. This would include investment in spa facilities and other services and facilities for which there is growing market demand and for which Barbados' conditions might be particularly suitable. This could be combined with eco-tourism, which was identified as having high potential also. Eco-tourism can provide a basis for the country's relatively undeveloped inland tourism.

Strengths and Weaknesses

The major strengths identified by the local respondents were climate/weather, safety, friendliness of people, accessibility and infrastructure. According to the data from the UK Tour Operator Survey, the major strengths of Barbados are airline connections, its beaches and the friendliness of its people. Accommodation, safety and security, and service follow as the other strengths. In terms of weaknesses, 46% of the tour operators indicated that Barbados was an expensive destination while 27% mention the poor level of service. However 35% of the tour operators thought that the quality of service was a strength.

Figure V-11. Top Types of Holidays with Potential for Barbados

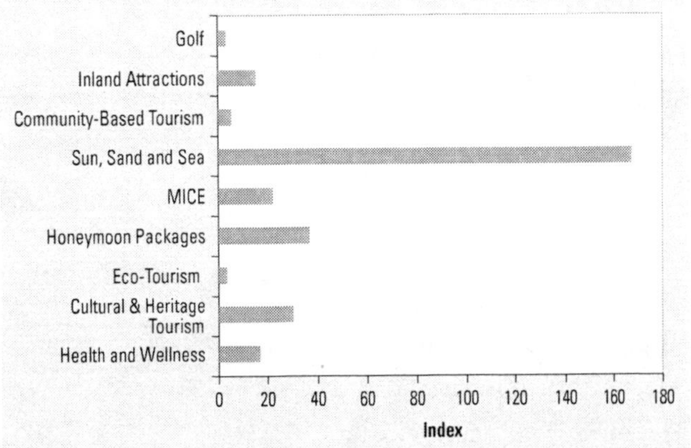

Source: Tourism Intelligence International Tour Operator Surveys, 2005.

There were only three main weaknesses identified by

the respondents: poor quality of service (62.5%), expensiveness of destination (43.8%) and an ageing product (25%). These results reflect the perceptions of local operators and other stakeholders, whose perceptions appear to be more critical than those of external operators. They indicate a consciousness locally of the need for improvements in service levels in order to provide exceptional experiences that will help visitors to feel that visiting Barbados provides value for money. This consciousness is an important prerequisite for consensus building on policy and strategy to improve the industry, and for the commitment to take the necessary action.

Figure V-12. Top Types of Holidays with Growth Potential—All Tour Operators

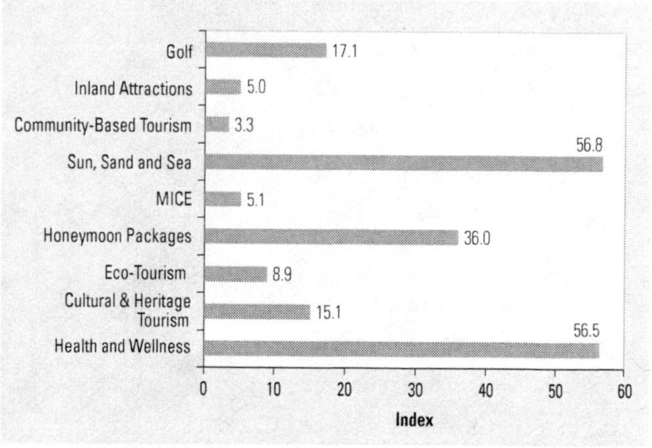

Source: Tourism Intelligence International Tour Operator Surveys, 2005.

Barbados has many strengths on which to capitalize: airline connections, friendliness of people, beaches, accommodation, and safety and security. However it needs to continue to rejuvenate its product and train its human resources in order to enhance its competitive edge over those who provide the same "sun, sand and sea" experiences. The country needs to be innovative and to create new experiences. At the same time, there is a real potential to develop the health, wellness and honeymoon markets. Notably, these are the very markets in which St. Lucia, a major competitor to Barbados, has developed special strengths.

Figure V-13. Strengths Identified within the Destination Survey

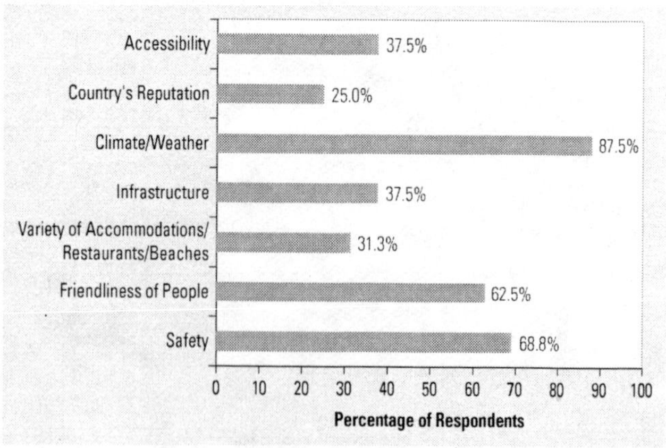

Source: Tourism Intelligence International Tour Operator Surveys, 2005.

E. Conclusions and Recommendations

Lucrative Market Niches

Survey results show that Barbados is still ranked high in the minds of local stakeholders, visitors to the island and tour operators that service the destination. "Sun, sand and sea" is, and will continue to be, the key driving force for tourist arrivals in Barbados. Nonetheless, it is important for Barbados to look beyond sun, sand and sea for avenues to future growth. The development of other, related niche markets and products is expected to be a key source of such growth.

The surveys in Barbados' main generating markets shed some key insights. The spa and wellness sector shows good potential as an area for development in the view of tour operators. Another area identified as having leading potential is the honeymoon market. Culture and heritage and the MICE market were also identified by Barbadian respondents as having potential for development within the Barbadian tourist industry.

Figure V-14. Strengths Identified within the U.K. Tour Operator Survey

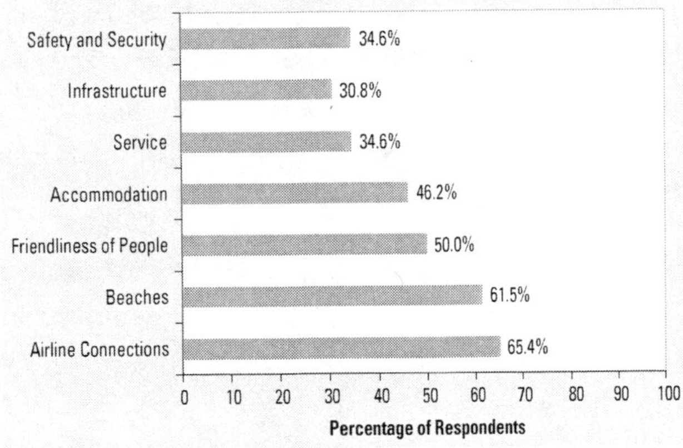

Source: TII UK Tour Operator Survey, 2005.

Table V-5. SWOT* Matrix

Strengths	Weaknesses
Airline Connections Friendliness of People Beaches Accommodation Safety and Security	Ageing Product Poor Service Quality Levels Value for Money
Opportunities	**Threats**
Health and Wellness Market Honeymoon Market	Competition—Regional and International Natural Disasters

*SWOT = strengths, weaknesses, opportunities, and threats.

Recommendations for Increasing Competitiveness

Barbados has to examine ways in which to position itself within the health and wellness niche, paying attention to the infrastructure needed for hospital, health facilities, spas, etc. In addition, an examination of the key competitors in this segment (e.g., Thailand) can provide insights about future marketing strategies as well as product development.

It is critically important for Barbados to explore fully the potential of the health and wellness sector. But which specific niches in this sector will be most suitable for future development in Barbados? With which partners? In which ailments, if any, should Barbados specialize? These are among questions that need to be answered.

The further development of the wedding and honeymoon market needs to be fostered with greater marketing and promotion. In this regard, key competitors are St. Lucia and Jamaica as well as the Sandals chain of hotels throughout the Caribbean.

The MICE market also has great potential. However, this potential needs to be exploited, particularly with regard to the existing conference facilities at Sherbourne and the new Hilton Hotel. More research is needed on this market, specifically addressing group size, choice of facilities, linkages with other sectors and hotel facilities. Out of this research should come a detailed product and market development plan for this sector.

Finally, for the bread-and-butter "sun, sand and sea" market, it is critically important to develop and improve on attractions and create more—and more interesting—things to do in Barbados. What is really needed here is the movement of the product from mere attraction to the creation, orchestration and delivery of exceptional experiences.

Appendix 1 – References

1. Annual Statistical Digest 2004 – Central Bank of Barbados
2. Barbados Cruise Passenger Survey April–June 2004
3. Barbados Cruise Passenger Survey January–March 2004
4. Barbados Economic and Social Report 2002
5. Barbados Stayover Visitor Survey January–March 2004
6. Barbados Stayover Visitor Survey October–December 2003
7. Barbados Travel & Tourism Forging Ahead – The 2004 Travel & Tourism Economic Research – World Travel & Tourism Council
8. Barbados: Agriculture's Competitiveness, Final Report Feb. 2005 – Reed Hertford
9. Business Barbados 2005
10. Caribbean Hotel Trends 1994 – Pannell, Kerr, Foster Consulting
11. Caribbean Tourism Statistical Report 2002–2003
12. Financial Statement – Economic & Financial Policies of Government 2001 – Ministry of Finance and Economic Affairs, Barbados
13. Hotel Industry Study 1998 – Horwath Caribbean
14. Socio Economic Report for Barbados – Tourism Sector, 1992 – Dr. Auliana Poon
15. The Caribbean – The Impact of Travel and Tourism on Jobs and the Economy – World Travel & Tourism Council
16. Tourism Development Act, 2002–7
17. Worldwide Hotel Industry Survey 1999 – Horwath

Appendix 2 – List of Sources Consulted

- Ministry of Tourism
- Barbados Hotel and Tourist Association
- Central Statistical Office (CSO)
- Caribbean Tourism Organisation (CTO)
- The Internet
- International Association of Conventions and Visitor Bureaus (IACVB)
- Barbados Tourism Authority (BTA)
- Central Bank of Barbados
- Ministry of Finance and Economic Affairs
- Tourism Intelligence International
- Travel Agent Handbook
- Travel Agent Magazine
- Travel Weekly
- Travel and Tourism Intelligence
- Travel Industry Association
- World Tourism Organisation (WTO)
- World Travel and Tourism Council (WTTC)

Annex I

Some Public-Policy and Institutional Issues

The Case of the Agricultural Sector in Barbados

A. Strategic Vision and Policy Framework

In recent years, governments have initiated a process of transforming their role. In this new posture, they aim to:

- adopt a coordinating and facilitating as opposed to an implementation role;
- reduce their intervention and involvement in the market;
- be more all-inclusive and participatory; and
- concentrate its regulatory role to trade and food safety issues.

The Barbados Government is currently in this process. However, its rate of change is influenced by the country's traditional commercial, social and political realities as they impact on the agricultural and rural sectors and the need to preserve its fragile ecosystem. For example, the Government had to intervene directly in the sugar industry to prevent a crisis in the financial sector, and by extension, the economy, when a number of plantations were on the brink of bankruptcy.

In the current international environment, the Government may wish to increase the rate of this transformation. However, this must be accompanied by an intensification of efforts in education, including policy formulation, and informatics and technological development. This would enable it to smoothly and painlessly transfer some of its responsibilities to the private and civil society and simultaneously, be reasonably assured that Barbadian agri-entrepreneurs can compete in an environment that is free and fair even if unprotected by high tariffs.

This transformation should be complemented by a redirection—not reduction—of Government expenditure. In addition, state and para-government agencies involved in agricultural and rural development must be subjected to intra- and inter-reorganization so as to maximize the benefits accruing from their interventions.

The Government is currently completing the preparation of a Framework Document for the periods, 2002–2012, which is likely to set out its Vision and Strategy for the "new" Agriculture and its preferred role. The Programmes and projects detailed therein could benefit from the elements of the Jagdeo Initiative[1] and thus be consistent with initiatives to reposition agriculture in the entire region.

Recommendation #1 – *Government should complete and publicize its policy framework (2002–2012) for agricultural and rural development. This would facilitate effective dialogue with all relevant stakeholders so as to get their "buy in".*

B. Public Resources and the Agricultural Institutions

Public Resources

Throughout the period, 1989–90 to 2001–02 total agriculture expenditure (excluding "allied agencies involved in agricultural and rural development) ranged between 2.5 and 2.9 percent of total GDP. However, expenditure in 2001 was 28 percent of the agricultural GDP (Table A-1). This was considerably larger than that the percentage for each of the five selected Latin American countries. However, the actual and relative small size of Barbados, where fixed costs would represent a reasonably high percentage of total costs, may be exacerbating the difference.

Targeted development projects, which include a miscellany of programs, such as investments in marketing infrastructure, 'land-for-the-landless", and AIDS prevention training for staff of the Ministry of Agriculture and Rural Development (MARD), attracted the most resources (35.7%). This was followed by integrated rural development (15.2%), natural resources conservation (13%), research and extension (12.4%), health/protection (12.2%), internal program support (9.4%) and agricultural planning/development plus information services (2.1%).

When compared to the other countries, Barbados spent more on natural resources conservation. This would be in response to its fragile ecosystem, particularly its shallow soils, and the need to protect its beaches and reefs, which are critical for its important tourism sector. On the other hand, expenditures on research and extension and planning and information were relatively low. In the context of repositioning the agriculture sector where new and appropriate technology and more intense agri-entrepreneurial organization and

---

[1] A proposal led by CARICOM's Lead Head for Agriculture, President Jagdeo, that aims to operationalize the Regional Transformation Programme for Agriculture (RTP) by identifying ten constraints to reversing the declining importance of agriculture. Its implementation was approved by the CARICOM Heads of Government in July 2005.

Table A-1. Six LAC Countries: Public Expenditures in Agriculture by Object, Plus Indicators of the Scale of Agricultural Expenditures, circa 2001

	Barbados	Uruguay	Chile	Argentina	Peru	Colombia
Public Expenditure						
Agric. Planning/Development and Info. Services	2.1	5.7	5.6	n.a.	2.3	3.8
Research, Extension	12.4	21.6	8.5	56.5	1.0	29.7
Natural Resources Conservation	13.0	3.0	1.5	2.0	4.8	6.7
Health/Protection	12.2	14.0	16.5	11.1	2.5	7.2
Targeted Development Projects*	35.7	10.3	48.3	9.5	81.9	3.7
Integrated Rural Development*	15.2	5.7	2.8	20.6	0.0	23.0
Internal Program Support**	9.4	39.7	16.8	0.3	9.5	25.9
Total	100.0	100.0	100.0	100.0	100.0	100.0
Indicator						
Government Agric. Expenditures/Agric. GDP	28.0	10.8	7.0	1.5	5.0	0.7
Government Agric. Expenditures/ All Government Expenditures	2.5	2.6	2.5	0.4	1.8	0.5

Sources: M. Sader, *Gasto publico agrario en el Uruguay en el periodo 1985–2001* (Montevideo, Uruguay: OPYPA, 2003); G. Kerrigan, *Gasto publico hacia el sector agricola y desarrollo de áreas rurales: tablas por países* (Rome: FAO, 2001). Value added data are taken from the World Bank World Development Indicators. Public expenditures for countries other than Barbados are from the International Monetary Fund, International Financial Statistics. For Barbados, the data are based on the preceding table and data from the Ministry of Agriculture and Rural Development for the Financial Years 1999–05.

* Definitions are provided later in the sub-section.

** These include programs implemented by the responsible ministry, but not dealt with in other line items of public expenditure.

training, as well as greater public sensitization, would be required, this level of expenditure needs to be examined.

Agricultural Institutions

There are four allied agencies involved in agricultural and rural development. These are the Rural Development Commission (RDC), the Barbados Agricultural Development and Marketing Corporation (BADMC), the Barbados Agricultural Management Company (BAMC) and the Agricultural Development Fund (ADF). A brief description of their mandates and functions follows:

- The RDC has a mandate to work chiefly in the areas of road construction, home improvement and replacements, street light installation, investment capital for micro-enterprises (to date, almost 600 loans have been approved for about B$5.0 million), and the training of small entrepreneurs.

- The BADMC is charged with managing agricultural development projects and with some marketing functions. A proposal for its restructuring, which is under consideration, should also include the determination of appropriate criteria for its involvement in projects and marketing.
- The BAMC was established to manage a number of privately owned sugar plantations which were heavily indebted to the commercial financing houses and would have been foreclosed were it not for Government's financial and other intervention. Currently, it manages the majority of these plantations and the remaining factories. In the context of Government's plans to move from a sugar to sugar cane industry, the role, and functions and operations of the BAMC will need to be reviewed so as to minimize the current level of Government's support of Bds$20 million annually.
- The ADF, which was created in December 2001 and capitalized in 2002 with Bds$30 million, covers technical assistance and loans for working capital and equipment in agriculture in the Bds$50,000 to Bds$1.0 million range. Currently, the interest rate charged is 6.0 percent. Through February 2003, its loans totaled Bds$9.7 million—the poultry industry has been the largest borrower, with 12 percent of this total—and grants totaled Bds$12.5 million. It is managed by the Enterprise Growth Fund Limited (EGFL), and the MARD provides technical evaluations of all project applications.

The functions and responsibilities of these organizations appear to overlap. For example, both BADMC and ADF have loan functions. These Allied Agencies, along with the MARD, should be subjected to a comprehensive assessment so as to achieve greater synergies, coordination and cost benefit and, consequently, provide more streamlined support and service to the agricultural community.

In addition to MARD and the allied agencies, the following agencies support the activities within the agriculture and rural sectors:

- the Caribbean Agricultural Research and Development Institute (CARDI), a regional body;
- the Inter American Institute for Corporation on Agriculture (IICA) and the Pan American Health Organization (PAHO), both hemispheric bodies; and
- the United Nations Development Programme (UNDP) and the Food and Agriculture Organization (FAO), both international agencies.

There is also a long-standing, partially government-financed farmers' organization, the Barbados Agricultural Society (BAS). In recent years, it has embarked on a process of restructuring and a program to more readily embrace all segments of the agri- entrepreneurial sector.

Recommendation #2 – *In view of the importance of agriculture to the sustainability of the tourism sector, the key engine of growth, the Government should actively consider increasing its agriculture allocation as a percentage of total GDP. Similarly, in its leadership role to fashion a "new" agricultural sector that is knowledge-based, technologically driven and people-focused, MARD should allocate a greater percentage of its available resources to research, extension, planning and public-awareness programs.*

Recommendation #3 – *Within its policy framework and the annualized priorities the MARD, through the National Agricultural Commission, should lead the process of dialogue with the allied agencies, regional, hemispheric and international institutions and agri-entrepreneurial groups to ensure that their programs of work are complementary, supportive, and consistent with national policies and programs as set by the MARD through the National Agricultural Commission.*

C. Major Current Policies and Programs in Agriculture

This section describes: (i) a major program, Sugar Cane; (ii) some support services - agricultural health and food safety (AH&FS), research and extension, irrigation, marketing facilities and credit; and (iii) rural development programs, including Scotland District and Praedial Larceny.

Sugar Cane

As stated previously, the economic importance of the sugar industry has declined drastically. This situation was accepted by the Prime Minister in his 2003 Budget Speech when he stated that: ". . . it is pellucidly clear that the sugar industry in its present form as a producer of a primary commodity for export is doomed."

The continuing loss of trade preferences within the EU market has not been the sole factor for the decline in Barbados' sugar industry. Compared to other sugar producing countries, Barbados' sugar industry is small, production per factory is low whilst its field and employee productivity are acceptable. Further, at the current price (US$0.22 per pound of sugar) received, the Barbados industry covers its variable costs, but not all of its fixed costs. With the proposed 39% cut in prices over a three-year period, the economic position will worsen. However, because of the continuing significant social and environmental importance of the sugar cane plant to the national well-being, the Government has embarked on a program to find uses of the sugar cane plant that are viable and complementary to sugar. The sources of funds for the implementation of this program are, "targeted development projects"; BAMC for out-of-crop planting; a Cane Replanting Incentive Scheme; and a mechanism of price support for independent estates and small farmers.

The above schemes appear geared towards maintaining the farm production of sugar cane and do not explicitly address the development of new products, such as ethanol and fuel cane for electricity. These costs are probably subsumed in "targeted development projects" since work is ongoing. For example, in 2004, the BAMC launched a project to cultivate high-fibre sugar canes to provide Biomass to be used as a source of renewable energy. This would substitute for fossil fuels, which are currently used for electricity generation. At the projected yields, approximately 12,500 acres (5580 hectares) of "fuel cane" will be needed. With a vigorous planting program, it is estimated that this target, which represents 70% of 2002 planted acreage, could be reached in 2008.

However, the field logistics and techniques of having cane matured and harvested throughout the year (a requirement for electricity generation) and/or the possibility of using hydrocarbon fuels during the period of the year when sugar-based fuel is unavailable would have to be determined. This determination should be made as early as possible, as there are other benefits to be derived. For example, the significant reduction in hydrocarbon emissions as compared to electricity generated by fossil fuels would be more environmentally friendly and therefore attract "carbon credits". In addition, the juice derived in the extraction process (at projected 2008 average) would yield annually 11,000 tons of sugar, 50,000 tons of molasses or up to 25 million liters of ethanol.

There is no reported examination of the production of ethanol as another prime alternative commodity. However, since only 70% of the current planted acreage is needed for the cogeneration of electricity, and there is need to protect the landscape, most if not all of the remaining sugar cane lands could be used for ethanol production. Thus, there is need to urgently place ethanol production under the same scrutiny as was done for "fuel cane".

Although hard numbers have not been made available, circumstantial evidence suggests that revenues from the fuel and sugar or molasses or ethanol produced from an acre of sugar cane would be greater than that earned from sugar alone. Very rough estimates (Hertford 2005)[2] of this new model suggest that with petroleum prices at US$40.00 per barrel the net return per acre of fuel cane would be appreciable.

In October 2004, in an effort to achieve full participation, as was done for the reorganization of the rum industry, the Prime Minister met with many interested parties including representatives of the Barbados Light and Power Co. He urged them to proceed rapidly with the development of the sugar-cane industry. With the recent EU pronouncement on the cut in sugar prices, the Prime Minister's call is even more urgent. Further delays would result in additional uncertainty and damage to the agricultural sector and wider economy.

---

[2] Op. cit.

Recommendation #4 – *The Government should move rapidly to finalize (if not already done) the feasibility study and plan of action and move into the implementation stage. Further, because of the severe negative implications of a "failed" sugar industry to at least eight Caribbean countries, the regional and hemispheric development banks should actively consider the provision of concessionary loan and/or equity funding.*

Support Services

The major support services to the sector are AH&FS, research and extension, credit, marketing and irrigation facilities.

Agricultural Health and Food Safety (AH&FS)

As noted earlier, the Government spends about 8% of its agricultural budget on agricultural health—veterinary services, regulatory services, chiefly pesticide management and quarantine services, and food safety—Government Analytical Services, (GAS), MARD-administered laboratories that include food chemistry, food microbiology, water microbiology, inorganic chemistry, pesticide residues and trace organics, and related environmental projects, for example, sewerage projects. A brief description of these services follows:

Agricultural Health

Veterinary Laboratory. The main client of the veterinary laboratory is the poultry industry. However, the laboratory also deals with other animals, both wild and companion, including monkeys, that are a unique export for Barbados. For the poultry industry, which is the largest livestock industry in Barbados, the laboratory runs checks on all new birds for known and exotic pests and diseases. However, a recent study by the Caribbean Poultry Association revealed that the Barbadian poultry industry is not as competitive as its counterparts in the other poultry-producing countries in CARICOM, viz, Guyana, Jamaica, and Trinidad and Tobago, and also Brazil and the United States. This has implications for the sustainability of the industry within the CSME and the FTAA, if it were to be established, and in turn, the projected use and capitalization of the Veterinary Laboratory. The laboratory is staffed by six professionals; it requires more floor space; and many pieces of equipment require upgrading or replacing.

The Plant Protection Laboratory performs pathological and entomological determinations and provides support to plant quarantine and the Pesticide Control Board. The Laboratory identifies new pests and diseases, provides recommendations for chemical control of pests and for selected crops, and prepares and disseminates relevant literature. It has a staff of

34 – including four with a M.Sc and three with a B.Sc. Unfortunately none of the staff are accredited "specialists" who could produce accreditation for the Laboratory.

Plant Quarantine Services are available at three international ports – Grantley Adams Airport and the Bridgetown and St. Charles Seaports. These services provide surveillance, inspection, and other services to protect agriculture and its flora from harmful, exotic pests and disease. It has collaborated with CARICOM countries to develop phytosanitary protocols for trade in fresh agricultural produce and with Customs to broaden inspections to non-plant materials, wood products, and handicraft. It has also performed phytosanitary inspections and certifications of compliance for exports of local agricultural produce in accordance with the WTO's sanitary and phytosanitary standards (SPS) agreements, and it has worked for the importation of clean plants and related materials, including turf grass and sand, for Barbados' premier golf courses. It is reported as being short-staffed.

The Pesticide Control Board (PCB) was created in 1975 to regulate the use of agricultural chemicals for the control of pests and diseases. From 1975 to 2004, the number of agricultural chemical suppliers has dropped from eight to two. This reduction is said to be due to the absence of scale economics for agriculture chemical use and the reported ineffectiveness of the PCB. With respect to the latter, the practice of licensing approved pesticides for use for only one year has been questioned, having regard to the approval process and the time lag between approval and order and arrival in the country. The level of staffing is also reported to be a problem.

Food Safety

The Government Analytical Services (GAS) has five sections. The *Food Chemistry* Section of GAS performs analyses to satisfy quality control requirements of importing countries. Numerous specialized analyses are also performed on request (e.g., a characterization of cranberry cocktail products for Customs). *Food Microbiology* checks the wholesomeness of food, analyzing the presence of bacteria in samples provided by environmental health inspectors and other public and private agencies. The *Water Microbiology* Section checks ground-, surface-, marine-, and waste-water samples for the Barbados Water Authority, the Environmental Engineering Division, and businesses and other entities seeking ISO certification for their water. The *Inorganic Chemistry* laboratory does similar work on water, foliage, fertilizers, and sediment samples brought to it by a host of organizations. Over 7,500 samples are analyzed in a given year. The *Pesticide Residues* and *Trace Organics* Section conducts analyses of samples for pesticide residues, oils and grease, petroleum hydrocarbons, gasoline, diesel-range organics, and fuel oils.

The mandate of the Food Chemistry Section should be expanded to support better inspections of imported and other foods that are locally consumed, as well as food and food products for export. Although equipment for testing pesticide residues is available, training is needed for staff with post-graduate degrees working such equipment, as well as for staffers that can help them hasten the development and implementation of related methods and general quality assurance/quality control procedures. Maximum pesticide residue limits are clearly specified in Codex for the European Union; those, in turn, lead to definitions of "good agricultural practices" that should be widely disseminated on the Island.

What Needs to Be Done

More than ever the consumer is requiring safe food. It is the responsibility of the Government to ensure this compliance. This is particularly true for Barbados with its critically important tourism sector. In addition, sanitary conditions are essential for the facilitation of trade. Further, the greater movement of people and transport equipment increases the possibility of the introduction of invasive alien species (IAS)—plant and animal—that could threaten a country's agriculture and its biodiversity. An efficient, responsive, agile and respected AH&FS system/authority with adequately and appropriately trained staff, facilities and equipment is a necessity. In the context of the CARICOM Single Market (CSM), collaboration with the proposed Caribbean Agriculture Health and Food Safety Agency will be required. Consequently, the following recommendation is made:

Recommendation #5 – *The Government should expedite its plans for the establishment and operation of a National Agricultural Health and Food System/Authority. Within this context it should:*

- *Conduct an analysis of the current and future demand for these services;*
- *Rationalize the role, functions and staffing of the many existing facilities so as to ensure reduction or duplication in order to optimize the use of available resources;*
- *Seek to have, as far as possible, all of the facilities at one location;*
- *Develop a phased program for all facilities to conform to ISO-17025 standards;*
- *Implement a system in which the users will pay partially or totally for these services so as to reduce the financial burden on the Government;*
- *Approach development financial institutions to support the provision of financing to implement this program.*[3]

[3] The IDB has provided assistance to the Belizean Government for the establishment of a similar agency.

Agricultural Research and Extension

The public-sector expenditure data on agriculture showed agricultural research and extension activities to be fourth-ranked in Barbados (Table A-1). Furthermore, Barbados was seen to be spending far less of its agricultural budget on research and extension than were Argentina, Colombia, and Uruguay among the countries shown. Nonetheless, it should be pointed out that the data presented are expenditures only of the MARD and, in Barbados, agricultural research and extension are conducted in several places, in addition to MARD.

A significant amount of agricultural research is financed and performed by MARD, although it is more applied and adaptive than basic like that of the UWI. There is no "Director of Research". This function is assumed by the Chief Agricultural Officer in MARD. One of his deputies serves as Director of Crops Research and another as the Director of Livestock Research. Fisheries research in the Department of Fisheries is supervised by the Permanent Secretary of MARD.

Operating out of the Central Agronomic Research Station (CARS), crop research covers three general areas of work: food crops, non-food crops, and plant protection, including entomology, pathology and plant quarantine. Current work in food crops includes hot peppers (the target is yield increases), herbs and spices (where new seed materials are being screened, assessed and evaluated in local growing conditions), onions (yields are being improved through varietal selection and irrigation), and root crops, potatoes, sweet potatoes, and yams (where the target is yield increases through plant density changes and alternative fertilizer applications).

The chief accomplishment cited by crops researchers since 2001 is the better understanding of the management of key aspects of the hot-pepper production system. In addition, a good stock of pepper germplasm has been accumulated. There are eight professionals plus 36 support staff researching these food crops. They have some linkages with the Asian Vegetable Research and Development Center (AVRDC), and, occasionally, the International Potato Center (CIP) drops in to look at their potato research.

Livestock research and fisheries research involve three and four professionals, respectively. The livestock work has emphasized the introduction of artificial insemination for dairy cattle, pigs, and sheep, as well as the identification of feasible forage/roughage production systems and the testing of feed and forage samples for livestock. The fisheries work has included research to assess the impacts of changes in commercial fish traps; the improvement of catch-and-effort statistics; and surveys of the dive and the long-line fisheries of Barbados.

Some of the most basic work is being conducted at the University of West Indies (UWI) Cave Hill Campus, which probably doubles the capacities of the MARD agricultural research program. Most research relating to agriculture takes place in the Biological and Chemical Sciences Department of the Pure and Applied Sciences Faculty, which has about

615 graduate and undergraduate students, with 50 working at the postgraduate level alongside 44 faculty. Most faculty have Ph.D.s and are earning competitive salaries in reasonably well-furnished facilities. Connections with researchers outside Barbados are spotty, yet well developed in some instances. Research in agriculture is being conducted on yam, pepper, tomato, onion, anthurium and papaya.

Most interesting is the work UWI is undertaking with the Caribbean Agricultural Research and Development Institute (CARDI), with partial financing from the Barbados National Council on Science and Technology. This research is culminating in a regional project for the development of hot peppers in the Caribbean, as a new entrant into the "fiery foods" industry, a rapidly growing industry with US sales of US$3.5 billion annually. A thoroughgoing strategic plan has been prepared and priority research has been identified in the areas of breeding to develop new varieties; studying water/plant relationships for best yields and lowest costs; developing cultivars to resist Whitefly/Gemeni virus and Aphid/Poty virus; and integrated pest-management strategies for mite, thrip, whitefly and aphid.[4]

The West Indies Sugar Cane Breeding and Evaluation Network (WISBEN), one of the oldest research efforts on sugar in the world, together with the Sugar Association of the Caribbean (SAC), is performing world-class research on sugar in Barbados. Five researchers are involved on a full-time basis. In addition, the Barbados Agricultural Management Company (BAMC) is supporting two researchers working on post-harvest sugar technologies and another three working on crop commodities in an Agronomic Research and Variety Testing Unit (ARVTU). While the human capital of these operations is impressive, WISBEN is not focused on Barbados alone and ARVTU is researching commodities other than sugar cane. With the need to rapidly transform the sugar industry, this excellent research capacity must translate into meaningful results at the commercial field level.

Tissue Culture Laboratories—There are two tissue culture laboratories in Barbados, one operated by CARDI and the other by MARD. Food crops and ornamentals, including cut flowers and foliage, are subjects of both. The CARDI laboratory produces and conducts research on a regional basis in crops that include musaceae, root crops, and ornamentals, like anthurium. The MARD Laboratory concentrates on production and protocol adaptation for local farmers and growers. It also cooperates with the Organization of American States (OAS) in the Mini-Plant Project, which produces tissue culture novelties for sale to the tourist sector, as well as with the Plant Health Institute of the UWI/Cave Hill. Anthurium improvement and the production of plantlets for hobbyist breeders of orchids constitute their work program.

---

[4] Biological and Chemical Sciences, UWI/Cave Hill Campus. 2002. *A Framework for the Development of a Hot Pepper Industry in the Caribbean: A Strategic Plan.* Cave Hill, Barbados: University of the West Indies.

Plant propagation work is conducted at MARD's facility at the Bullens Agricultural Station for field crops and foliage plants. Another propagation unit is at the Scotland District headquarters unit, which produces fruit tree planting material for island-wide distribution. Seedlings, budding, and grafting are done either in the shade houses or special mist houses.

The commodity selections and problem foci for research are the result of a conference in 2001, which brought together all relevant players in the sector, including representatives from CARDI and IICA. The conference identified specific problems that constitute the core of today's research program. It appears appropriate for the results of this 2001 Conference to be revisited, not so much from the perspective of commodity selection and the research areas but rather from that of the conduct of the research. In this regard, the civil service structure and policy on PhD training that governs the operation of MARD must be assessed to ensure that they facilitate the flexibility required for the implementation of a dynamic research program.

The above narrative highlights the following;

(i) For developing countries, such as Barbados, to benefit from trans-border transfer of technology, they must be proactive. In this regard, Barbados must use its involvement with CARDI, IICA and FAO to ensure that it benefits from technology generated regionally, hemispherically and globally, respectively.

(ii) There are apparent overlap and/or duplication (at worst) and inadequate coordination and/or collaboration (at best) among the various institutions involved in agricultural research. These are undoubtedly factors that limit the achievement of optimal benefits from the resources dedicated to technology generation and/or adoption.

(iii) There is a difference in perception between the public and private sectors as to the direction and/or value of research currently undertaken. This difference could be minimized with improved communication between the two sectors, followed by such adjustments to the structure and procedures that drive the research machinery in MARD as are necessary.

Recommendation #6 – *To address these issues it is proposed that, through the National Agricultural Commission, MARD develop a five-year (2006–2010) agricultural research program that would:*

1. *prioritize the commodities on which research would take place. This prioritization process would include the participation of agri-entrepreneurs and could benefit from the analysis described in Chapter V.*

2. *identify the responsibilities of each of the institutions involved in agricultural research and the time frame for achieving same. It is mandatory that these research responsibilities be expanded past the farm gate, that is, it must involve value-added research, and therefore include commercial (private-sector) entities.*
3. *require each institution to report on an annual basis the results of its work and the financial and human resources utilized.*
4. *be flexible enough to make adjustments to the scope and rate of implementation of the program and to recommend to the various institutions possible changes to their structure and process in order to improve implementation.*

Facilities

The major facilities available to the agriculture and rural development sectors in Barbados are irrigation, marketing and credit. These are described briefly below.

Irrigation—Over the period, 1988–2000, Barbados received an average of 49.2 inches of rain per year with a range of 35 to 71 inches. In addition, there were four periods—1989, 1993–94, 1997 and 2002—which experienced less than 44 inches per annum and were described as periods of drought. Hertford (2005)[5] estimated that on average crop production was reduced by 11%. Although distribution data were not presented, with the relatively modest rainfall, and based on the 1988–2000 data, 33% expectancy of drought and the estimated negative impact on crop productivity, one sees an apparent need for irrigation water.

Currently, irrigation is used mainly for vegetable and root crops. Sugar cane is not usually irrigated. The major users of irrigation water are schemes operated by BADMC, the estates managed by BAMC, plantations with privately licensed wells and smallholders and backyard gardeners with water obtained from the Barbados Water Authority (BWA) . The BADMC appears to be the major institution providing water for irrigation. Between 1993 and 2004, it invested some Bds$3 million.

The 1989 Agriculture Census listed 3,000 acres of irrigated farmland or 6 percent of total agricultural lands. However, by 2004, the MARD farmer registration program recorded 5,207 irrigated acres (including 1,100 acres within BADMC's Land for the Landless Programme), or an average growth of 3.7% per annum.

As non-sugar crops become more important in the crop mix, more irrigation water would be required and the rate of growth in the availability of irrigated water would need to be increased. The investment required could best be by both the private and public sectors and should promote better management—storage and use—of rainfall water. With

---

[5] Op. cit.

respect to the latter, the MARD should consider encouraging the use of on-farm collection and distribution systems, such as, the ferro-concrete tanks recently introduced by IICA, particularly for intensive, up-scale technology production of vegetable and food crops for the hospitality and similar markets. Appropriate incentives, such as those given in the past when solar energy apparati were introduced, could be provided to encourage their use. In addition, for the largest commercial schemes, greater organization of the farmers, possibly into water users' associations, is suggested so as to expand their involvement in the development and implementation of, and eventually investment in, the expansion and/or improvement of the schemes.

Recommendation #7 – *As Barbados must increase the rate of growth of irrigated land, the investment for implementation of the programs must be shared by both the public and private sectors. In this regard, it is recommended that:*

1. *through the use of appropriate incentives, the MARD promotes the use of on-farm rainfall storage and use systems for intensive vegetable and food crop production; and*
2. *the development of water users' associations be organized and strengthened in order to allow for farmers to have increased involvement in the development, implementation and oversight of the larger commercial irrigation schemes and ultimately the investment in the improvement and/or expansion of such schemes.*

Marketing—BADMC's agricultural marketing division is the main entity involved in marketing. Currently, it operates two retail outlets at the Grantley Adams International Airport. In addition, it imports 314,000 lbs and 931,800 lbs of chicken and turkey wings and onions, respectively. MARD also is responsible for marketing programs that are confined to the development, repair and maintenance of infrastructure facilities for the public markets, both general markets and fish markets. The Barbados Agricultural Society (BAS) also operates a retail outlet at its headquarters for its members' products. There are also a number of small operators who retail food crops, primarily vegetables and root crops. On a limited scale, they are also involved in imports (mainly from CARICOM countries) and exports.

There is a proposal to restructure BADMC in a way that will "emphasize investment opportunities in agriculture". The restructuring would aim to revive Barbados' agricultural export program with emphasis on hot peppers. The proposal also supports the processing and marketing of fish products; the availability of information to facilitate investment and marketing decisions; access to and development of new markets; the coordination of agri-entrepreneurs in their activities to develop new products for all markets; the arrangement of possible partnership and supply options with CSM partners to obtain supplemental raw products; and the intensification of linkages between the agricultural and tourism/hospitality sectors. These are developmental functions that would require public financing at least in the initial stages.

However, the proposals by BADMC must be fully supported by the private sector, and greater emphasis must be placed on full use of the markets provided by the tourism/hospitality sector. With respect to the latter, much greater effort should be expended by both the agricultural and tourism sectors to link local agricultural food and handicraft production with the island's hotels, plus the cruise ship passengers, 800,000 in 2004. Highest demand from the hotels and cruise ships is thought to be for herbs, spices, vegetables, onions, and root crops.

However, for this action to be successful, there must be a "hands-on", practical, long-term program agreed to in advance by both the agricultural and tourism sectors. This program must: (a) receive the total commitment of all parties concerned; (b) have an agreed set of commodities; (c) be phased with incremental and achievable targets, including product quantity and quality; and (d) be managed by a steering committee comprising representatives of the farming community, the hospitality entities involved and MARD and/or its allied institutions.

BAS and the Barbados Hotel and Tourism Association should be made aware of the activity and provide their blessings. However, their inclusion in the Steering Committee is not considered mandatory.

The proposal for phasing the "adopt a community" model that has been successfully pursued in Jamaica and St. Lucia could be adopted.

When this program is substantially operational, a decision could be taken as to the need for other facilities, such as a market information website, centralized marketing, etc.

Recommendation #8 – *The restructuring of BADMC should be completed taking into consideration the functions, as agreed to by the MARD and its National Agriculture Commission, but which should reflect both the current trend to reduce the involvement of Government entities in agricultural marketing and the reality of the willingness and/or capacity of the private sector to be involved in all aspects of marketing required by a repositioned/new agriculture.*

Recommendation #9 – *The establishment of a phased, defined and properly managed program that links the actors in the agricultural and hospitality/tourism sectors and recognizes the peculiarities of the former and the requirements of the latter.*

Agricultural Credit

There are three major sources of agricultural credit, viz., the Rural Development Commission (RDC), the Agricultural Development Fund (managed by the Enterprise Growth Fund Limited (EGFL) and commercial banks. Previously, Barbados National Bank was a major supplier of agricultural credit, until the financial challenges of the sugar industry in the mid-1990s damaged its financial integrity and forced the closure of that "window".

The RDC provides loans of up to Bds$50,000 with an interest rate of 1 percent per annum, to small agri-entrepreneurs primarily through the Rural Enterprise and Livestock Development Fund and also a Fruit Orchard Development Fund. Through 2004, it had provided 572 loans, valued at Bds$ 47 million, at concession interest rates of 1.5 percent per annum.

The ADF provides loans in the range of Bds$50,000 to $1.0 million, at an interest rate of 6 percent per annum, to individual agri-entrepreneurs and organizations. Its target is to be able to provide loans totaling Bds $10 million annually. Of this, Bds$6 million would be dedicated for the sugar industry. As of February 2003, ADF's loan portfolio amounted to Bds $9.7 million with the poultry industry being the largest beneficiary with Bds $1.2 million. It had also disbursed Bds $12.5 million in grants.

As shown in Table A-2, commercial bank lending to agriculture, as a percentage of total lending, declined from 2.3 percent in 1989 to 1.8 percent in the first six months of 2002. The absolute amounts were greater than 15 percent of the annual agriculture GDP, which was reported to be generous when compared to other Latin America and Caribbean (LAC) countries. Not unexpectedly, the percentage of agricultural lending to the sugar industry declined by almost 50 percent.

Both the RDC and ADF provide support to improve institutional capacity and technological understanding. For example, the RDC proposes to train 9,000 agri-entrepreneurs over a five-year period, starting 2001.

Taking into consideration the quantum of loan funding from both the public and private sectors, one has difficulty understanding the perception of the farming community that credit is unavailable. Perhaps the problem may be accessibility and not availability. Inaccessibility may be due to the requirements imposed by the financial institutions because of

Table A-2. Barbados: Distribution of Commercial Bank Credit to Agriculture, Sugar Cane, Livestock, and Food Crops, Three Selected Years, 1989–2002

Credit Type	1989	Calendar Year 1995	June 2002
Total, Commercial Banks ($ millions)	1,198	1,522	2,876
Total Agriculture, Commercial Banks ($ millions)	27.4	37.1	51.5
Total Agriculture/Total, Commercial Banks (percent)	2.3	2.4	1.8
Share for Sugar Cane (percent)	45.3	29.3	25.4
Share for Livestock (percent)	36.4	42.4	52.8
Share for Food Crops (percent)	8.7	4.0	7.8
Share for Other Agriculture (percent)	9.6	24.3	14.0
	100.0	100.0	100.0

Source: Central Bank of Barbados, *Economic and Financial Statistics* (Bridgetown, Barbados: Central Bank of Barbados, Research Department, 2004).

their limited human and technical capacity and/or understanding of the biological characteristics of agriculture. This has resulted in the consolidation of their position as to the high risk inherent in agricultural activities. This level of risk to the financial institutions could possibly be reduced if there was an adequate level of equity to complement loan financing. However, the agricultural community reported that venture capital or equity funding is an "extremely scarce commodity". Perhaps, this situation could be ameliorated, where appropriate, by the Government's quantifying the technical assistance that it provides to the enterprises and "using" that assistance to buy special shares that the private-sector owners would redeem in time from the profits earned.

It is imperative that the financial (banking, insurance and credit unions) and agricultural sectors should enter into serious dialogue to foster the investment needed for the agricultural sector to be restructured and the integrity of the financial institutions to be maintained. This dialogue would be formalized with the appointment of representatives of the financial sector to the Minister's National Agricultural Commission.

Recommendation #10 – *Even though the reports indicate that the quantum of loan funds made available to the agricultural sector is of an acceptable level, there is a perception of unavailability and/or inaccessibility. In addition, there is a recognized shortage of equity/venture capital. Therefore, it is recommended that the Minister invite representatives of financing institutions to be members of his National Agriculture Commission so as to effect dialogue and improve inter-sectoral understanding.*

Rural Development

This sub-section describes (a) the programs, mainly operated by the Government to foster development of the rural areas, (b) a community or district program, the Scotland District, that aims to optimize and/or catalyze efforts at rural development, and (c) a major deterrent to agriculture and rural development, praedial larceny.

Rural Development Programs

As shown previously (Table A-1) rural development is the second largest beneficiary of Government expenditure. It receives 15 percent of the expenditure on all MARD programs and, in this respect, is well placed amongst LAC countries. The responsibility for utilizing these resources resides with the RDC, which was established in mid-1996, and reports to MARD. The major programs of the RDC are: roads, housing, rural credit and management training.

Through 2003, RDC completed 110 roads and installed 6,000 street lights in rural districts. It also made major investments in house construction and repairs, wells and sceptic tanks, electrical and water installation, etc.

The training program, which commenced in 1998 with 20 persons, had benefited approximately 1,500 persons by 2004. In collaboration with the Barbados Small Business Association, the major courses, which are bookkeeping, records management and cost accounting, are provided at 11 locations throughout the country. The credit program has been described earlier.

Other agencies, such as BASand IICA, provide limited training programs to build institutional and technical capacity amongst individuals and groups.

Recommendation #11 – *Opportunities for strengthening linkages between the rural development program and mainline agriculture should be further exploited (for example, in the area of management training) to ensure sustainable economic outcomes, accelerate agricultural and rural development, and contribute to sector competitiveness.*

Scotland District—An Example of Rural Development

The Scotland District occupies about 6,127 hectares or, about 14 percent of Barbados' landmass. There are 1,200 hectares in arable crops, distributed amongst almost 1,600 individual holdings, and 2,200 hectares dedicated to improved and/or native pastures and shrubs.[6] In addition, there are 2,700 beef and dairy cattle, 3,500 sheep, 2,500 pigs and almost 500 goats.

The project was started in the mid-1950s in an effort to conserve soils following a series of land slips and slides that have occurred since the beginning of the 20th century. This effort was accompanied by a desire to develop tourist sites to complement existing ones. However, currently the roads and bridges are generally in various stages of disrepair.

In recognition of the potential of the Scotland District, MARD commissioned two studies in 1999–2000. The first determined the demography and topography of the area. The second, done by FAO, built on the first and prepared a five-year program to rehabilitate the District's agriculture. The cost for implementation was Bds$61 million, with Bds$38 and $15 million for land conservation and water-resource development, respectively. The remaining Bds $8 million was used for increasing production and productivity through the development of marketing systems and linkages with other sectors, improvement of infrastructure and institutional capacity and the development of required policies and of a legislative framework. Further evidence of the importance of Scotland District to the Government is the Bds $6.8 million committed in the 2004–05 budget and the Prime Minister's stated determination in his 2003 budget speech to provide monies "over and above the amount (already) being spent".

---

[6] Ministry of Agriculture and Rural Development (MARD). 2002. Draft Agricultural Development Plan for the Scotland District. Bridgetown, Barbados: MARD.

There may appear to be an imbalance in the relative amount of funds allocated to conservation compared to that for water-resource development and increased production/productivity. However, this probably reflects a very cautious response to ensuring that the very fragile pedological structure is not further threatened and to the possibility of any economic and social activity evaporating. However, in this regard, a few steps suggest themselves. Firstly, this project must be considered as a first phase, and once the topography is reasonably stabilized, more resources must be placed into water resource development and into the enhancement of production and productivity. Secondly, the District should be divided into sub-districts (based on the demographic and topographic information available) and these must be prioritized for actions.

These actions would result in an acceleration of economic returns from the program and provide opportunities for multiplier effects and a follow-the-leader(s) paradigm. These actions should fit into an overall objective of making the Scotland District a sustainable community (economically, socially and environmentally) with the major enterprises being agriculturally derived. These must include a strong agro-/eco-tourism component that makes full use of the natural biodiversity and topography.

However, for this proposal to be successfully implemented, there has to be strong inter-ministerial collaboration, involving particularly MARD and the Ministry of Tourism; there must be abundant community participation resulting in an effective public/private/civil partnership; the technical extension programs must transcend the entire commodity chain and include group dynamics and collaborative initiatives. Indeed, the Scotland District lends itself most readily to be an in vivo crucible for agro-tourism linkages and for validation of the concepts of rural territories and "clusters".

Recommendation # 12 – *The Government should revisit the elements of the second study and phase its implementation in terms of time and geographic space. This approach should be characterized by strong inter-ministerial collaboration, total community participation that would result in effective partnerships and total "ownership".*

Praedial Larceny—A Constraint on Development

As for the rest of the Caribbean, praedial larceny continues to be a major constraint to the successful development of agriculture in Barbados. It causes a reduction in revenue because of theft and, where resources are available, an increase in costs occasioned by heightened security measures. In an attempt to reduce the incidence of praedial larceny, some farmers opt for cultivating commodities that are less "theft friendly" but that may not be ideal for the particular ecological situation. Consequently, there is a reduction in profits and hence in the quantum of funding available for reinvestment.

It also causes uncertainty in the decision-making process of new investors. About 12 years ago, the police, in consultation with the farmers, made far-reaching recommendations to the Ministry of Agriculture, which accepted them and incorporated them into legislation. The resulting laws now provide that any person found conveying produce on any street must produce a certificate showing from whom the produce was obtained and the quantity and value involved. The police were also given powers to stop persons transporting produce and to carry out the necessary checks to determine whether the goods are stolen.

However, the impact of this legislation on the reduction in praedial larceny is not evident. It has been suggested that farmers themselves and the authorities have not fulfilled their respective responsibilities.

The National Commission on Law and Order has recommended that:

- the police should aggressively seek to enforce existing legislation designed to prevent and detect the theft of growing crops and produce;
- agricultural inspectors be appointed by the Ministry to carry out inspections to ensure that the provisions of the legislation are being complied with;
- legislation be amended (if necessary) to provide for inspection of business places to ascertain whether the provisions of the Act are being complied with; and
- the Ministry of Agriculture should educate the public about the problems of praedial larceny, and inform those engaged in the sale and purchase of produce about their responsibilities.[7]

What is now required is for a campaign supported and "owned" by the authorities and the farmers. For example, the police should stop and search vehicles suspected of being used to transport stolen produce and the farmers must religiously issue the certificates. Failure to produce the necessary certificate should lead to the confiscation of the produce and the lodging of appropriate charges. Further, the registration by and of farmers should become mandatory.

Recommendation #13 – *In view of the gravity of praedial larceny and its impact on the redefining of the scope and extent of the agriculture sector, the Government should set out to vigorously implement the recommendations of the Commission on Law and Order placing special emphasis on public education.*

MARD should also review the proposals developed in other countries, including Caribbean countries, to determine their level of success and their possible suitability for adoption in Barbados.

---

[7] Government of Barbados. 2004. *Report of the National Commission on Law & Order*. Bridgetown, Barbados: Government of Barbados.